GW00696916

Fiscal Policy Reforms in India Since 1991

Fiscal Policy Reforms in India Since 1991

By

S.M. Jawed Akhtar
and
Sana Naseem

New Century Publications
New Delhi, India

NEW CENTURY PUBLICATIONS
4800/24, Bharat Ram Road,
Ansari Road, Daryaganj,
New Delhi – 110 002 (India)

Tel.: 011-2324 7798, 4358 7398, 6539 6605
Fax: 011-4101 7798
E-mail: indiatax@vsnl.com • info@newcenturypublications.com
www.newcenturypublications.com

Editorial office:
LG–7, Aakarshan Bhawan,
4754-57/23, Ansari Road, Daryaganj,
New Delhi – 110 002

Tel.: 011-4356 0919

First Published: **2013**

ISBN: **978-81-7708-346-0**

Published by New Century Publications and printed at Salasar Imaging Systems, New Delhi.

Designs: Patch Creative Unit, New Delhi.

PRINTED IN INDIA

About the Book

The external payments crisis of 1991—which led to the initiation of economic reforms in India—was the result of deteriorating fiscal situation during the latter half of 1980s. Fiscal imbalance was identified as the underlying cause of the twin problems of inflation and the difficult balance of payments position. Hence, fiscal consolidation constituted a major objective of the policy response. This consolidation was planned to be achieved through reduction in the size of budget deficit and public debt in relation to Gross Domestic Product (GDP). For this purpose, it became necessary to: (a) enhance tax and non-tax revenue, (b) curtail current expenditure growth, (c) restructure public sector undertakings, including disinvestment, (d) improve fiscal-monetary co-ordination, and (e) deregulate financial system.

The need for improvements in budgetary practices led to the enactment of the Fiscal Responsibility and Budget Management (FRBM) Act, 2003 which ushered the Indian economy in an era of fiscal consolidation based on fiscal policy rules.

This book provides a vivid account and analysis of reforms in India's fiscal policy during the post-liberalization (1991 onwards) period.

About the Authors

Dr. S.M. Jawed Akhtar is currently Associate Professor in the Department of Economics at Aligarh Muslim University, Aligarh. He was awarded gold medals for securing first position in B.A (Hons.) and M.A (Economics) examinations of the same university. He has been actively engaged in teaching and research for the last two decades. He has to his credit a good number of publications in various reputed national and international journals. He is a recognized research guide and several Ph.D. degrees have been awarded under his guidance. He is an active member of several academic bodies.

Dr. Sana Naseem completed her Ph.D. in Economics in 2011. She has published research papers and articles in reputed journals. She is a visiting fellow at many management colleges.

Contents

Preface

The external payments crisis of 1991, which led to the initiation of economic reforms in India, was the result of deteriorating fiscal situation during the latter half of 1980s. This period was marked by high and persistent fiscal deficits, accompanied by large revenue deficits. This had led to a significant enlargement of Government borrowings from financial intermediaries and increased financing of Government deficit through automatic monetisation which aggravated price rise. When the Indian economy faced an unprecedented macroeconomic crisis in 1991, fiscal consolidation constituted a major objective of the policy response. This consolidation was to be achieved through reduction in the size of budget deficit and public debt in relation to GDP. For this purpose, it became necessary to: (a) enhance tax and non-tax revenue, (b) curtail current expenditure growth, (c) restructure public sector undertaking, including disinvestment, (d) improve fiscal-monetary co-ordination, and (e) deregulate financial system.

Apart from these reforms aimed at fiscal consolidation, a number of institutional measures were also taken during the 1990s. Public sector restructuring and disinvestments were undertaken with a view to increase the efficiency of the public sector undertakings and also to provide additional resources to the Government. The need for improvements in budgetary practices led to the enactment of the Fiscal Responsibility and Budget Management (FRBM) Act, 2003 which ushered the Indian economy in an era of fiscal consolidation based on fiscal policy rules.

Tax reforms introduced by the Government since mid-1991 have helped to build a structure which is simple, relies on moderate tax rates but with a wider base and better enforcement. Historically, rates of income tax in India have been quite high, almost punitive. For example, in 1973-74, the maximum marginal rate of individual income tax was as high as 97.7 percent. When high rates proved counter-productive from revenue angle, the Government initiated a series of rate reductions with the result that the top rate for individual taxpayers declined to 30 percent.

Multiple rates of commodity taxes have long been considered a weakness of the indirect tax system of India. Thus, in a landmark move, the Finance Minister announced in his 1999-2000 Budget a triple rate excise structure. In other words, the then existing 11 major *ad valorem* rates were reduced to 3, viz. a central rate of 16 percent, a merit rate of 8 percent and a demerit rate of 24 percent. The initiative of the Finance Minister to rationalise the rate structure of excise system was widely appreciated.

In mid-l991, Government began the process of reducing import duties. The Finance Act (No. 2), 1991, reduced the *ad valorem* rate of basic plus auxiliary duties of customs to a maximum of 150 percent where it was more than that. Thus, tariff peaks above 150 percent were eliminated with the exceptions of duty on imported alcoholic beverages and passenger baggage. The Finance Act, 1992, lowered the peak level of import duties to 110 percent with the exception of passenger baggage and alcoholic beverages. The Finance Act, 1993, made a significant simplification in the import tariff by merging auxiliary duty with basic duty, and also by reducing the maximum rate of import duty from 110 percent to 85 percent. After successive downward revisions, the peak rate of import duty on non-agricultural products stands at 10 percent at present.

Tax reforms since June 1991 have helped in correcting structural imbalances in the tax system. They are *soft* on industry with a view to create new investment climate and make India internationally competitive. By lowering the tax rates, the Government expects speedy industrial development and hence buoyancy in tax revenues.

The country is keenly awaiting implementation of the Goods and Services Tax (GST) and the Direct Tax Code

(DTC). GST is India's most ambitious indirect tax reform. Lack of political consensus is holding up progress and the Government has already missed the April 1, 2012 deadline of implementing GST.

Apart from tax reforms, a number of institutional measures were taken during the 1990s. Public sector restructuring and disinvestments were undertaken with a view to increase the efficiency of the Public Sector Undertakings (PSUs) as also to provide additional resources to the Government. The Ahluwalia Committee Report on Fiscal Transparency (2001) underscored the need for improvements in budgetary practices, which prepared the ground for the enactment of the Fiscal Responsibility and Budget Management (FRBM) Act, 2003.

Expenditure reforms in the context of liberalisation have two aspects: (a) consolidation so as to reduce the quantum of expenditure, and (b) restructuring with a view to changing the composition of government expenditure, i.e. shift towards growth-inducing expenditure on infrastructure and human resource development and reduction in unwarranted subsidies.

Government has taken various initiatives in recent years to streamline public expenditure management. The focus has shifted from financial outlays to outcomes for ensuring that the budgetary provisions are not merely spent within the financial year but have resulted in intended outcomes. At the same time, steps have also been taken in the form of austerity instructions to reduce expenditure in non-priority areas without compromising on operational efficiency.

Aligarh **S.M. Jawed Akhtar**
November 2012 **Sana Naseem**

Abbreviations/Acronyms

APM	Administered Price Mechanism
BIFR	Board for Industrial and Financial Restructuring
BPL	Below Poverty Line
CAG	Comptroller and Auditor General of India
CCF	Contingency and Compensatory Financing
CCFF	Compensatory and Contingency Financing Facility
CEM	Country Economic Memorandum
CENVAT	Central Value Added Tax
CPI	Consumer Price Index
CRR	Cash Reserve Ratio
CSO	Central Statistical Organisation
DTEC	Direct Taxes Enquiry Commission
DvP	Delivery versus Payment
ERC	Expenditure Reforms Commission
FRBM	Fiscal Responsibility and Budget Management
GDP	Gross Domestic Product
GFD	Gross Fiscal Deficit
GNP	Gross National Product
HDI	Human Development Index
IFL	Incremental Financial Liability
IMF	International Monetary Fund
KTF	Kelkar Task Force
LDC	Less Developed Countries
LPG	Liquefied Petroleum Gas
LTFP	Long-Term Fiscal Policy
LTUs	Large Tax-payer Units
MANVAT	Manufacturing Stage Value-Added Tax
MAT	Minimum Alternative Tax
MODVAT	Modified Value-Added Tax
MOUs	Memorandums of Undertakings
MTNL	Mahanagar Telephone Nigam Limited
NAS	National Account Statistics
NDCCR	Non-debt Creating Capital Receipt
NDTL	Net Demand and Time Liabilities

NRF	National Renewal Fund
NSSF	National Small Saving Fund
PEM	Public Expenditure Management
PIT	Personal Income Tax
PSBR	Public Sectors Borrowing Requirement
PSEs	Public Sector Enterprises
PSUs	Public Sector Undertakings
RBI	Reserve Bank of India
R&D	Research and Development
SLR	Statutory Liquidity Ratio
STT	Securities Transaction Tax
TEC	Taxation Enquiry Commission
TIN	Tax Information System
TRC	Tax Reforms Committee
UK	United Kingdom
USA	United States of America
VAT	Value-Added Tax
VCFs	Venture Capital Funds
VCUs	Venture Capital Undertakings
VRS	Voluntary Retirement Scheme
WMA	Ways and Means Advances
WTO	World Trade Organization

1

Fiscal Policy: An Introduction

1.1 Meaning of Fiscal Policy

Fiscus (in Latin) refers to a purse and 'fisc' (in English) is a royal or state treasury. Mrs. Hicks says that fiscal policy is concerned with the manner in which all the different elements of public finance, while still primarily concerned with carrying out their duties (as the first duty of tax is to raise revenue), may collectively be geared to forward the aims of the economic policy (Hicks, U.K.,1968). [1] The crux of a good and effective fiscal policy lies in keeping its ingredients like expenditure, loans, transfers, tax revenues, income from property, debt management, and the like in a proper balance so as to achieve the best possible results in terms of the desired economic objectives.

Usefulness of fiscal policy lies only if it facilitates in achieving socio-economic objectives of the society. But it must not be forgotten that fiscal policy is only one of the many sets of weapons in the hands of the Government. It should also be emphasized that fiscal policy tries to achieve its objectives by regulating the working of market mechanism (while in contrast some other weapons may by-pass it). The extent of its success, therefore, largely depends upon the response of market forces to various policy steps initiated by the Government. The fact that fiscal policy can be a potent tool in the hands of the authorities came to be recognized only slowly. For decades, both official and academic thinking favoured laissez-faire and balanced budgets.

This policy, obviously, had its own drawbacks. As Keynes pointed out, an attempt to balance the budget results in its imbalance and vice versa. In spite of these problems, the appropriateness and usefulness of fiscal policy came to be recognized only during 1930s and later. The significance of fiscal policy as an instrument of economic control was first emphasized in the mid-1930s by Keynes *General Theory of Employment, Interest and Money.* Keynes showed clearly the direct and indirect effects of fiscal action on aggregate spending in the community and its influence on economic activity and gave a new importance to the budgetary policy of the Government as a weapon of economic management.

1.2 Tools of Fiscal Policy

Fiscal policy has three important tools: taxation, public expenditure, and public debt management. The tax system of the country, of course, is meant to bring in revenue to the Government but it can also be used to encourage or restrict private expenditure on consumption and investment. Public expenditure of the Government may take various forms-normal government expenditure (on civil administration, defence, etc.), expenditure on public works (such as road, parks, etc.), expenditure on relief works, subsidies of various types, etc., while taxes reduce the income of the general public (they transfer income from the general public to the Government), public expenditure transfers income from the Government to the general public. Finally, Government borrowings and public debt influence the volume of liquid assets with the public, for example, subscription to a Government loan would transfer liquid funds from the general public to the Government, while repayment of a public debt would mean transfer of funds from the Government to the general public.

All these three tools of fiscal policy—tax policy, public expenditure, and public debt management—are significant to maintain economic stability and for influencing the level of economic activity. It is now generally accepted that the main problem of industrial or high income economies is stability in business conditions and maintaining full employment, while rapid economic progress and increase in employment are the basic needs of less developed countries. Fiscal policy has come to assume significance as effective means of stabilization in an advanced economy and, therefore, for high income countries.

It is now generally held that no other measure of economic planning is better than adoption of a correct fiscal policy. Some fiscal theorists argue that fiscal policy may not be effective in an underdeveloped economy, since modern economic and financial institutions are not as well developed. Even then, fiscal policy has a positive and significant role to play in an underdeveloped economy.

In the first instance, the state is called upon to play an active and important role in promoting economic development, especially through control and regulation of economic life; it is argued that fiscal policy is the most powerful and the least undesirable weapon of control which the state can employ to promote economic development. Secondly, capital accumulation is the key problem of an underdeveloped economy and this can be done through taxation. Finally, fiscal policy has an important role to play under democratic planning; financial plan is as much important as physical plan and the implementation of the financial plan will obviously depend upon the use of fiscal measures.

Fiscal policy may be taken to embrace all government transactions which have as their objective the support of general economic policy. In an advanced country (at least of the welfare state type) general economic, as distinct from political, policy is geared to promote growth with stability and to increase welfare through a more equal distribution of available (spendable) incomes. In an advanced country fiscal policy very largely operates on the expenditure side of the account, through widespread social expenditure and through selective incentives directed to particular industries or localities which it is desired to encourage.

These are both long term fields of operation. Expenditure policy is also extremely important in respect of short-term stability (compensatory finance), because of the ease with which alterations can be brought about in social expenditure, or, more precisely, in the balance between social expenditure and social taxation (insurance contributions). Main reliance for income redistribution falls, however, on the tax side of the account. By controlling the available incomes of the rich and by redistributing capital assets through taxation, a far greater equality of spending power is obtained than results from the productive process. Increasingly also, on the side of production, attempts are made to write into tax formulae (especially of profits taxes) incentives for investment, both general and selective. These too can be varied over time in the interests of stability.

Thus, fiscal policy in an advanced country comprises a large supply/armoury of weapons, some concentrating mainly on welfare effects, others on considerations of economic growth with stability; some aiming mainly at short-term effects, others at long-term development. But no means all these objectives are consistent. For instance, redistribution carried out too violently, or a stability policy which reaches the point of long-term disincentive, are both inimical to growth. Subsidies to certain industries (particularly to agriculture, which are the most general) may counteract an income redistribution policy by forcing consumers to pay more for their food, thus injuring the poor more than the rich.

In a developing country, the main emphasis of general economic policy will be on growth, with sufficient stability to prevent recurrent crises which would cause development to slow up or even retrogress, and hence give rise to losses on investments already made. With different emphasis in different countries, it will probably also be desired to use fiscal policy to reduce the very large gap between the incomes of the few rich and many poor. On the expenditure side there is not likely to be a great deal of opportunity for a policy either of income distribution through social expenditure or of stabilization through compensatory variations in public outlay. In all lines of expenditure growth must have the priority. Hence, the heaviest responsibility both for stability and for income redistribution must fall on the tax side of the account (Hicks, U.K., 1965). [2]

1.3 Objectives of Fiscal Policy

The chief objective of the fiscal policy in the developed countries is to counteract cyclical fluctuations arising out of the dips and spurts in the level of aggregate effective demand. As such, the Keynesian fiscal recommendations hinged on the ways to regulate the level of aggregate effective demand and the total flows of purchasing powers are well suited to the needs of these economies. But growth being the primary goal of the underdeveloped countries, the fiscal policy in their case has to be tailored to the needs of rapid economic growth. Further, the very fact that these countries have a low propensity to save and a high propensity to consume, an inversion of Keynesian fiscal measures is called for in their case. Thus, whereas the maintenance of stability is the key-note of fiscal policy in developed countries, and this key-note of the fiscal policy in underdeveloped countries has to be the fostering of an accelerated rate of economic growth.

Fiscal policy seeks to influence the economy through a double-barrelled course; by the magnitude of public income that could be raised, and by the volume and direction of the public expenditure. The latter, of course, to large extent depends on the former. The magnitude of fiscal revenue pre-eminently determines the availability of resources with the government to finance economic development. The government has access to three important fiscal means through which resources can be raised, viz., taxation, public borrowing and credit creation. A successful operation of the fiscal policy requires a harmonious combination of these three means. Only then it can engender rapid economic growth with stability. However, taxation remains the most effective instrument of fiscal policy. As such, the actual efficiency of fiscal policy largely depends on the country's tax system. Within the framework of general programme for accelerated development, fiscal policy in general and taxation policy in particular should be so attuned and used as to accomplish the following main objectives of developing countries.

1. **Mobilization of Resources:** Developing economies are characterized by low levels of income and investment, which are linked in a vicious circle. This can be successfully broken by mobilizing resources for investment energetically.
2. **Acceleration of Economic Growth:** The government has not only to mobilize more resources for investment, but also to direct the resources to those channels where the yield is higher and the goods produced are socially accepted.
3. **Minimization of the Inequalities of Income and Wealth:** Fiscal tools can be used to bring about the redistribution of income in favour of the poor by spending revenue so raised on social welfare activities.
4. **Increasing Employment Opportunities:** Fiscal incentives, in the form of tax-rebates and concessions, can be used to promote the growth of those industries that have high employment generation potential.
5. **Price Stability:** Fiscal tools can be employed to contain inflationary and deflationary tendencies in the economy.

The main objectives of fiscal policy in developed countries are the following.

1. **To Raise the Level of Investments:** The main objective of fiscal policy in a developed county should be to raise the volume of production keeping in view the fact that the level of production should not be higher than the level of consumption. Now to increase production, it is essential to raise the level of investment. The level of production should be increased by increasing effective demand.
2. **To Check the Fluctuations in the Effective Demand of Money:** In developed countries there exists irregular unemployment. If the people do not like to work in spite of

the available opportunities of work or if they possess so much income that they can lead healthy life even without doing any work, it will lead to irregular unemployment. The manpower will become idle. Now to control irregular unemployment, it is essential to check fluctuations in the effective demand of money.

3. **To Control the Automatic Process of the Market:** Today, all the economists are of the opinion that on reaching the developed economy at the top, it cannot be left alone. This fact has been verified by 1930 worldwide depression. The worldwide depression has disturbed the economy of world badly. Hence, in order to avoid the uncertainty of the market, effective control is needed.
4. **Proper Direction to Government Investments:** In order to have effective coordination between demand and supply, the Government investments are required to play an important role. Hence, proper direction should be given to Government investments.
5. **Determination of Suitable Taxation Policy:** In order to establish short-term and long-term balance in the economy, it is essential that there must exist complete coordination between taxation policy, credit creation policy, lending policy, and resources mobilization policy of the Government. Unless there is a mutual coordination between them, it is not possible to bring about stability in developed economy. Prof. Musgrave pointed out the following objectives of fiscal policy in a developed economy:

- To secure adjustment in the allocation of resources;
- To secure adjustment in the distribution of income and wealth; and
- To secure economic stabilization (Kumar, N. and Mittal, R., 2002). [3]

1.4 Evolution of India's Fiscal Policy

The objective of economic policy in India during the

1950s and 1960s was mainly to increase the growth rate of the economy through increasing public investment and overall economic planning. Taxation was used as an instrument for reducing private consumption and investment and for transferring resources to the Government to enable it to undertake large-scale public investment in an effort to spur economic growth. Furthermore, taxation policy was geared towards achieving the economic objectives of promoting employment through grant of tax incentives to new investment; reducing inequality through progressive taxes on income and wealth; reducing pressure on balance of payments through increase of import duties; and stabilizing prices through tax rebate in excise duties on consumption goods.

Fiscal policy during the 1970s consciously focused on achieving greater equity and social justice and both taxation and expenditure policies were employed towards this end. Accordingly, income tax rates were raised to very high levels, with the maximum marginal rate of income tax moving up to 97 percent and, together with the incidence of wealth tax, it even crossed 100 percent. Over the years, in addition to the commitment towards a large volume of developmental expenditure, the Government's expenditure widened to include rising subsidies. Large interest payments on growing debt and downward rigidity in prices further contributed to increased current expenditure. Current revenues, on the other hand, were less buoyant leading to the emergence of sizeable revenue deficit in the Central Government budget from 1979-80 onwards, complicating the task of monetary policy.

During the 1980s, Indian public finances were in a state of disarray with the fiscal pattern destabilizing the relationship between the economy and the budget. This resulted in persistently large deficits which were seemingly intractable. Considerable fiscal deterioration took place during the 1980s and eventually became unsustainable, though the growth rate did rise significantly with enhancement in public investment in infrastructure. During this phase, expenditure of the

Government was seen as an instrument having a bearing upon aggregate demand, resource allocation and income distribution. The Government sought to reduce its deficit through tax increases. Custom duties were hiked to augment revenue and to protect domestic industry. There was a structural change in the Government budgets during the 1980s. The emergence of revenue deficit in 1979-80 in the Centre's budget continued to enlarge during the 1980s, raising concerns over the rising public debt and interest payments and the consequent constraint on the availability of resources for meeting developmental needs. The 1980s witnessed a steady increase in market borrowings along with an increase in Reserve Bank's support to such borrowing, thus compromising monetary policy.

During 1990s, the structural adjustment programme and the consequent economic reforms gave a fresh dimension to fiscal system which focused not only on the various instruments of fiscal policy and issues of debt but also on the overall fiscal sustainability in the context of an open economic framework. Although the first half of the 1990s witnessed some fiscal correction, its retraction during the second half of the decade underlined the need for a consistent and sustainable fiscal consolidation process. The Government, therefore, formulated and enactment the fiscal responsibility legislation which signalled a new dawn in fiscal consolidation.

The performance of the Indian economy in recent years has attracted increasing international interest. An interesting feature of the record of economic growth in India is that it has experienced a sustained slow acceleration in growth since independence. Growth has been accelerating gradually since the 1950s, except for an interregnum between 1965 and 1980. Thus, the current observed acceleration in growth has to be seen in the context of this long record of consistent growth, which has been accompanied by a relatively continuous increase in savings and investment rates over the years. What is remarkable in recent years is the very substantial steep increase in the rates of savings and investment.

It is widely believed that Indian economy witnessed near stagnation in real GDP growth till the late 1970s. A closer review of the performance of the Indian economy, however, suggests a continuing increase in real GDP growth over each decade since independence, interspersed with an interregnum during the 1970s. Interestingly, growth of manufacturing production, in terms of decadal averages, was roughly constant at around 5.6-5.9 percent in the first five decades after independence, except for the 1970s. There are two other features of India's growth history that are notable. First, agricultural growth has been subject to large variation over the decades. The 1970s interregnum is particularly marked by the severe deceleration in agricultural growth, followed by a marked recovery in the 1980s, and a slowdown thereafter. Second, until the 1990s, little note had been taken of growth in the services sector. A glance at the acceleration in growth in services over the decades, that had earlier been ignored, that really accounts for the continuous acceleration in overall GDP growth, once again, except for the 1970s interregnum.

The slowdown of growth witnessed during the 1970s was reversed during the 1980s; the pick up benefited from the initiation of some reform measures aimed at increasing domestic competitiveness. Since the early 1990s, growth impulses appeared to have gathered further momentum in the aftermath of comprehensive reforms encompassing the various sectors of the economy. There was some loss of the growth momentum in the latter half of the 1990s, which coincide with the onset of the East Asian financial crisis, setbacks to the fiscal correction process, quality of fiscal adjustment, slowdown in agriculture growth affected by lower than normal monsoon years, and some slackening in the pace of structural reforms. The slowdown could also be attributed to the excessive enthusiasm and optimism in regard to investment plans in domestic industry following deregulation, which was followed by significant problems experienced in viability and competitiveness.

Monetary tightening in the face of inflationary pressures is also believed by some to have contributed to the slowdown over this period. Since 2003-04, there has been a distinct strengthening of the growth momentum. Restructuring measures by domestic industry, overall reduction in domestic interest rates, both nominal and real, improved corporate profitability, a benign investment climate amidst strong global demand and commitment rule-based fiscal policy have led to real GDP growth averaging close to 9 percent per annum over the four-year period ended 2006-07; growth in the last two years has averaged 9.3 percent per annum (Mohan, Rakesh, 2008). [4] The statistical analysis shows that the average real GDP growth in India during 1990-91 to 2007-08 has been 6.23 percent, while the compound annual growth rate has been 4.7 percent during the same period.

The sustained acceleration in real GDP growth of the Indian economy has been associated with a secular up trend in domestic savings and investment over the decades. Gross domestic savings has moved up from an average of 9.6 percent of GDP during 1950s to 17.5 percent during 1970s, and further to 23.4 percent during 1990s.Gross domestic savings improved marginally from 23.5 percent in 2001-02 to 37.7 percent in 2007-08.Similarly, the domestic investment rate has increased continuously from 10.8 percent in 1950s to 24.5 percent in 1990s. The gross domestic investment increased from 28.2 percent in 2003-04 to 37.5 percent in 2007-08. The remarkable feature of these trends in saving and investment rates show that India's economic growth has been financed predominantly by domestic savings. The recourse to foreign savings equivalently, current account deficit has been rather modest in the Indian growth process. However, the two decades, 1960s and 1980s, when the current account deficit increased marginally towards 2 percent of GDP, were followed by significant balance of payments and economic crises (Mohan, Rakesh, 2008). [5]

The average of gross domestic savings and investment is 26.65 and 26.95 percent respectively during 1990-91 to 2007-08. The co-efficient of variance of savings is found to be 19.10 percent which is higher than the co-efficient of variance of investment which is 17.20 percent during the same period. The standard deviation of savings and investment is 5.01 and 4.63 respectively, meaning thereby deviation in gross domestic saving is higher than gross domestic investment, and CAGR of gross domestic savings and gross domestic investment is 2.8 and 2.21 percent respectively reflecting marginal difference in their annual growth pattern during the same period.

However, Government's ability to invest has been declining continuously since the late 1980s because of its deteriorating fiscal position. What is encouraging, of course, is the increase in private corporate sector investment levels subsequent to the 1991 reforms. The reforms have therefore succeeded in encouraging higher level of private investment as envisaged. But further increases are constrained by declining public investment levels. Today concentration is now on the rapid deterioration of the fiscal balance both at central and state levels. The key deterrent for achieving higher economic growth in the country lies in its deteriorating fiscal performance. The key threat to substantial economic growth and to economic security is the substantial decline in investment expenditure made by the Government.

The growing fiscal imbalances of the 1980s spilled over to the external sector and were also reflected in inflationary pressures. Along with a repressive and weakening financial system, this rendered the growth process of the 1980s increasingly unsustainable. The external imbalances were reflected in a large and unsustainable current account deficit, which reached 3.2 percent of GDP in 1990-91. As the financing of such a large current account deficit through normal sources of finance became increasingly difficult, it resulted in an unprecedented external payment crisis in 1991 with the foreign currency assets dwindling to less than US$ 1 billion. The financing problem was aggravated by the fact that the deficit was largely financed by debt flows up to the late 1980s, reflecting the policies of the time, which preferred debt flows to equity flows. Indeed, equity flows were almost negligible till the early 1990s.

Moreover, a significant part of the debt flows during the late 1980s was of a short-term nature in the form of bankers' acceptances; such flows could not be renewed easily in view of the loss of confidence following the balance of payments crisis. In response to the balance of payments crisis, a programme of macroeconomic stabilization and structural adjustment was put in place. Fiscal consolidation constituted a major plank of the policy response to the macroeconomic crisis; however, public sector savings continued to deteriorate during the 1990s, and even turned negative over the five-year period 1998-2003 owing to sharp deterioration in savings of the Government administration.

The progress on fiscal correction was mixed during the 1990s at the central level. While there was some reduction in the Centre's fiscal deficits up to 1996-97, the process was reversed over the next few years under the impact of the industrial slowdown and the Fifth Pay Commission award. Furthermore, fiscal consolidation, which was envisaged to be achieved through revenue enhancement and curtailment in current expenditure growth, was however, brought through compression of capital expenditures from 5.6 percent of GDP in 1990-91 to 3.1 percent in 1996-97, with consequential effects on growth and infrastructure constraints in ensuring years.

In view of the deterioration in fiscal deficits over the period 1997-98 to 2002-03 and rising public debt, and its adverse impact on public investment and growth, a renewed emphasis was laid on improving the health of public finances on a durable basis. In order to achieve this objective, fiscal consolidation has been guided by the Fiscal Responsibility and Budget Management (FRBM) Act, 2003 at the Centre level.

Since 2002-03, significant gains have been witnessed in the fiscal consolidation process at the Centre, partly as a result of the implementation of the rule-based fiscal policy at the Centre. A major factor contributing to the durability of the fiscal consolidation process under way in India in recent years has been the buoyancy in the revenues accompanied by some reprioritization of expenditure with a focus on outcomes, unlike the expenditure compression strategy in most other countries as also the experience in India in the 1990s. The revenue augmenting strategy encompassed moderating the tax base and broadening the tax base through expansion in the scope of taxes, specifically service tax, removal of exemptions, some improvement in tax administration with a focus on arrears recoveries.

However, India's persistently large fiscal imbalances raise three concerns. First, the upward trend in the interest burden on public debt threatens the sustainability of the current macroeconomic stance. In particular, it threatens the current mix of growth and inflation. Assuming that real interest rates are equal to the GDP growth rate, solvency requires that in the long-run the primary (non-interest) public sector surplus be sufficient to finance the interest service on net outstanding public sector liabilities. This would avoid an explosive situation in which new debt is issued to cover the interest payments on the mounting stock of old debt. Because a large share of the public debt has been contracted at interest rates well below current ones, and this debt will take time to mature and be rolled over at the higher current rate, India is far from such a situation.

However, in the absence of a serious adjustment in India's tax or spending patterns, this situation will eventually materialize forcing either inflation to increase or growth to decline. Secondly, from a public finance angle, servicing the country's public debt puts large claims on public resources, which reduce the government's capacity to spend on key development activities. In addition, it also creates a need for higher taxation, which undermines efficiency. Third, the large fiscal imbalances pose a risk to macroeconomic stability as the financial sector is further liberalized. Since a large portion of the outstanding public debt stock carries interest rates well below current market rates, the overall interest bill will increase as these obligations mature and have to be rolled over at the higher current market rates. This convergence of the average rate to the marginal rate will have a sizeable impact on public finances (Prasad, C.S., 2005). [6]

1.5 Economic Reforms and Fiscal Policy

In recent years many countries have adopted economic programs aimed at adjusting their economies because of the large macroeconomic disequilibria characterized by inflation, balance of payments difficulties, and increasing debt obligations. By and large, adjustment has aimed at reducing the rate of inflation, improving the balance of payments, and promoting economic growth. Adjustment requires many policy changes, including devaluation, opening of the economy, financial reforms, reduction of excessive regulations and removal of price controls. All these adjustment programs adopted by countries (whether supported by the IMF or the World Bank or undertaken without outside support) have required that substantial attention be paid to the fiscal situation. The reason for this is obvious. In countries facing major macro-economic difficulties, the public finances are often in substantial disequilibrium. A reduction of the disequilibrium becomes a necessary condition for improving the macroeconomic situation.

The need for fiscal reform is now widely recognized but at the same time it has been experienced that the fiscal reform is very difficult. In fact, it has been found to be the most difficult of the various policy changes required in adjustment programs. The difficulties are partly political, partly institutional, and partly conceptual. Dealing with fiscal deficits remains today one of the most difficult problem for the majority of developing countries. For many, growing fiscal deficits led to money creation as the main source of financing followed by increasing inflation, an erosion of the tax base, and even larger fiscal imbalances. Even counties that contained their fiscal deficits usually did so at great costs mainly by indiscriminate expenditure cutting.

According to the World Bank, Country Economic Memorandum (CEM) on India, economic crisis which triggered the reform process in 1991 itself was diagnosed as the consequence of the severe fiscal imbalance that afflicted the economy throughout the 1980s, a detailed review of achievements and challenges of fiscal adjustment efforts is opportune. Fiscal reforms must therefore be analyzed from the perspective of whether and to what extent they have helped to achieve economic growth.

The Indian economy has undergone a gradual transformation during the post-independence period. The pace of such transformation, however, being relatively rapid since the last decade. The structural transformation that occurs in the Indian economy over the decade is the consequence of the development process witnessed since the beginning of planning in 1951. This is reflected in the growth rate and in the changing sectoral composition of the GDP. With the Indian economy shifting to a high growth path during the 1980s it was evident that the economy has emerged from a phase of stagnation, which has set in since the mid-1960s. However, the impressive growth performance of the 1980s was also associated with steady deterioration in a number of macroeconomic indicators.

In the early 1991, a major economic crisis surfaced in India. Most economists are now conceived that the crisis in the economy was the worst that this county had experienced since independence. However, the situation is much less unstable than it was two decades ago. Over the past two decades, the Government has followed a policy of macroeconomic stabilization and has introduced certain structural reforms. So far these policy measures have not shown any spectacular results and whether in future these neo-liberalization measures will ensure economic growth with equity cannot be said a priori.

The problems of the economy which assumed crisis proportions in 1991 did not develop suddenly. The origin of the crisis is directly attributable to the careless macro-management of the economy during the 1980s which led to large and persistent macroeconomic imbalances. The strategy of development, notwithstanding its limitations, cannot be blamed for this crisis. The widening gap between the revenue and expenditure of the Government resulted in growing fiscal deficits which had to be met by borrowings at home. Further, the steadily growing difference between the income and expenditure of the economy as a whole resulted in large current account deficits in the balance of payments which were financed by borrowings from the abroad.

The internal imbalance in the fiscal situation and the external imbalance in the payments situation were closely related, through the absence of carefulness in the macro-management of the economy. The fiscal situation, which had been under mounting pressure throughout 1980s, assumed crisis proportions by the beginning of the 1991-92. The twin crises were reflected through an unmanageable balance of payments crisis and a socially intolerably high rate of inflation that were building up in the 1980s and climaxed in 1990-91. The Gulf crisis in the late 1990s sharply accentuated macroeconomic problems. There was also political instability in the country at this juncture. All these developments together eroded international confidence in the Indian economy and as a result, this country's credit rating in the international capital market declined steeply.

However, it has to be recognized that the problems of the economy did not assume crisis proportions abruptly. These problems, in fact, were very much there for years destroying the capacity of the economy to cope with any internal or external shocks. The two OPEC shocks of 1973 and 1979 hurt, but did not have a sustained impact on the economy. The external shocks administered by the loss of remittances and the expenditures incurred to rescue workers in the aftermath of the invasion of Kuwait in August 1990 certainly accentuated the fiscal crisis at the end. But the crises was certainly 'home made'.

This was the context in which a newly elected Government took office in June 1991 and set about the difficult task of launching a programme of economic reforms. The Government initiated a programme of macroeconomic stabilization and structural adjustment with the support of the IMF and the World Bank. To some extent the urgency was derived from the gravity of the crisis because the day of reckoning could not be postponed any further. There was also the performance record of the 1980s which clearly pointed towards speeding up the pace of structural reforms while setting the fiscal house in order without any loss of time. Fiscal stabilization was begun with a view to bring about macroeconomic stabilization.

The regular budget for 1991-92 took a bold step in the direction of correcting the fiscal imbalance. It envisaged a reduction in the fiscal deficit by nearly two percentage points of GDP. This magnitude of fiscal correction can be considered unprecedented in as much as only eight months of the current fiscal year remained to accomplish the task. The budget laid stress on fiscal stabilization being supported by essential reforms in economic policy and management. While it contained proposals for raising additional revenue, most of the reduction in fiscal deficit was sought to be achieved through reduction in non-plan expenditure.

The reform process was comprehensive. The initial reforms focused on fiscal reforms, policy paradigm shift from physical control regime to the one relying more on market forces and trade related reforms. Subsequently, reforms were extended to cover financial sector and to put in place law and regulatory framework compatible with a market system. The full impact of the reform measures edges into view over a long span of time (Sarma, A. and Gupta, M., 2002). [7] In India, over the last several years, public debate with respect to fiscal policy reforms has proceeded at three distinct levels:

1. At the *microeconomic level*, where discussion has cantered on the base and structure of tax rates and the distribution of Government expenditures across alternative end uses,
2. At the *administrative level*, where concern has been expressed with respect to the quality of Government expenditures, the delivery of its services and the inefficiencies inherent within its tax collecting bureaucracies, and
3. At the *macroeconomic level*, where attention has focused on the size of the Government's fiscal deficits (and its various counterparts) and the implications this carries for real interest rates, inflation, investment and growth (Mishra, V., 2001). [8]

Fiscal reforms at the Centre covered:

- Tax reforms.
- Expenditure reforms.
- Restructuring of PSUs.
- Coordination between monetary and fiscal policies.
- Institutional measures.

The structuring of the tax system constitutes major components of fiscal reforms with the aim of augmenting revenues and removing anomalies in the tax structure. The main focus of the reform was of simplification and rationalization of both direct and indirect taxes drawing mainly from the recommendation of the Tax Reforms Committee headed by R.J. Chelliah in 1991. Since the rates were very high and structure of indirect taxes was highly complex, it was considered undesirable to augment revenues merely by raising tax rates. The Committee had recommended adoption of a small number of simple broad-based taxes with moderate and limited number of rates and with very few exemptions and reductions. Accordingly, the tax rates were significantly rationalized and progressively brought down to the levels comparable to some of the developed economies. The concern with tax rationalization has been reflected in the appointment of a number of Committees to review the tax system in the last few years.

Since 1991, several efforts have been made through the annual budget process to achieve tax reforms. These have focused on : expanding the tax base by including services (not previously taxed); reducing rates of direct taxes for individuals and corporations; abolishing most export subsidies; lowering import duties (covered below by us under structural reforms relating to trade policies/external sectors); rationalizing sales tax and reducing the cascading effect of central indirect taxes by introducing a modified value-added tax (MODVAT) and later on value-added tax (VAT); rationalizing both direct and indirect taxes by removing unnecessary exemptions; providing for tax incentives for infrastructure and export-oriented sectors, including setting up special economic zones; and simplification of procedures and efforts for improving the efficiency of the tax administration system specially through computerization.

The Central Government has included a lot of measures to curb built-in growth in expenditure and to bring about structural changes in the composition of expenditure in successive budgets during 1990s. These included subjecting all ongoing schemes to zero-based budgeting and assessment of manpower requirements of government departments. These measures, by and large, focused on downsizing government and reducing its role and administrative expenditure. The process also involved review of all subsidies with the view to introducing cost-based user charges wherever feasible, review of budgetary support to autonomous institutions and encouragement to PSUs to maximize generation of internal resources.

Further, as an institutional arrangement, the Government

also constituted an Expenditure Reforms Commission (ERC) to look into areas of expenditure correction. The ERC constituted to suggest measures for rationalizing public expenditure and made the following important recommendations which are at different stages of implementation:

1. Food subsidy should be reduced and should be allowed only to population below the poverty line. For this purpose, the State Governments should identify below poverty line population.
2. Fertilizer subsidies which have grown over the years should be withdrawn in a phased manner. This will require dismantling of the control system over time to make fertilizer industry completely decontrolled.

Since there is excess staff in the Government, for optimizing the Government staff strength, a cut of 10 percent on the staff strength as on January 1, 2000 should be carried out by the year 2004-05. There should be complete ban on creation of new posts for two years.

The public sector was originally intended to be the engine of self-sustain economic growth. It was also conceived to hold the commanding heights of the economy. In order to fulfil these roles, it was necessary for the public sector to generate adequate investible surpluses. No doubt public sector contributed significantly to the expansion of the industrial base. However, it has failed to generate sufficient internal resources for its further expansion and, as a result, has now become major constraint on economic growth.

Under structural reforms, the Government has decided to give greater managerial autonomy to public enterprises to enable them to work efficiently. On careful consideration, it becomes clear that managerial autonomy is of great importance to improve the performance of the public enterprise. During the reforms period there has been a distinct change in the public perceptions in favour of reducing the size of public sector and improving private participation. Hence, a two-pronged strategy was adopted by the Central Government—reduction in budgetary support to the PSUs and privatization of PSUs.

Another objective of the reform process has been to improve fiscal-monetary coordination. This involved steps to ensure wider participations in the Government securities market so as to facilitate elimination of automatic monetization and pre-emption of institutional resources by the Government. During the 1990s, the RBI undertook a series of steps towards widening Government securities market.

In the second half of the 1980s, when the Government had pursued expansionary fiscal policies to support growth from the deficits contributed to the foreign exchange crisis in 1991 which then prompted the far-reaching economic reforms. The combined deficit then declined until 1996-97, but increased again in the following years. Net dis-savings of general Government peaked in 2001. The Government was then absorbing almost half of the nation's saving in order to finance its own consumption outlays. In addition, the Government was borrowing to finance its investment, capital transfers and loans to state-owned enterprises.

As a result, the borrowing requirement (fiscal deficit) of State and local Governments had reached nearly 10 percent of GDP by 2001 and public debt was rising significantly. In order to end this unsustainable situation, the Central Government enacted legislation to improve fiscal discipline. After close to three years discussion, the Fiscal Responsibility and Budget Management (FRBM) Act was adopted in August 2003. This Act sets a medium-term target of achieving a balance between current revenue and current spending (i.e. a zero-revenue deficit) by 2008 and limits the overall fiscal deficit for the Central Government to 3 percent of GDP. By 2006 the Central revenue deficit had only been reduced to 2 percent of GDP, but the fiscal deficit has been reduced by 3.5 percent of GDP. The 2007 budget confirms the faster adjustment of fiscal deficit, which is only slightly greater than the target for 2008 incorporated in the FRBM Act.

However, the revenue deficit is expected to be 1.5 percent of GDP, indicating that a very sharp reduction would be necessary to meet the target of the FRBM for this balance. In effect, the Central Government has not been able to stem the increase in current expenditure as much as had been planned and, consequently, the hope–for increase in the extent of investment, which would have raised the fiscal deficit relative to the current deficit, has not materialized.

The FRBM Act also improved the transparency of budgetary policy. The Act provides that the Government has to lay three documents before parliament every year: one with an assessment of economic prospects, another with its strategy with regard to taxation and expenditure, and the final one giving a three-year rolling target for the revenue balance and the overall balance.

Fiscal reforms were the integral and perhaps the most critical part of the macroeconomic stabilization and reforms initiative taken by the Government after the 1991 economic crisis. The fiscal consolidation measures taken immediately after the crisis situation yielded significant positive results in terms of reduction in fiscal deficit, control in expenditure and marked changes in the fiscal system particularly in the financing pattern of the deficits through reduction in monetization.

However, the continued structural imbalances in terms of falling tax buoyancy, nature of fiscal correction in terms of reduction in investment expenditure, increased interest burden owing to borrowing at market related rates, impact of enhanced salary of Government employees, compulsions of increased defence expenditure etc. were some of the major factors which reversed the situation such that at the end of the decade the combine fiscal deficit of Centre and States was almost at the same level as was at the beginning of the reform measures.

The emerging situation has led economists to suggest that

the second generation of reforms should constitute a program of action aimed at preventing another major economic crisis and should stimulate rapid economic growth in the country during the new century. In fact, in the strategy outlined by the Finance Minister in his budget speech in February, 2000, declaring the next 10 years as 'India's decade of development' one of the elements is to establish a credible framework of fiscal discipline. Many economists in their surveys have even warned that unless substantial fiscal consolidation is achieved continued fiscal deficits pose India's greatest risk to future destabilization (Deshmukh, H., Chaudhari, K., Powar, Y., Parhar, A and Shejwal, A., 2006). [9]

To sum up, the need for comprehensive fiscal reforms in India was apparent during the late 1980s, as there was rapid deterioration in Government finances. During this period, the expenditure of the Central Government rose much faster than its revenue leading to a steep rise in the Centre's fiscal deficit to GDP ratio. The sharp increase in revenue deficit of the Central Government and the emergence of such deficits in State finances happened to be the most worrisome developments in the fiscal scenario during the 1980s.

Economic and fiscal reforms undertaken from the early nineties brought fresh air and released clogged up economic energies. Growth rates accelerated and the economy went through a major structural shift in the composition of output. The poverty ratio fell tangibly in the high growth years. If there is one vulnerable part of these otherwise sound developments, it is the disarray in the fiscal scenario. Comprehensive economic and fiscal reforms were initiated in the early nineties leading to a substantial rise in the overall growth rate by the mid-nineties. The nineties witnessed momentous changes in the macroeconomic scenario of India in terms of economic growth, changes in the sectoral composition of output, public finances, and the overall policy environment that characterized and influenced the macroeconomic outcomes.

Towards the close of the decade, reforms appeared to have slowed down even as industrial recession seriously beset the economy for three consecutive years towards the end of the decade. Several events in the latter part of the nineties clouded the gains from the fiscal reforms of the initial years, leading the public finances of the Centre as well as the States to exhibit chronic imbalances showing themselves up in the form of large revenue and fiscal deficits. Important among these was the revision of salaries of Central and State Government employees in the wake of the recommendations of the Fifth Central Pay Commission.

A second reason was a substantial rise in the nominal and real interest rates, with low inflation rate. A third reason was the onset of recession that led to a fall in Government revenues relative to GDP and large fiscal imbalances, with Government expenditures adjusting much less than revenues. The new crisis led to new responses. The Centre and many State Governments emerged with fiscal responsibility legislations and medium term adjustment programmes.

End Notes

1. Hicks, U.K. (1968), Public Finance, Cambridge Economic Handbook, 3rd edition, p. 274.
2. Hicks, U.K. (1965), Development Finance, Planning and Control, Clarendon Press Oxford, pp. 61-62.
3. Kumar, N. and Mittal, R. (2002), Public Finance: Theory and Practice, Anmol Publication Pvt Ltd., New Delhi, pp. 167-168.
4. Mohan, Rakesh (2008), "Growth Record of the Indian Economy, 1950-2008: A Story of Sustained Savings and Investment", *EPW*, May 10, pp. 61-62.
5. Mohan, R. (2008), *op.cit.*, p. 62.
6. Prasad, C.S. (2005), "The Centrality of Fiscal Adjustment" in C.S. Prasad (ed.) *India: Economic Policies and Performance*, New Century Publications, New Delhi, pp. 53-55.
7. Sarma, A. and Gupta, M. (2002), "A Decade of Fiscal Reforms in India", International Studies Program, Working Paper 02-04, Georgia State University, Andrew Young School of Policy Studies.

8. Mishra, V (2001), "Fiscal Deficit and Fiscal Responsibility Act", Economic and Political Weekly, February, Mumbai, p. 609.
9. Deshmukh, H., Chaudhari, K. and Powar, Y., and Shejwal, A. (2006), Fiscal Consolidation in India, www.it.iitb.ac.in.

2

Studies on Fiscal Policy: A Review

Tripathi, R.N. (1966) [1] in his study of tax structure in developing countries opined that the high rates of taxes on commodities with a high income elasticity of demand are quite effective in siphoning a substantial proportion of increase in output into the resources of the public sector needed for development financing and a stiff rate of commodity taxes on luxury articles tends to introduce an element of progressiveness in an otherwise predominantly regressive tax structure in developing countries.

Chelliah, R.J. (1969) [2] in his study of fiscal policy attempted to analyze the fundamental problems of fiscal policy in less developed countries, the basic structure of public finance with emphasis on tax structure and fiscal policies, against the background of planned economic development. The greater part of his work is carried on with special reference to India. He has also observed that the fiscal policy appropriate for a country will depend, apart from many other factors, on the stage of its development and on the social grounds.

Jain, M.M. (1969) [3] is of the view that the Indian tax structure was found to be highly buoyant with respect to income. Analysing the tax yields through log linear functions for the period 1955-56 to 1965-66, he found that while the buoyancy co-efficients were greater than unity for both direct and indirect taxes, indirect taxes had a much higher co-efficient than direct taxes, reflecting the tax efforts which were largely in the form of commodity taxes or taxes on transactions. However, a tax-wise analysis showed corporation tax to have the highest co-efficient of buoyancy. The built-in flexibility of the tax system was also found to be high which is attributed to the additional taxes imposed during the Second and Third Five-Year Plans.

Musgrave, R.A. (1969) [4] in his study of fiscal policy examined the essential characteristics of fiscal system in the content of certain key features of economic life. His study deals with the adoption of fiscal systems to the requirement of centrally planned and decentralized market economy. He also examined the interaction between fiscal systems and economic development and compared the tax structure of a number of highly developed countries. In his study he also raised the issues like fiscal centralization versus decentralization, the formulation of a budget plan, the impact of government forms on fiscal behaviour, social security and transfer systems, and the structure and management of public debt.

Shaws, G.K. (1981) [5] in his study of the concept of fiscal policy in developing countries suggested a relatively homogeneous body of fiscal instruments applicable to such countries and perhaps more important that public finance and fiscal policy in developing economies constitute an academic discipline distinct from its counterpart in the more advanced economy. Both notions are certainly false, the former being contradicted by the greater diversity in conditions pertaining to third world countries when compared with the more integrated advanced economies, whilst the latter encounters the objection that policy objectives, fiscal instruments and both political and administrative constraints are in principal the same.

Gowda, K.V. (1987) [6] in his work has criticized the long term fiscal policy (LTFP) that it has placed exclusive reliance not on fiscal policy with all its various segments. It does not touch on expenditure policy, monetary policy, debt management and international economic policy but on tax policy.

In his study, he explains how fiscal policy instruments are to be integrated with all other instruments of macro-economic policy in order to realize the desired results and underlines the complications of pursuing fiscal policy in isolation.

On the issue of tax elasticity, Shome (1988) [7] found the tax system to be lacking the design that would automatically yield higher tax revenue with growth in gross domestic product. He felt that in the event of low tax elasticity, even the discretionary measures may fail to evoke the desired response in the form of improvement in tax-GDP ratio. According to him, the improvement in tax elasticity would call for expansion of coverage, a regular adjustment in rates on inflation and reasonable progressively in the system as a whole. Removal of various exemptions in income tax would be critical for improving elasticity. For tax on goods and services, a broad-based general sales tax or value added tax would yield a higher elasticity.

Singh, S.K. (1988) [8] examined the nature of the fiscal crisis in India and evaluated long-term fiscal policy (LTFP) as a response to this crisis. The study explains that since 1975-76, the tax ratio has kept pace with the expenditure ratio resulting in the long run imbalance between Government revenues and expenditures. This gap which widened during the Sixth Plan became much larger during the Seventh Plan. Thus, the Central Government has to borrow even to meet its current expenditure. His analysis indicates that the LTFP, as a response to the challenging problem of fiscal crisis, has failed to offer any clear direction in two vital areas, namely: (i) how to restrain the increase in non-plan expenditure on revenue account, and (ii) how to augment the surpluses of PSUs. Finally, he has warned that without proper advance in these areas the fiscal crisis will persist.

Rakshit, M. (1991) [9] in his work studied the fiscal roots of macroeconomic imbalance in India, and found that during 1980, fiscal imbalance assumed alarming proportions due to widening gap between revenue and expenditure. In his work he has discussed macro-economic adjustment programme introduced by the government to resolve the fiscal crisis. Finally, he raises a number of important issues regarding viability of fiscal management.

Buiter and Patel (1992) [10] found the state of Indian public finance to be perilous. They observed the rising trend in public debt as ratio to GNP and also in monetized deficit. This disturbing trend, as they found, started in 1970s but accelerated significantly in 1980s. They also make it clear that this deterioration cannot be explained in terms of some external shocks like OPEC I and OPEC II (when oil prices were increased substantially in early 1970s and late 1970s) and 1990 Iraqi occupation of Kuwait and subsequent war. They blame public sector for the crises. Far from being a channel for mobilizing national saving and stimulating domestic capital formation, the public sector has become a drain on nation's investable resources. Public consumption growth has steadily out paced the growth of current revenue.

Mundle and Rao (1992) [11] analyzed the nature of fiscal crisis in India in 1990 and related issues in the growth and composition of public expenditure, the tax system and mobilization of tax revenues and non-tax revenues. They have shown that the fiscal imbalance was mainly a reflection of the increasing gap between revenue receipts and revenue expenditure. There was a spurt in spending mainly on account of interest payments, subsidies, plan and non-plan grants to State Governments, defence and failure of public sector undertakings etc. on the other hand, the growth of tax and non-tax revenues was stagnated. Finally, they have endorses the fiscal stabilization measures initiated in 1991.

Buiter and Patel (1993) [12] basically updated their earlier analysis (Buiter and Patel 1992) and extended the period of it up to 1992-93. They concluded that considering the magnitude of the crises the fiscal correction measures were insufficient. Debt-GDP ratio would continue to rise. They calculate that a permanent increase of primary surplus to about 4.5 percent of GDP is required for the stabilization of debt-GDP ratio, which demands both revenue enhancement and expenditure control. To achieve this, it recommends the widening of tax base for both direct and indirect tax. On expenditure side, they emphasized the pruning of Government wage bill, food and fertilizer subsidies and subsidies to public sector enterprises. They opine that currently implemented food subsidies normally benefit other than those who are subject to malnutrition or under- nourishment. Therefore, target-oriented subsidies should be used as anti-poverty instrument.

Chhibber and Mansoor Dailama (1993) [13] argued for a need for a broader approach to the relationship between fiscal policy and private investment in developing countries. Such an approach needs to emphasize the role of fiscal policy and stabilization, the competitiveness between public and private investment and the taxation of income from capital. While these issues have long been recognized in the literature in the context of both developed and developing countries, they have assumed particular urgency and importance in the context of the ongoing liberalisation and privatization trends evident in most developing countries.

Cornia and Stewart (1993) [14] reviewed changes in the fiscal policy of developing countries undergoing economic adjustment during 1980s. Macro choices in the areas of overall taxation, government expenditure and fiscal deficit are first examined. It appears that although a few countries managed to combine raising government expenditure per head and a falling budget deficit thanks to increase in the ratio and/or to overall growth, in the majority of the countries analyzed, traditional fiscal policy emphasizing rapid reductions in budget deficit through expenditure reductions compounded the negative effects of falling incomes on the welfare of the poor. Finally, they concluded that the main elements of fiscal policy approach are aiming at protecting the poor during adjustment.

De Melo Martha (1993) [15] proposed the use of a sustainable deficit concept to estimate the minimum fiscal adjustment required in a high debt country. The sustainable deficit is defined to be compatible with a sustainable debt, which the borrower is willing and able to service. His work provides empirical estimates of the need for fiscal adjustment in a small group of high debt countries in the mid 1980s. Their experience is compared to that of small group of low debt countries to distinguish the differences in the adjustment required and its determinants during this period. The results illustrate the extent to which the appropriate size of fiscal deficit depends on the macro-economic content.

Faini, R. and Jaime (1993) [16] take a look at the evidence of fiscal adjustment in developing countries. They found that, while on an average, developing countries were successful after 1985 in cutting their primary deficits, rising interest costs and stagnant fiscal revenues implied limited progress towards reducing fiscal imbalances. Most of the improvement on the fiscal front was achieved by cut in capital expenditures. Then they have focused on issues such as the size of fiscal adjustment, the macroeconomic impact of deficit reduction and choice between expenditure cut and tax increases.

Gulati (1993) [17] dealt with some questions concerning the growing burden of internal public debt in India. These questions that have lately been raised with a stridency not noticed before focus on reducing the fiscal deficit, a term that hardly ever figured in the lexicon of fiscal policy in India.

Kapila, U. (1993) [18] in her analysis of public finances of India opined that the fiscal policy situation which was under strain throughout the 1980s, reached a critical situation in 1990-91. Throughout the 1980s, all the indicators of fiscal imbalances were on the rise. The unabated growths of non-plan expenditure and poor returns from investments made in the public sector have been the main contributory factor in the fiscal crisis. Government initiated the fiscal stabilization and intended to continue it. She has also suggested that for the realization of the fiscal stabilization, it is imperative to restrain the rise of expenditures. Fiscal discipline is also necessary on the part of PSEs to hasten the process of fiscal correction.

Mookherjee, D. (1993) [19] analyzed the fiscal stabilization reforms in the Indian economy. In this work, he has highlighted that at the term of the eighties into the nineties, serious action on the fiscal front was urgently needed to correct the macro-economic imbalances. The principal instruments of fiscal stabilization in 1991-92 were plan expenditure and subsidies on exports and fertilizers. Disinvestment of equity holding in central public sector enterprises also provided a cushion. Initially government succeeded in its determined effort at fiscal stabilization and brought the fiscal deficit down.

Mundle and Hiranya Mukhopadhyay (1993) [20] in their study analyzed the impact of alternative fiscal policies on macro-economic performance of the Indian economy. The most important lesson emerged from their work is that in reducing the deficit, greater revenue mobilization would be preferable to expenditure compression. This should be attempted through tax reform rather than raising rates. There are, however, limits to how far tax reforms can raise the buoyancy of tax revenue. Hence, fiscal correction will have to depend in part on public expenditure compression. They have shown that in the post-reforms period expenditure on almost all items except interest payments have been cut in real terms. However, the sharpest cuts have fallen on those items of expenditure which ought to be protected.

Tanzi, V. (1993) [21] observed that fiscal reform has proven difficult to implement for political, institutional and conceptual reasons. In his work he has discussed the determination of the correct size of the fiscal adjustment needed, the problems in measuring fiscal disequilibrium, the desired fiscal measures and the sequencing of the required fiscal reforms. Finally, he argues that fiscal reform require time to be successful.

Taylor, L. (1993) [22] attempted to study fiscal policy issues that arise during macroeconomic stabilization in developing countries. His work is based on the study of stabilization episodes in eighteen countries. He observed that the effects of fiscal stabilization and adjustment on income distribution are less clear cut and stabilization programme should take into account specific country conditions.

Thirsk, W.R. (1993) [23] observed that many countries have overhauled their tax systems during the past decade. His work reviews the profile of a typical developing country tax system prior to recent wave of reforms. A detailed description of tax reforms in several developing countries is presented. Comparisons across countries indicate an emerging consensus on the desirable characteristic of a tax system: neutrality and the adoption of a more uniform system of taxation, the progressive abandonment of special tax distinctions and exemption and simple tax design.

Bagchi and Stern (1994) [24] noted that the early results of fiscal policy were quite striking. Breaking out of the stagnation of the preceding fifty years Indian economy grew about 4 percent per annum in the first two plan periods. Per capita income grew at 1.8 to 2 percent. But this momentum was not maintained. What was more, financing of public sector proved increasingly difficult, leading to larger and larger recourse to market borrowing and deficit financing (borrowings from the central bank) with all their attendant consequences. Before the decade of 1980s had drawn to a close, it was evident that the Government budgeting in India was in a crisis. Apparent reason for the imbalance in Indian public finances was not other than the faster growth of Government expenditure than the revenues.

Thus, a fiscal correction was inevitable. Although the move towards fiscal adjustment in India was discernible in the pronouncements made as part of long term fiscal policy announced in the mid 1980s, a comprehensive fiscal reforms programme at the Central Government level was initiated only at the beginning of the 1990s as part of the economic adjustment programme initiated in 1991-92. The fiscal reforms were aimed to achieve a reduction in the size of fiscal deficit and debt in relation to GDP and were affected through rationalization of tax structure expenditure pruning, restructuring of PSUs and better coordination between monetary and fiscal policies.

Shand Ric and Kalirajan (1994) [25] in their study indicated that the reforms implemented in India since 1991-92 have been yielding the anticipated positive results. Though the reform process has been gradual, it is becoming increasingly clear that sustainability is not in question. The study concludes that Indian economy may be evolving a new paradigm of growth which could be relevant to other developing countries with similar structural linkages.

Bhattacharya (1995) [26] in his work evaluated the factors responsible for fiscal imbalance in 1990 and analyzed the performance of fiscal stabilization measures. He has shown that the basic problem of the fiscal stabilization in India was that the government expenditure was rising faster than the government income. As a result all the measures of deficit such as fiscal deficit, revenue deficit, primary deficit, etc. have rising trends. Finally, he suggested that the fiscal deficit should be reduced by slowing down growth of non-plan and wasteful expenditures on the one hand and improving direct tax revenue and surplus of public enterprises on the other.

Ghosh and Sen (1995) [27] observed in their study that during 1980s not only the revenue receipt have been rather inelastic but the expenditure accounts particularly of the non-plan outlays have also gone up quite rapidly. This has been termed by them as the main cause of the fiscal imbalance. They have also suggested that it requires to be attended with policies to reduce the non-plan expenditure drastically.

Rao, Sen and Ghosh (1995) [28] analyzed in their study that after 1980-81, expenditure growth was higher than that of revenue receipt. Within total expenditure, revenue expenditure grew at rates higher than that of capital expenditure. Growth of revenue expenditure was particularly sharp in the case of interest payments, subsidies, wages and salaries, while those on maintenance of capital assets lagged behind. So fiscal imbalance became inevitable by the end of 1980s. The analysis also points towards the difficulty in achieving fiscal equilibrium in the short and medium term context. So long as the interest groups succeed in securing a large and increasing share of expenditures on categories beneficial to them compression of fiscal deficit become difficult.

Nayak (1995) [29] in his work revealed that in the fiscal sector, government expenditure had been far outpacing revenues for more than a decade, leading the government to resort to substantial borrowings, both internal and external. As a result interest payments become largest expenditure head of the Central Government budget. Non-essential expenditure continues to grow unabated. He has also observed that the tax to GDP ratio is already reasonably high and the prospect of increasing it further appears to be limited at least in the short run. So, there is not much choice left and expenditures have to be cut in several vital areas.

Mc dermott, John and Wescott (1996) [30] in their study tried to use the fiscal expansion and consolidation experiences of the industrial countries over the period 1970 to 1995 to examine the interplay between fiscal adjustments and economic performance. A key finding is that fiscal consolidation need not trigger an economic slowdown, especially over the medium-term. Fiscal consolidation that concentrates on the expenditure sides, especially transfers and government wages, is more likely to succeed in reducing the public debt ratio than tax-based consolidation. Also, the greater the magnitude of the fiscal consolidation, the more likely it is to succeed in reducing the debt ratio.

Chakraborty (1997) [31] attempted to examine whether lowering the rates of direct and indirect taxes in recent years has resulted in higher tax mobilization. The study concludes that compared to indirect taxes, direct taxes were more buoyant during the post-reform period. It has been observed by the author that generally reduction in tax rate cannot make a tax more buoyant instantly. There is a time lag involved.

Shome (1997) [32] attempted to assess the state of fiscal

stabilization in the post-reforms period.

He has shown that after an initial improvement in the fiscal deficit, the government faced difficulty in controlling the fiscal deficit-GDP ratio.

The tax-GDP ratio also declined and the Central Government passed down certain expenditure responsibilities to State governments, thereby managing to reduce the expenditure-GDP ratio to some extent.

His work focuses on the performance of the fiscal sector and the direction for future policy imperatives.

Mohan (2000) [33] analyzed the trends in State and Central Government revenues and expenditures and suggested ways to climb out of debt trap.

He has observed that rapid economic growth is the only solution to the problem of poverty and such growth is not possible without significant fiscal correction.

The key objective of fiscal reform has to be a reduction in public debt service payments.

Rao, M. Govinda (2000) [34] advocated that there have been major changes in tax systems in several countries over the last two decades for a variety of reasons. The objective of his study is to analyze the evolution of the tax system in India since the early 1990s.

He describes and assesses the introduction of new forms of direct and indirect taxes, their revenue and equity implications and the successes achieved in their implementation. He concludes that after eight years of reforms, improving the tax system remains a major challenge in India.

Rakshit (2000) [35] is a critique of the whole approach of fiscal policy pursued during 1990s. He points out that adverse effects of it could be found in many macroeconomic variable like declining aggregate capital formation and stagnant saving, low agricultural growth alongside sharp fluctuations in food output, deceleration of industrial growth during second half of 1990s and ultimately the rise in fiscal deficit itself. He also argued that not only deficits, but revenue and expenditure also need to be redefined for the specific purposes as they generate different effects on different macro variables.

For example, he favours the expenditure and health to be taken out from revenue expenditure and receipts from disinvestments cannot be equated with tax revenue as former reduces the future non-tax receipts. He thus argues that 'Fiscal Gap' rather than fiscal deficit is the better measure for measuring sustainability of public debt. It is also critical of the shift in financing the deficit towards high interest borrowing instruments.

Kopits, G. (2001) [36] assessed the potential usefulness of fiscal policy rules for India in the light of rapidly growing international experience in this area. As part of his assessment, he explores various design options and institutional arrangements that seem relevant for India in the context of the Fiscal Responsibility and Budget Management Bill. He also outlines preparatory step for successful implementation.

Karnik, A. (2002) [27] addressed the question that can fiscal policy play a key role in the revival of the economy? He argued that the problem is that this question has had to be posed in the context of deteriorating fiscal balances of the Centre and the States, whose combined deficit is today slightly worse after 10 years of reform. The States' gross fiscal deficit has deteriorated significantly. It is absolutely necessary, therefore, for the Centre to be fiscally prudent, which will be a signal to the states of the Centre's seriousness in regard to fiscal management. A contrary signal will undermine any restraint that the Centre can bring to bear on the States.

Peter, M., Kerr, I. and Thorpe, M (2002) [38] in their study said that the tax reforms of recent years in India are based on Chelliah's recommendations of simple broad-based taxes with a moderate and limited number of rates. The reduction in direct tax rates in the economy has not only increased revenue collection but also accelerated economic growth. Their aim is to investigate the effect of India's tax policy on private capital formation. A time series analysis of data for the economy for the period 1950-51 to 1994-95 reveals that a one percent increase in the direct tax ratio has led to a reduction of 0.12 percent in the ratio of private capital formation to GDP. They also examine whether there is any gain in opting for an expenditure tax to promote savings and capital formation in the economy. The major problem facing the Indian direct tax system is evasion of income taxes. They concluded that an expenditure tax is powerful tool to combat evasion.

Sarma, A. and Gupta, M. (2002) [39] in their paper opined that the year 1991-92 was one of the toughest years for the Indian economy. All the macroeconomic indicators became adverse. The overall economic growth slumped to a mere 1.1 percent. The gross fiscal deficit stood at 8 percent of the GDP and the revenue deficit on the current account at 3.5 percent in 1990-91. Prices shot up to 17 percent, an all time high level. In the external sector, the balance of payments with as little as US$ 1.1 billion foreign exchange reserves or barely enough to meet two weeks' import bill became precarious.

The shortage of foreign exchange apart from inducing import squeeze for industrial production led the country by June 1991 to face a hard option of defaulting on international commitments such as debt servicing or accepting IMF structural adjustment and stabilization programme. The new government decided to adopt in June 1991 programme of macroeconomic stabilization to restore viability to fiscal balances and the balance of payments and to contain prices. At the same time it undertook a far reaching programme of structural reforms involving bold initiatives in external trade, exchange rate, industrial policy and so on, higher growth trajectory through infusing efficiency and international competitiveness.

It also aimed at integrating the Indian economy with the global system and enhancing its robustness through wider access to better technology and benchmarking with the global performer. The reform process was relying more on market forces and trade related reforms. Subsequently, reforms were extended to cover financial sector and to put in place law and regulatory framework compatible with a market system. The full impact of the reform measures edges into view over a long span of time. Nevertheless, a decade since the introduction of the reform process is a long enough period to make visible the results of the reform measures.

It is in this background that this paper addresses itself to a vital area of reforms, viz., fiscal reforms. It attempts to evaluate the impact of fiscal reforms on the public finances of the Union and State governments. The paper starts with the outcome of the reform process as reflected in different measures of balances and then proceeds to examine the performance of the process variables that determine the aggregate balances. To form a view of the effectiveness of fiscal reforms, they have examined the performance of some of the important fiscal variables in an inter-temporal context. To be more specific, they have compared the performance of fiscal variables in the post-reform decades with that of the proceeding decades.

Bhattacharya, B. and Sabyasachi, Kar (2004) [40] examined the nature of relationship between aggregate economic growth and fiscal and external balances in the Indian economy. Acceleration in aggregate GDP growth can lead to worsening of fiscal deficit which is to be financed by other sources. Investment and productivity capital is further prerequisites for acceleration of GDP. This study examined the inter-linkages between the production sector, the fiscal and external sectors.

Lahiri, Ashok and Kaman (2004) [41] in their study examined the sustainability of fiscal deficits, the differences between monetary versus debt financing of fiscal deficits, the increasing importance of revenue deficits. According to them, high fiscal deficits are not exclusive to India but high sustained deficit are quite unique, especially in the content of relative stability of the external balance of payments. The authors allude to two factors to explain sustainability: that the interest rate has been more or less consistently below the rate of growth of nominal GDP and the deficit has been mostly financed domestically rather than through external savings.

Mohan, R. (2004) [42] in his paper examined the trends in Central finances over a three decadal period beginning from the 1970s. It is found that there is lack of buoyancy in all the major sources of revenue of the Central Government. This calls for devising new methods of revenue mobilization. There are political economic limits to the premise that direct taxes with its simplified rate structure and administrative reforms will make good the losses from the cuts in customs duty revenue. The analysis of the issues involved would require an examination of the influence of dominant classes on the State. Very recently however, the thrust of the tax reform seems to be on introduction of a Central value-added tax (VAT).

Total expenditure of the Central Government as a proportion of the gross domestic product (GDP) has not increased during the 1990s when compared to the 1980s. But the composition of expenditure has shifted more towards revenue expenditure. An emphasis on expenditure allocation with targeting at a detailed level and innovative tax reforms aimed at more revenue mobilization are necessary to achieve qualitative fiscal correction, but this is often stymied for political economic reasons. Procrustean fiscal correction aiming merely at deficit targeting is not a very desirable method. His study finds that the main problem in achieving fiscal consolidation at the Central level is falling revenue and tax receipts during the 1990s.

C. Rangarajan (2004) [43] Chairman of the Twelfth Finance Commission, Government of India, emphasized on current fiscal situation, fiscal deficit and its adverse impact on the economy. Raising debt results in raising interest payments, fall in the growth rate of development expenditure, serious implications of balance of payments and low investment. Debt-GDP ratio is needed to be reduced and tax-GDP ratio has to be picked up considerably by introducing VAT. Raising revenues for accelerated flow of development expenditures are leading to improved socio-economic growth.

Raju, S. (2004) [44] in her study examined that deficits measure the excess of government spending over revenues and reflect the fiscal health of an economy. Fiscal consolidation has been the focus of the reform process initiated in 1991-92. Fiscal reforms have seen tax reforms, rationalization and restructuring of the tax structure to augment revenues as well as expenditure management which in turn can influence deficit containment. Interdependence between revenues and expenditures can lead to ambiguous impact on deficit and the efforts to contain the deficit. Our results indicate bi-directional causality between total government expenditures and tax revenues and revenue receipts. Instantaneous causality is observed for all variants of revenue.

Rakshit, M. (2005) [45] attempted to examine some analytics and empirics of fiscal restructuring in India. The study concluded that TFC's focus on growth as a key element of its fiscal reform strategy is well taken. Also eminently sensible are its recommendation for performance budgeting; doing away with the distinction between plan and non-plan expenditure; and transparency including elimination of all hidden subsidies. However, the major weakness of the strategy consist of not dovetailing demand management policies in a developmental programme; ignoring the saving-generating impact of investment in an economy where rural and informal sectors are characterized by considerable underutilization of resources even while the formal sector may not have much slack; treating education, health and other social sector expenditures as current; and absence of optimality considerations in respect of allocation of expenditures, and of alternative modes of their financing, taking into account their short- and long-term effect on growth, equity and government finances.

Bagchi, A. (2006) [46] is of the view that deficit reduction has had the adverse fallout for public spending on health and education in several states, forcing shrinkage of the public sector's involvement in the social sector. Policy-makers are now seeking an escape route by getting the fiscal and revenue deficit targets relaxed. While there can be valid arguments against inflexible targets, abandoning the discipline underlying fiscal responsibility legislation, as has been suggested, is questionable. For, at base, the fiscal problems of democracies have their origin in the short time horizon of governments and their penchant for promising the moon to electorate while showing an extreme reluctance to tax.

Kochhar, K. (2006) [47] examined both the evolution of India's fiscal imbalances since the early 1990s and the key developments in major macroeconomic variables—inflation, external balances, interest rates, and growth—in order to assess the macroeconomic implications of the growing fiscal imbalances and rising public debt-GDP ratio reflects a weakening in revenue mobilization, persistent deficits at both the Central and State levels and narrowing of the gap between the real interest and growth rate. Deficits of the States have become increasingly large relative to that of the Central Government.

After exploring why fiscal imbalances have not led to serious macroeconomic problems, she then explores their hidden costs on the economy in terms of the foregone potential for even higher economic growth than that has recently been experienced. In effects, by its high fiscal deficits, productive public expenditure has been crowed out, the scope for further structural reforms and liberalization has been constrained, and room for macroeconomic policy manoeuvre has been narrowed. Kochhar argues that time is running out for India to address these fiscal imbalances in a way that does not result in enhanced vulnerability to macroeconomic crisis. She advocates stronger revenue mobilization efforts and a reorientation of expenditure away from subsidies and toward physical and social infrastructure projects.

Rao, M., Govinda and Singh, Nirvikar (2006) [48]

examined recent and potential reforms in India's fiscal federal system. They summarized key federal institution in India, including tax and expenditure assignments, and mechanisms for Centre-State transfers. They discuss the institutional process by which reforms can and do take place, including the role of academics, political influences, and especially institutions such as the Finance Commission. In contrast to the past, recent Commissions have played a greater role in articulating an agenda for fiscal federal reform, which then proceeds through political bargaining. This change has taken place in the context of broader economic reforms in India.

Gurria, A. (2007) [49] examined areas of government spending, taxation and fiscal federalism where further reforms are desirable to reduce economic distortions and improve the provision of public services. As to government spending, it finds that a large share is used to subsidize commercial undertakings, agriculture and food distribution and that there is much room to improve the quality of spending and target it better to reduce poverty. On taxes, which have undergone major reforms since the early 1990s, it points to the large number of loopholes and suggest that a broadening of the tax bases would allow further reductions in tax rates and make the system simpler and more efficient.

Reforms of indirect taxes should focus on creating a common market within India so that goods can move between States without border controls. India's federal structure has led to a well-developed system of tax-sharing and transfers, both through constitutionally empowered bodies and delivered through the annual budget. Overall, this transfer system has worked well; moving resources towards the poorest States, but the system has become very complex and, in the past, weakened fiscal discipline. Furthermore, it has not been able to create an effective local government system; this would be important for improving account ability and responsiveness to citizen needs as three-quarters of the population live in States with over 50 million inhabitants.

Mohan, R. (2008) [50] in his paper opined that the performance of the Indian economy in recent years has attracted increasing international interest. His paper focuses on the role of fiscal and monetary policies in the evolution of the Indian economy over the years, with particular attention being given to the reforms undertaken in these policies since the early 1990s. The coordination of fiscal and monetary policies has been crucial in the sequencing of the economic reform process carried out since the early 1990s. Monetary policy aims to maintain a judicious balance between price stability and economic growth. With the opening up of the Indian economy and the spread of financial sector reforms aimed at functional autonomy, prudential strengthening, operational efficiency, and competitiveness of banks, considerations of financial stability have assumed greater importance in recent years alongside the increasing openness of the Indian economy. The biggest challenge facing the conduct of fiscal and monetary policy in India is to continue the accelerated growth process while maintaining price and financial stability.

Therefore, the self-imposed rule-based fiscal correction at both the national and sub national level has to be consolidated and carried forward. The existence of a high level of fiscal deficit also contributes to the persistence of an interest rate differential with the rest of the world, which then also constrains progress toward full capital account convertibility. The success achieved in revenue buoyancy through tax rationalization and compliance has to be strengthened further.

End Notes

1. Tripathy, R.N. (1966), *Public Finance in Developing Countries*, The World Press, Calcutta, p. 200.
2. Chelliah, R.J. (1969), *Fiscal Policy in Under-Developed Countries*, George Allen and Unwin (India) Pvt. Ltd, Bombay, p. 17.
3. Jain, M.M (1969), "Income Elasticity of Indian Tax Structure: 1955-56 to 1965-66", *Economic and Political Weekly*, May 3, Mumbai.
4. Musgrave, R.A. (1969), *Fiscal Systems*, Yale University Press,

London.

5. Shaw, G.K. (1981), "Leading Issues of Tax Policy in Developing Countries: The Economic Problems", in A. Peacock and F. Forte (ed.) *The Political Economy of Taxation,* Blackwell, Oxford, p.148.
6. Gowda, K.V. (1987), *Fiscal Revolution in India: A Macroeconomic Analysis of Long-Term Fiscal Policy,* Indus Publishing Company, New Delhi.
7. Shome, Parthasarthy (1988), "On the Elasticity of Developing Country Tax System", *Economic and Political Weekly*, August 20, Mumbai.
8. Singh, S.K. (1988), "Long-Term Fiscal Policy and The Fiscal Crisis" in R.K. Sinha (ed.) *Long-Term Fiscal Policy and Planning in India*, Deep and Deep Publications, New Delhi.
9. Rakshit, M. (1991), "The Macro-economic Adjustment Programme: A Critique", *Economic and Political Weekly,* Aug.24, Mumbai, pp. 1977-1988.
10. Buiter, W.H. and Patel (1992), "Debt, Deficit and Inflation: An Application to the Public Finance in India", *Journal of Economics,* Vol. 47, March.
11. Mundle, S. and M.G. Rao (1992), "Issues in Fiscal Policy", *NIFP (mimeo),* New Delhi.
12. Buiter, W.H. and Patel (1993), "Indian Public Finance in 1990s: Challenges and Prospects", *World Bank Working Paper*, Washington, D.C.
13. Chhibber, A. and Mansoor Dailami (1993), "Fiscal Policy and Private Investment in Developing Countries: Recent Evidence on Key Select Issues", in Faini, R. and J. de Melo (ed.) *Fiscal Issues in Adjustment in Developing Countries*, St. Martin's Press, New York.
14. Cornia, G.A. and F. Stewart (1993), "The Fiscal System, Adjustment and The Poor", in Faini, R. and J. de Melo (ed.) *Fiscal Issues in Adjustment in Developing Countries,* St. Martin's Press, and New York.
15. De Melo M. (1993),"Fiscal Adjustment in High Debt Countries", in Faini, R. and J. de Melo (ed.) *Fiscal Issues in Adjustment in Developing Countries*, St. Martin's Press, New York.
16. Faini, R. and J. de Melo (1993), "Fiscal Issues in Adjustment: An Introduction", in Faini, R. and J. de Melo (eds.) *Fiscal Issues*

in Adjustment in Developing Countries, St. Martin, Press, New York.

17. Gulati, I.S. (1993), "Tackling the Growth Burden of Public Debt", *Economic and Political Weekly*, May1, Mumbai, pp. 883-886.
18. Kapila, U. (ed.) (1993), *Recent Development in Indian Economy with Special Reference to Structural Reform*, Academic Foundation, Delhi.
19. Mookherji, D. (1993), "*New* Economic Policies", *NIPFP (mimeo),* New Delhi.
20. Mundle, S. and H. Mukhopadhyay (1993), "Stabilization and the Control of Government Expenditure in India", *NIPFP*, New Delhi.
21. Tanzi, V. (1993), "Fiscal Issues in Adjustment Programs", in Faini, R. and J. de Melo (ed.) *Fiscal Issues in Adjustment in Developing Countries*, St. Martin's Press, New Delhi.
22. Taylor, L. (1993), "Fiscal Issues in Macroeconomic Stabilization: A Structuralist Perspective", in Faini, R. and J. de Melo (ed.) *Fiscal Issues in Adjustment in Developing Countries,* St. Martin Press, New York.
23. Thirsk, W.R. (1993), "Recent Experience with Tax Reform in Developing Countries", in Faini, R. and J. de Melo (ed.)*Fiscal Issues in Adjustment in Developing Countries*, St. Martin's Press, New York.
24. Bagchi, A. and N. Stern (1994), *Introduction in Tax Policy and Planning in Developing Countries,* Oxford University Press, Delhi.
25. Shand, R. and K.P. Kalirajan (1994), "India's Economic Reforms: Towards a New Paradigm?", *Economic Division Working Papers No.94/1, Research School of Pacific and Asian Studies,* Australia.
26. Bhaattacharya, B.B. (1995), "Fiscal Management: Key Issues and Policy Options", in *Fiscal Management and Fiscal Discipline in India in Recent Years*, IIDS, The New Book Stall, Calcutta.
27. Ghosh, A. and R.K. Sen (1995), "Fiscal Management: Issues and Policy Option", in *Fiscal Management and Fiscal Discipline in India in Recent Years*, IIDS, The New Book Stall, Calcutta.
28. Rao, M.G., T.K. Sen and M. Ghosh (1995), "Uneven Growth of Government Expenditure in India: An Analysis of the Trends

between 1974-75 and 1990-91", *Journal of Indian School of Political Economy*, April-June, pp. 256-276.
29. Nayak, P.B. (1995), "Some Key Issues in India's Recent Economic Crisis", in *Fiscal Management and Fiscal Discipline in India, IIDS*, The New Book Stall, Calcutta.
30. Mc Demott, C. Johan and Robert F. Wescott (1996), "An Empirical Analysis of Fiscal Adjustments", *IMF Staff Papers,* Vol. 43, No. 4, December.
31. Chakraborti, P. (1997), "Tax Reduction and their Revenue Implications: How Valid is the Laffer Curve?" , in *Economic and Political Weekly*, April 26, Mumbai, pp. 887-890.
32. Shome, P. (1997), "A Critical Assessment of the Public Finances and a Future Agenda for Reform", *NIPFP (mimeo),* New Delhi.
33. Mohan, R. (2000), "Fiscal Correction for Economic Growth, Data Analysis and Suggestion", in *Economic and Political Weekly*, June10, Mumbai, pp. 2027-2036.
34. Rao, M.G. (2000), "Tax Reform in India: Achievements and Challenges", *Asia-Pacific Development Journal,* Vol. 7, No. 2, December, p. 59.
35. Rakshit, Mihir (2000), "On Correcting Fiscal Imbalances in Indian Economy", *ICRA Bulletin*, July-September.
36. Kopits, G. (2001), "Fiscal Policy Rules for India?", *Economic and Political Weekly*, March 3, Mumbai, pp. 749-756.
37. Karnik, A. (2002), "Fiscal Policy and Growth", *Economic and Political Weekly,* March 2, Mumbai, pp. 829-831.
38. Peter, M. V. and Kerr Alan and Thorpe (2002), "Tax Policy in India", *Asian Journal of Public Administration,* Vol. 24, No. 1 June, pp. 111-138.
39. Sarma, A. and Gupta, M. (2002), *op.cit.*
40. Battacharya, B.B and Sabysachi Kar (2004), "Nexus between Growth and Fiscal and External Balances: A Macro-Econometric Evaluation of Post-reform India", in D.M. Nachane, Romar Corea, G. Anantha Padmanabhan and K.R. Shanmugam (ed.), *Econometric Models: Theory and Applications*, Allied Publishers Pvt. Ltd, New Delhi.
41. Lahiri, K. Ashok and R. Kannan (2004),"India's Fiscal Deficits and Their Sustainability in Perspective", in Favaro, M. Edgardo and Ashok K. Lahiri (ed.) *Fiscal Policies and Sustainable Growth in India*, Oxford University Press, New Delhi.
42. Mohan, R. (2004), "Central Finances in India-Alternative to

Procrustean Fiscal Correction", Working Paper 365, p. 4, www.cds.edu.

43. Rangarajan, C. (2004), "Some Aspects of Fiscal Federalism", in D.M. Nachane, Romar Corea G. Ananitha Padmanabhan and K.R. Shanmugam (ed.) *Econometric Models: Theory and Applications* Allied Publishers Pvt. Ltd, New Delhi.
44. Raju, S. (2004), "Government Expenditures and Receipts: A Causality Analysis for India", Department of Economics, University of Mumbai, Vidyanagari, Mumbai, p. 1.
45. Rakshit, M. (2005), "Some Analytics and Empirics of Fiscal Restructuring in India", *Economic and Political Weekly*, July 30, Mumbai, pp. 3440-3448.
46. Bagchi, A. (2006), "India's Fiscal Management Post-Liberalization Impact on the Social Sector and Federal Fiscal Relations", *Economic and Political Weekly,* September 30, Mumbai, pp. 4117-4121.
47. Kochhar, K. (2006), "India: Macroeconomic Implications of the Fiscal Imbalances" in Peter S. Heller and M. Govinda Rao (ed.) *'A Sustainable Fiscal Policy for India',* Oxford University Press, New Delhi, p. 2.
48. Rao, M.G. and Singh, Nirvikar (2007), "The Political Economy of India's Fiscal Federal System and its Reform", University of California, Santa Cruz Munich Personal RePEc Archive (MPRA) Paper No. 1279, posted 7 November.
49. Gurria, A. (2007), "Improving the Fiscal System", *OECD Economic Survey 2007,* New Delhi.
50. Mohan, Rakesh (2008), "The Role of Fiscal and Monetary Policies in Sustaining Growth with Stability in India", *RBI Monthly Bulletin*, December, p. 2093.

3

Role of Fiscal Policy in Economic Development

3.1 Keynes and Functional Finance

Lord Keynes threw out the traditional doctrine of the neutrality of public finance- held since the time of Adam Smith- and laid the foundations of the "functional finance". He insisted that Government finance should be adjusted to the changing conditions of the economy, to fight inflationary pressures and deflationary tendencies. By assuming that fiscal policy can influence the level of individual and corporate incomes, many economists have recommended the use of fiscal policy to:

1. Achieve optimum allocation of economic resources.
2. Bring about equal distribution of income and wealth.
3. Going for rapid economic growth. Under the influence of Keynes, the promotion and maintenance of full employment was regarded as the most important objective of fiscal policy.

The concept of fiscal policy in developing countries suggests a relatively homogeneous body of fiscal instruments applicable to such countries and also, perhaps more important that public finance and fiscal policy in developing economies constitutes an academic discipline distinct from its counterpart in the more advanced economy. Both notions are certainly false, the former being contradicted by the greater diversity in conditions pertaining to third world countries when compared with the more integrated advanced economies, whilst the latter encounters the objection that policy objectives, fiscal instruments and both political and administrative constraints are in principle the same (Shaw, G.K.,1981). [1]

For developed countries which experienced the process of

economic development over two centuries ago under conditions of frugality and dexterity—self-finance by economic units was the primary source of capital accumulation. For the present-day developing world, time is of essence. Rising aspirations place pressures on limited savings and there is a broader role for credit in investment and in entrepreneurial development. Unlike in developed countries where market forces help to evolve financial institutions and instruments, developing economies have to make deliberate efforts to promote and nurture diverse institutions and instruments as part of the process of development. With the system of physical controls and regulations gradually losing its hold, banking industry and financial system in developing countries will have a larger role in establishing investment and production priorities (Malhotra, R.N., 1991). [2]

The importance for economic development of a comprehensive integrated and efficient fiscal policy in general and taxation policy in particular is undoubtedly pivotal. However, in the context of underdeveloped countries the fiscal measures need to be reformed in such a way as to achieve a number of accepted objectives-which are primarily related to the basic goals of rapid economic development and establishment of a desired pattern of distribution.

The role of fiscal policy in the process of economic development occupies a dominant place among all the special tools of the government employed to direct and control the economic affairs of a country. But fiscal theories propounded with reference to developed countries do not, generally, suit to the requirements of under-developed economies, mainly due to peculiar economic conditions prevailing in these countries. The classical economists followed the principles of 'fiscal neutrality, and advocated to slim the size of public sector and to reduce the functions of government to the minimum possible extent in order to have a free play of market mechanism. They advocated a tax structure which disturbed the pricing system as little as possible including the pricing of factors of production (Hansen, A.H., 1941). [3] In modern times, classical ideas are irrelevant in case of advanced as well as under-developed countries as fiscal policy has to play an important role in the fields of economic growth and economic stabilization in these countries.

The theory of national income and employment, originally developed by Keynes, shed new light on the relation of Government finances to the level of income and employment in the economy. It was realized then that Government finances could be manipulated to influence the level of economic activity, by influencing the level of effective demand. This is the genesis of the modern concept of fiscal policy in advanced economies. Its underlying notion is that the revenue and expenditure programmes of the Government should be so adjusted as to produce and maintain a stable and high level of economic activity (Chelliah, R.J.,1960). [4] The fiscal policies advocated by Keynes and Lerner are, generally, concerned with achieving 'short-term stability' in the economy. Keynes regarded fiscal policy "as a balancing factor" (Keynes, J.M., 1936) [5] which would "bring about an adjustment between the propensity to consume and inducement to invest" (Ibid). [6]

He visualized the operation of a fiscal policy in the context of a static model in which skill and quantity of labour, technique, degree of competition and tastes and habits of consumers, etc. were assumed constant and a certain rate of growth was assumed. According to him, "The economy tends to fall below this rate of growth because investments do not equate themselves with the potential savings of the system" (Ibid). [7] Keynes advocated increase in effective demand and reduction in savings and these factors made his theory irrelevant to economic development in under-developed countries.

For achieving economic development in under-developed countries, it is necessary to use fiscal policy for restraining propensity to consume and thus raising propensity to save.

Keynes advocated a rise in the level of investment in order to increase national income and employment. This rise was restricted to a level which utilizes all the potential savings of the economy. But, in underdeveloped economy if the volume of investment is limited to savings, it would tend to stay stable at a level of underdeveloped equilibrium as savings constitute a comparatively much lower proportion of its national income.

Two important implications of this concept of fiscal policy are worthy to note here. First, the finances of the Government should be conducted on a 'functional' basis, and revenues and expenditures should not be considered as being occasioned solely by the requirement of securing collective consumption. This view of public finance may be called 'functional finance'.

Secondly, the budget needs not always be balanced. Under conditions of less than full employment, for instance, a deficit would be desirable (Chelliah, R.J., 1960). [8] It is the concept of functional finance which constitutes the real revolution in point of view. If the Government's expenditure and tax programmes are to be treated on a functional basis, the simple analogy with private finance no longer holds good. Expenditure may be incurred not mainly for the sake of its direct benefit, but for the sake of the indirect effect it produces in the form of a rise in employment; and revenue may be raised not to meet a proposed expenditure, but to curtail effective demand.

It follows that taxation no longer can be looked upon merely as a means of finding the money for the state; it becomes one of the primary weapons in the hands of the Government to promote stability and progress. Functional finance, thus deliberately aims at unbalancing the budgets with a view to attaining and maintaining full employment level in a developed economy. In an underdeveloped economy, however, the main problem is not one of full employment but that of rapid economic growth. In a developing economy, thus, the functional aspect of fiscal policy is to be conceived in the context of a planned process of economic development. In the words of Tripathi, "The requirements of economic growth demand that fiscal policy has to be used for progressively raising the level of investments and savings and thus the criteria of fiscal policy in developing economy are different from those of functional finance" (Tripathi, R.N., 1964). [9]

In the early Keynesian era, the preoccupation was with the problem of short-run stability and with counteracting cyclical fluctuations. Attention was given mainly to the perfecting of a counter-cyclical policy. Pressing short-run problems the depression of the thirties and the inflation of the First World War and post-War years absorbed all attention, to the neglect of the long-run problems of growth. More recently, however, condition for long-run equilibrium in a dynamic economy have been analyzed, and the possibility of the emergence of long-run disequilibrium has been pointed out, calling for a shift in emphasis in the goal of fiscal policy. The goal postulated now is that of insuring conditions of stable growth (Chelliah, R.J., 1960). [10] Mr. Harrod (Harrod, R.F.,1948) [11] and Professor Domar (Domar, E.D.,1957) [12] have been in the forefront of the economists who have tried to study the requirements of steady growth in an economy.

The growth models developed by Harrod and Domar gave a strategic importance to capital accumulation in the process of economic growth. They emphasized that investment has a dual character: on one hand investment creates income and on the other, it augments the economy's productive capacity by enlarging its capital stock. According to Harrod's model, if equilibrium is to be maintained in an expanding economy at the level of full employment, the actual rate of growth must correspond to the warranted rate of growth. The rate of growth required to maintain full employment without inflation is referred to as the required rate of growth (Musgrave, R.A., 1959). [13] Musgrave assigned the similar rate to fiscal dynamics in economic growth of advanced economics. According to him, the problem of fiscal dynamics in economic growth is "one of securing a growing level of capacity income at stable prices" (Ibid). [14]

3.2 Harrod-Domar Growth Models

Harrod-Domar growth models assume an economy at an advanced stage of economic development and with a high rate of capital accumulation. In such an economy, if unemployment develops, this is due to deficiency of effective demand and the situation can be remedied by raising the rate of investment expenditures in money terms. In under-developed countries the problem of ensuring the purchase of growing output at stable prices is not very important because there is always pressure of money demand on the limited productive capacity of the economy. Thus, fiscal policy has to play distinct roles in the process of economic development in case of advanced and under-developed countries. Broadly speaking, "Whereas the maintenance of stability will be assigned the first priority in an advanced economy like the United States, capital accumulation would have to be assigned first priority in an under-developed economy, like India" (Chelliah, R.J., 1969). [15]

Fiscal policy has an important role to play in regard to accumulation of human capital and promotion of education and skills. Human resource development is a vital element in social welfare activities of the state; and transfer payments for purposes of development of education and skills, health and family welfare- as also housing- constitute an important part of government's social expenditure. The modern concept of human development index (HDI) has attracted considerable attention and may be considered. The total quantum of allocation of budgetary funds for providing education, health facilities and the various factors that contribute to improvement in standards of living of the masses is a prime determinant for improving HDI.

Fiscal policy has an important role to play in determining not only the overall volume of funds, but also in channelizing these funds in the manner best calculated to maximize human capital accumulation. An important aspect of budgetary formulation is the decision to allocate available funds between various areas of research: military research, nuclear and space development; scientific research; industrial, medical and other research. It follows that if budgetary allocations in accordance with the government policy give primacy and direct large funds to military research, and funds for industrial or other research are inadequately provided for, it could have an impact upon development of industrial technology and the competitive capacity of industry.

Fiscal policy has an important role to play in the development of infrastructure. The quantum of funds to be allocated every year for development and maintenance of infrastructure are decided by the finance ministry on basis of requisition for funds from the concerned ministries. However, the total allocation would depend upon the availability of funds in the budget. The bulk of infrastructure in many developing countries is provided by the state. In many cases, there is an element of subsidy, often implicit, in the prices that are charged to consumers.

This imposes a burden on the budget and deprives other sectors of the economy of resources. Actually, the government should endeavour to increase user-charges to reduce the gap between cost and charges, so as to reduce budgetary deficit. Budgetary policy has also to determine expenditure allocation among and within infrastructure sectors: between irrigation, power, transport and communication; on new construction or maintenance of existing works; between rural and urban sectors; and between different districts and regions. So, it may be observed that allocative efficiency of resources is increased, provided infrastructure services are efficiently delivered (Kothari, S.S., 2001). [16]

The process of economic development accompanied by a large amount of investment tends to be, inherently inflationary because it tends to generate additional effective demand in the economy without an immediate and corresponding increase in the output of consumption goods. Therefore, the methods adopted by the government for financing its development plans must ensure that mobilization of adequate volume of resources is compatible with the maintenance of a reasonable measure of economic stability. Fiscal policy can play important role in counteracting inflationary tendencies and in influencing the structure of relative prices in the interest of economic development. The progressive tax structure is an effective fiscal stabilizer as it has a built-in-flexibility. Thus, if a tax structure has to work as an effective stabilizer, the marginal rate of taxation should be very high.

However, a highly progressive direct tax policy may adversely affect savings investment and output. Therefore, "Tax policy must be judiciously planned and it should discriminate in favour of essential production and consumption and against speculative investment and non-functional consumption" (Tripathi, R. N., 1964) [17] In under-developed countries like India, direct taxation covers very small segment of the population, therefore, progressive rates of commodity taxation work as better economic stabilizer. As economic development takes place larger part of income accrues to those persons who own means of production. Income is redistributed in favour of rich persons; hence a redistribution of income in favour of poor persons is required.

Any fiscal programme which involves improvement in the quality of manpower like education, training, health, housing, sanitation and subsidies on food and clothes, etc. generally benefits poor classes. To the extent that tax finances this process of human capital formation at the expense of lavish consumption and speculation, etc., it results in redistribution of income in favour of poor persons. Generally, it is argued that redistribution of income in favour of poor persons may adversely affect savings and investment by entrepreneur class. But high income in underdeveloped countries may, comparatively speaking, be derived from such sources and devoted to such uses that the disincentives effects are less damaging than in developed countries.

Through fiscal policy the Government creates and sustains the public economy consisting of the provision of public services and public investment; at the same time it is an instrument for reallocation of resources according to national priorities, redistribution, promotion of private savings and investments, and the maintenance of stability. Thus, fiscal policy has a multi-dimensional role. It particularly aims at improving the growth performance of the economy and ensuring social justice to the people.

Fiscal policy plays a central role in enabling a country to achieve its economic and social objectives, from macro-economic stability to sustainable growth and poverty reduction. Specifically, in the 1990s, fiscal policy has also assumed importance in the policy deliberations of most countries since concerns with fiscal dimensions, such as high unemployment, inadequate national savings, excessive budget deficits and public debt burdens have intensified. Looming crises in the financing of pension and health care systems are also putting pressure on fiscal policy management (Caron, Y., 2002). [18] In order to accelerate the growth of the economy, fiscal policy is used:

1. To mobilize the human and material resources of the economy and maximize their flow;
2. To promote savings in the economy and minimize current consumption;
3. To direct investment in the desirable channels both in the public and in the private sectors by providing suitable incentives;
4. To restrain inflationary forces in order to ensure economic stability;
5. To ensure equitable distribution of income and wealth in the country so that the fruits of development are fairly distributed. Reduction of economic inequalities and prevention of concentration of economic power become the major objectives of fiscal policy in developing countries; and

6. To protect the economy from unhealthy development abroad, i.e., to reduce the exposure of the economy to the ebbs and flows of world markets and to eliminate or reduce dependence on foreign food or foreign investments.

The role of fiscal policy can be likened to the driving of a car. While driving up a gradient (i.e. stepping up production and productivity), what is needed is an increase in power (promotion of higher saving and investment through fiscal measures). On the other hand, when it moves against the national interest it is necessary to control the supply of power (to combat inflationary and foreign exchange crises through higher taxation) and also to apply brakes judiciously to ensure that the vehicle does not slip out of control but keeps on moving all the same. The national exchequer should see that the brakes are not pressed so much as to bring the vehicle to a stop (Rastogi, K.M., 1965). [19]

A sound fiscal policy, responsible social spending and a well functioning and competitive financial system are the elements of good governance that are crucial to economic and social development.

Strategies for moving forward include, inter alia, disciplined macro-economic policies and fiscal policy, including clear goals for the mobilization of tax and non-tax revenues and responsible public spending on basic education and health, the rural sector and women. The Monterrey Consensus adopted at the International Conference on Financing for Development has recommended, inter alia, that developing countries and economies in transition should set up an effective, efficient, transparent and a accountable system for mobilizing public resources and managing their use by Governments as also emphasized the need to secure fiscal sustainability, along with equitable and efficient tax systems and administration, as well as improvements in public spending that do not crowd out productive private investment (Shende, S.N., 2002). [20]

3.3 Fiscal Policy and Resource Mobilization

Economic development has two main props—plan implementation and development financing. Planning and finance are interdependent with each other. One of the essential conditions for successfulness of planning is its financing. A plan, whether big or small in size, can be framed and implemented only when its scheme of financing is so well-devised that sufficient financial resources become readily available as and when required for meeting the development outlays of the process of planning. Availability of finance means mobilization of resources, entirely depends upon the extent of measures taken together for resource mobilization, refer to the scheme of collecting of funds for financing the plan. Hence, the term 'resource mobilization' stands for the collection of funds to allocate resources for meeting the plan outlays which covers not only taxation but the income from public services, public enterprises and public utilities (Gadgil, D.R.,1969). [21]

In other words, the task of mobilizing resources involves not only direct measures of taxation or changes in service charges, but also deliberate decisions on selection of major investments, control of expenditures, monitoring of performance and realization of planned levels of economic activity, in a broader view, prevention of tax evasion and tax avoidance and changes in the tax structure are, of course, crucial (Singh, Tarlok, 1947). [22] Mobilization of resources also means creation of 'economic surplus'. This is possible by mobilizing the existence of difference between the actual current output and actual current consumption in the economy and to continually enlarge it by curbing increments in consumption (Chelliah, R.J., 1969). [23] Mobilization of economic surplus would enable the Government to acquire funds with the help of which it can obtain resources and can direct them into developmental projects. Both direct and indirect taxes are instrumental for tapping such type of surplus.

Mobilization of resources in the monetized world means

raising of necessary finance for developmental purposes. Thus, finance is the mobilizer of resources. Mobilization of financial resources and economic development are synonymous with each other. The economic development is the function of mobilization of financial resources plus productivity of capital minus rate of inflation growth caused by excessive use of the technique of deficit financing. Resource mobilization is a direct means to the outcome of sustained growth. A decline in the resources mobilized may result in failure to attain the growth targets. It is for this reason that in a mixed economy inadequate resource mobilization manifests itself in internal and external instability.

The nature and extent of problem of resource mobilization is somewhat different in underdeveloped countries from the developed countries. For instance, in developed countries the income and the ratio of saving to national income is high while in underdeveloped countries, it is low as the "road to economic development is paved with vicious circles" (Higgins, B.,1959). [24] In underdeveloped economies where marginal propensity to consume is high, only a small part of income is saved for meeting the investment demands. Therefore, in order to raise the level of investment and saving in the underdeveloped economies it is imperative that the level of consumption must be curtailed. However, in such economies the level of consumption is already low due to low per capita income and it would be difficult to reduce it further. Since this task of capital formation cannot be shouldered by the private sector alone, in the developing economies the Government must come forward to hold this responsibility of raising the level of saving and investment.

The Government is expected to guide the economy by anticipating impediments to growth and providing necessary remedial action through institutional and other methods. As Jagdish Bhagwati remarks in this connection, "History seems to underline the importance of state action in engineering and assisting the process of take-off in developing economies. The more backward an economy when it proceeds to modernize itself, the larger tends to be the range of necessary action by the state" (Bhagwati, Jagdish,1966). [25] In fact, no country has made economic progress without positive stimulus from intelligent Government as has been the experience of England and the U.S.A" (Lewis,W.A.,1960). [26]

Resources can be raised both internally and externally which include revenue from taxation, public borrowing, surpluses of public enterprises and deficit financing and foreign aid, grants and loans from various foreign agencies respectively. The design or pattern of financing of a country is determined by these sources taken together having their distinct nature and contributions. Now, we may examine the nature, importance, extent, usefulness and defects of each source in order to mobilize the financial resources.

3.3.1 Taxation Policy: Taxation is an important instrument to achieve the objective of resource mobilization. As an instrument of resource mobilization for the development plan of the public sector, its principal function lies in raising the volume of public savings to be used for capital formation consistent with the growth in the rate of savings in the economy as a whole (Tripathy, R.N., 1964). [27] Emphasizing the importance of taxation Mrs. Ursula Hicks has rightly remarked, "Tax bankruptcy was an important contributory factor to the fall of the Roman Empire. Unjust and inefficient taxes set the French Revolution aflame. An important part of the explanation of the Germany's failure in the war of 1914-18 was her antiquated tax structure…inefficient taxes helped to lose Britain the American colonies" (Hicks, U.K., 1961). [28] Tax policy is, thus, a vital instrument in the hands of the public authority.

Taxation is used as the main policy instrument for transferring resources to the public sector. It can also assist in creating an atmosphere within which the private sector operates in conformity with national objectives. It has been argued by multilateral institutions, among others, that the tax system should be used only to raise finances that are sufficient for meeting the minimum necessary level of public expenditure, such as, to preserve territorial integrity, to maintain law and order, to provide various public goods and to regulate undesirable activities. From the efficiency viewpoint, it can be said that taxes provide the best means of financing the bulk of public expenditures. However, taxes impose three types of cost:

1. A direct cost or revenue forgone, as taxes, as taxpayers reduce their disposable income by paying the amount due;
2. An indirect allocative effect, or excess burden, which is the welfare cost associated with the economic distortions induced by taxes as they alter relative prices of goods, services and assets; and
3. An administrative/compliance cost, since tax forms, tax control, payment procedures and tax inspection are costly (Shende, S.N., 2002). [29]

The use of tax policy for the mobilization of development finance for the public sector in a developing country may be considered in two aspects: (i) static, and (ii) dynamic. In the static aspect, when the economy tends to stay at a stable level of underdevelopment equilibrium, taxation as an instrument of development finance should impinge on the consumption constitute of the aggregate output in such a way that work incentives are not unduly impaired. To the extent that taxation releases resources from non-functional consumption and unessential investment, its importance lies not so much in the reduction of over-all effective demand, but rather in the reduction of demand for certain resources which are thereby set free and made available to the public sector.

However, in its dynamic aspect, as the aggregate output tends to grow at a higher rate as a result of the initial efforts at planned development, tax policy must aim at preventing the increment in output from being consumed by deliberately siphoning an increasing proportion of it into the pool of investible resources of the public sector. Apart from the low level of per capita output, a number of factors of a purely technical nature operate in low income countries which make it very difficult for them to accomplish as large a proportionate resources transfer through taxation as high income countries. Their administrative mechanism is generally not very efficient partly due to the dearth of trained technical personnel.

As a result of a general lack of education among the tax payers, there exists difficult tax compliance conditions, including in many cases considerable taxpayer resistance and little moral disapproval of tax evasion. Due to the small size of the corporate industrial and commercial sector, it requires a larger proportionate investment of administrative resources to extract through taxation a significant proportion of the national income in low income countries as compared with the high income ones. Therefore, the tax structure is likely to show signs of strain at much lower rates of tax in the under-developed countries; and as a result, they may fail to utilize to the full, the existing tax potentials in their economies. Besides, the existence on a large scale of non-monetized sector also makes it difficult for them to tap the tax potentials of that sector through the usual forms of taxation.

Thus, the success of a developing country in diverting through the medium of taxation an increasing proportion of the national income into development financing depends partly upon the improvement of technical conditions such as improvement in tax administration, partly upon the spread of education, and upon the growing consciousness of the benefits flowing from larger development expenditure which will tend to diminish the psychological resistance of the tax payers (Tripathi, R.N., 1970). [30] As a U.N. Report puts it, "The problem of resource creation and deployment entails institutional innovation both in respect of the elaboration and use of fiscal machinery for stimulating saving and for raising the investment of public revenue and in respect of the organization and operation of a capital market for channeling savings into productive use in the private sector" (World

Economic Survey, 1965, U.N., 1966). [31]

In the early stages of the economic development of U.K. and U.S.A., their fiscal structure as a whole favoured the act of accumulation and capital formation and discriminated against the act of consumption. The economic development of these countries has been brought about largely by the efforts of a dynamic private enterprise; and to enable it to plough back its increasing incomes into investment, the structure of taxation was made highly regressive and the fiscal structure as a whole tended to redistribute the national income in favour of the investors and savers. According to the Colwyn Committee, "axation (in England) in 1818 hardly touched the saving power of the wealthy" (Report of the Committee on National Debt and Taxation, 1927) [32], and as a result, "all their savings were available for investment" (Hansen, A.H., 1941). [33]

In regard to the effect of taxation on the pattern of investment, it may so happen that taxes which reduce the rewards of successful investment may be a disincentive to risk-taking and this could have adverse effects on economic growth. The more people are encouraged to put their money into saving accounts or to keep in liquid form, the less entrepreneurship is there. Some of the empirical evidences also show that income and corporation tax have greater impact on the pattern of investment than on total savings and investment. But these adverse effects of taxation can be removed by appropriate public investment programmes and a combination of different type of taxes.

In underdeveloped economies, while making an effort at resource mobilization, the state is obliged to rely heavily on indirect taxation for collecting adequate revenue. The base for direct taxes is generally quite narrow and cannot be considered adequate for fiscal needs. In developed economies, however, no such generalization is possible. In their case while some economies rely more on direct taxes, other collect more revenue from indirect taxes. In U.S.A., for example, indirect taxes are only about 1/13 of direct ones, in Canada this ratio is about 1/2 in Belgium it is about 2/3, in Australia 3/2, and in Norway 7/2.

Taxes curtail consumption and thereby lead to forced savings and releases resources from consumption goods sector and make it available for the capital goods sector in the hands of the Government. In short, increase in taxation implies transfer of resources from household consumption to public sector investment. But, taxes should not amount to reduce output of consumption sector and create scarcity of wage goods, otherwise, it would mean an inflationary impact. Development rebate in taxation provides incentives to investment in the private sector. Similarly, indirect taxes also reduce consumption and increase saving for capital formation. Again taxation may lead to a change in the pattern of production by influencing allocation of resources in the various industries and regions. During inflation, direct taxes may be raised to seize excessive purchasing power and have economic stabilization.

Taxation is quite better than the other means of resource mobilization, i.e. deficit financing particularly in case of raising resources, promoting private investment, controlling inflation and securing an equitable distribution of burden of development finance on all sections of the community. Again, since some dose of deficit financing is desirable, a proper system of taxation is inevitable to control the adverse effects of the former. In this way, as matter of fact, taxation is both a substitute and a complement to deficit financing and for this the Government should be tough to taxation.

3.3.2 Public Borrowings: In modern public finance, developmental resources are also mobilized through public borrowings from internal and external sources, in order to meet increasing public expenditure. Government offers savings certificates, bonds, securities, etc. in order to borrow from the citizens and institutions like banks, insurance companies etc. It is referred to as internal public debt. Government may also raise loans from foreign international institutions like World

Bank etc. It is called external debt. Compared to taxation, a public debt has distinctive advantages such as:

1. Taxes are compulsory and pinching. While, public debt being voluntary, contribution to Government loans by the people depends on their will. Hence, no element of any psychological pinch or dissatisfaction is involved in public debt.
2. Taxes have no direct benefits. Loans confer direct benefits to the creditors like bond-holders.
3. Taxes may have adverse effect on desire to work, and save. Loans have no such disincentive effects.
4. Taxes are never refunded. Public loans are repayable. So, people always prefer public loans to taxation.
5. Taxes curb consumption by force which may adversely affect the standard of the people. Public loans also induce voluntary savings which, in turn, create an expansionary effect.
6. Public borrowings imply reallocation of resources from unproductive to productive uses.
7. Public borrowings can also serve as an anti-inflationary device, because they enable the Government to curb excessive purchasing power and utilize them for increasing the production.

Public borrowing is considered a better method of collecting public revenue than taxation (on the one hand Government will get sources for development programmes and, on the other, conspicuous consumption will be reduced). But it cannot substitute taxation completely because there are certain limitations to the use of this source of financing development. Firstly, public borrowing depends on the credit worthiness of the Government. Secondly, people do not want to lend to the Government because the rates of interest offered by the Government are lower than those offered by the borrowers in the private sector. And thirdly, if the prices are rising, people will not be interested in saving and lending because of depreciation in the value of money (Aggarwal,

Chawla, Medury, Uma, Mukherjee, Indira, Rao and Sopory, Aparna, 2008). [34]

However, for a successful programme of public borrowings, the Government security market should be strong. It requires well developed capital and money markets. Again, there is a problem of debt servicing. As such, the Government cannot resort to endless borrowings. Above all, public debt needs to be appropriately managed and fully redeemed in order to maintain the prestige and image of the Government.

3.3.3 Deficit Financing: Deficit financing as a method of resource mobilization has assumed an important place in public finance in recent time. It refers to means of financing the deliberate excess of expenditure over income through printing of currency notes or through borrowings. The term is also generally used to refer to the financing of a planned deficit whether operated by a government in its domestic affairs or with reference to balance of payments deficit. Keynes organized the idea of deficit financing as a compensatory spending meant to solve the problem of unemployment and depression. Modern economists prescribe deficit financing for development purposes.

The concept of deficit financing in the western countries implies financing of a deliberately created gap between public revenue and expenditure or a budgetary deficit. This gap is filled up by Government borrowings which include all the sources of public borrowings viz., from people, commercial banks and the central bank. In this manner idle savings in the county are made active. This increases employment and output. But deficit financing as used in the Indian context is resorted to when there are budgetary deficits. Government borrowing from public and commercial bank does not come under deficit financing as in the west. In Indian context, borrowings from the central bank of the country, withdrawal of accumulated cash balances and issue of new currency are included within the purview of deficit financing.

The technique of deficit financing has its historical origin in war finance. In war times, the Government tends to resort to deficit financing in order to quickly acquire a command over resources to meet the growing war expenses. As a rule, however, deficit financing is unproductive when it is used in the case of war finance. Deficit financing during war is always inflationary because monetary incomes and demand for consumption goods rise but usually there is shortage of supply of consumption goods. The use of deficit financing during times of depression to boost the economy got impetus during the great depression of the thirties.

It was Keynes who established a positive role for deficit financing in industrial economy during period of depression. It was advocated that during depression, Government should resort to construction of public works wherein purchasing power would go into the hands of people and thereby demand would be stimulated. This will help in fuller utilization of already existing but temporarily idle plants and machinery. Deficit spending by the Government during depression helps to start the stagnant wheels of productive machinery and thus promotes prosperity. Deficit financing for development, like depression deficit financing, provides stimulus to economic growth by financing investment, employment and output in the economy. On the other hand "development deficit financing" resembles "war deficit financing" in its effect on the economy.

Both are inflationary though the reasons for price rise in both the cases are quite different. When Government resorts to deficit financing for development, large sums are invested in basic heavy industries with long gestation periods and in economic and social overheads. This leads to immediate rise in monetary incomes while production of consumption goods cannot be increased immediately with the result that prices go up. It is also called the inflationary way of financing development. However, it helps rapid capital formation for economic development. Deficit financing in developing country is inflationary while it is not so in an advanced country. In an advanced country the Government resorts to deficit financing for boosting up the economy.

There is all-round unemployment of resources which can be employed by raising Government investment through deficit financing. The result will be an increase in output, income and employment and there is no danger of inflation. The increase in money supply leading to demand brings about a corresponding increase in the supply of commodities and hence there is no increase in price level. But, when, in a developing economy, the Government resorts to deficit financing for financing economic development the effects of this on the economy are quite different.

Public outlays financed by newly-created money immediately create monetary incomes and, due to low standards of living and high marginal propensity to consume in general, the demand for consumption of goods and services increases. But if the public investment is on capital goods, then the increased demand for the consumer goods will not be satisfied and prices will rise. Even if the outlay is on the production of consumption goods the prices may rise because the monetary income will rise immediately, while the production of consumer goods will take time and in the meanwhile prices will rise.

Though investment is being continuously raised (through taxation, borrowing and external assistance), most of it goes to industries with long gestation period and for providing basic infrastructure. Though there is effective demand, resources lie under or unemployed. Lack of capital, technical skill, entrepreneurial skills etc. are responsible in many cases for unemployment or underemployment of resources in a developing economy. Under such conditions, when deficit financing is resorted to, it is sure to lead to inflationary conditions. Besides, in developing economy, during the process of economic development, the velocity of circulation of money increases through the operation of the multiplier effect. This factor is also inflationary in character because, on balance, effective demand increases more than the initial increase in money supply.

Deficit financing gives rise to credit creation by commercial banks because their liquidity is increased by the creation of new money. This shows that in developing economy total money supply tends to increase much more than the amount of deficit financing, which also aggravates inflationary conditions. The use of deficit financing being expansionary becomes inflationary also on the basis of quantity theory of money. Deficit financing has proved to be conducive to economic development, especially in countries with acute shortage of capital. Deficit financing in developing economies can be regarded as a necessary evil which can be tolerated only to the extent it promotes capital formation and economic development. This extent of tolerance is known as safe limit of deficit financing.

To minimize the inflationary effects of deficit financing during the process of development, certain measures have to be taken like proper channelizing of investment in areas with low capital-output ratio, adoption of policies of physical control like rationing, import of only necessary capital equipment etc. In economies with low capital formation, deficit financing becomes a necessary and positive instrument if used with efficient and well executed plan of economic development (Aggarwal, Chawla, Medury, Uma, Mukherjee, Indira, Rao and Sopory, Aparna, 2008). [35]

Deficit financing can give a boost to development process. It makes optimum use of unutilized resources possible through effective mobilization in the country's economy. Again, deficit financing may cause a price rise and reduction in consumption. Thus, it implies a forced saving. Since poor countries lack voluntary savings, forced savings through deficit financing is much desirable phenomenon. When this forced savings leads to capital formation, productivity and output increase, and bring down the price level. Thus, inflation is in due course self-destructive. As IMF Staff Paper states, "the expansion of money supply within proper limits in a growing economy represents an increment of real resources for investment so long as the expansion of money supply (caused by deficit financing) is no more than enough to finance the larger volume of production, consumption, and investment at stable prices; it is not only non-inflationary, but is essential to the proper functioning of the economy.

With a view to mobilization of resources of the country these various instruments can be used as a complementary method to each other and the duty of an intelligent Government is to evolve a mutual and judicious combination of them for the required purpose. But, under certain circumstances, the policy of taxation is the most effective fiscal instrument for raising resources for the development of the public sector, accelerating development of private sector, controlling inflationary pressures and improving the even distribution of income and wealth. Taxation does not create any greater real burden on the community than would be caused by an equivalent amount of public borrowing owing to the fact that they do not raise the intense problem of repayment of interest on capital in the future.

Successive increment in public debt may accentuate inequality, dampen incentives to the entrepreneurs and create a big pressure of inflation on the smooth growth of the economy. The experience of post-war development in different countries show that the inflationary potential of a big development programme can be held within bounds by an appropriate degree of surplus budgeting on revenue account. In this way, taxation becomes indispensable both as a complement and a substitute to borrowing despite knowing the fact that taxation is unjust and harbinger of hardship to the people. A developing country can, therefore, escape from increased taxation only at its own peril (Mishra, B.,1978). [36]

Likewise, when we compare taxation and deficit financing, we find no compromise with deficit financing which is considered to be the most important cause of economic peril in the under-developed countries by sustaining pain of inflationary jerks. Deficit financing is a quicker technique to raise resources. Therefore, it can be asserted that "under the constraints of tax administration, taxes should be selected in a way that reflects the realities of the environment in which they are enforced, they must provoke the least resistance possible from taxpayers and establish through their multiplicity the necessary tax illusion which enables Government to increase its share in gross national product and effectively contribute to economic development.

3.4 Fiscal Policy and Allocative Efficiency

Economics deals with the efficient use of resources in best satisfying consumer wants. If the economy consisted of one consumer only, the meaning of efficiency would be quite simple. Robinson Crusoe would survey the resources available to him and the technologies at his disposal in transforming these resources into goods. Given his preferences among goods, he would then proceed to produce in such a way and such a mix of output as would maximize his satisfaction. In doing so, he would act efficiently. But the real world problem is more difficult. The economic process must serve not one but many consumers; and various outcomes will differ in their distributional implications. This calls for a more careful definition of what is meant by "efficient" resource use (Musgrave, R.A. and Musgrave, P.B., 1973). [37]

The Governmental operations basically involve the efficient provision of Government funds in maximizing the welfare of the community. The Government taxes the public and uses the amount in providing certain facilities and services considered essential by the people and the community. These facilities are such that they could not be provided by the people themselves (e.g., defence) or they could be provided but only at a high cost (e.g., education and medical facilities). Fiscal operations of taxation and public expenditure have the effect of transferring resources from the public which would have been used for consuming private goods to produce social goods which would satisfy collective wants. The objective of fiscal operations is to provide for the proper allocation of resources between private and social goods so as to maximize social welfare.

The primary task of fiscal policy in under-developed countries is to raise the ratio of savings to national income. The need is much more urgent than is generally recognized by policy makers in these countries. And there is reason to believe that well-devised policy measures can succeed in making available a larger flow of resources for economic development. This means that the role of fiscal policy in underdeveloped countries essentially has to be allocative. It is concerned with allocating more resources for investment and restraining consumption. By contrast, fiscal policy in developed economies is concerned mainly with regulating the total flow of purchasing power, with determining the level of total effective demand. Speaking of the United States, Arthur Smithies says, "fiscal policy aims primarily at controlling aggregate demand and leaves to private enterprise its traditional field the allocation of resources among alternative uses". It is obvious that in an underdeveloped country the emphasis has to be on allocation, that is, the broad allocation as between consumption and investment, and as between forms of investment. True, in a developed economy too, under certain circumstances, the rate of investment might have to be changed by public policy. But in the conditions prevailing in the developed economies at the present stage of their development maintenance of stability short-run and long-run remains the keynote of fiscal policy, whereas in the underdeveloped countries the keynote of policy must be acceleration of the rate of growth (Chelliah, R.J.,1960). [38]

Fiscal policy also influences growth performance of an economy through its effects on the allocation of resources. An efficient and rational allocation of resources will obviously be helpful in raising the rate of economic growth. Therefore, if fiscal policy favourably affects the efficiency of resource allocation, then in the process, growth performance of the economy is bound to improve. An indifferent fiscal policy adversely affecting the efficiency of resource allocation on the contrary retards the productive activity and thereby results in lower rate of economic growth.

Among the various instruments of fiscal policy perhaps tax policy is the most important determinant of the efficiency of resource use. It has been observed that the allocative effects of direct taxes are superior to those of indirect taxes. If a particular amount is raised through a direct tax like income tax, it would imply a lesser burden than the same amount raised through an indirect tax like excise duty. This is because an indirect tax involves an excessive burden since it distorts the scale of preference due to price changes caused by its imposition. Thus, in practice, the allocative effects of indirect taxes would be superior to those of direct taxes provided the Government chooses the indirect taxes judiciously.

In an underdeveloped economy, there is a need to shift the resources toward various priority industries and indirect taxes can be of help there. Even in a modern developed economy, there are usually numerous imperfections, monopolies and so on, as also a good deal of divergence between social and private costs on the one hand and between social and private benefits on the other. However, production of certain high priority goods may be lower not because resources invested in them are too few, but because due to market imperfections there are unutilized capacities as in the case of monopolies and monopolistic competition. The appropriate approach in breaking a monopoly is not to push more resources into it through taxation of goods produced by competitive industries and subsidizing the goods produced by competitive industries and subsidizing the goods produced by monopolies. Instead, steps should be taken whereby monopolies are forced to make use of their unutilized capacities.

Another reason on account of which a judicious use of indirect taxes turns out to be better than direct taxes in their allocative effects is the fact that it is rather difficult to have really proportional income taxation. The very concept of taxable income is an imprecise one and its definition differs from country to country and even within the same country from time to time. So, it is not easy to lay down exact standards by which to estimate the expenses for earning the income, or by which to estimate the depreciation. In a modern economy, due to changes in prices and other uncertainties, there are capital gains, windfall profits and casual incomes, which pose difficult problems of devising a system of proportional income taxation. In practice, the above comparison between the allocative effects of a proportional income tax with those of an equal-yield indirect tax is an academic exercise only, since a modern Government is expected to prefer a progressive direct income tax with an exemption limit to a proportional income tax.

Direct tax will have a resource allocative effect by changing the relative attractiveness of different sources of income. On this basis, therefore, supplier of labour would shift from one employment or industry to another if by so doing he can reduce his direct tax liability more than the reduction, if any, in his earning from the supply of his labour. If he finds that by shifting his employment, his tax liability remains unaltered, there would be no reallocative effect on existing labour supply in the economy.

If in general taxation reduces one's earnings from each type of investment substantially, then there will be a tendency for savings to go uninvested or get invested into those lines from which little or no income may be expected. Taxation of earnings from investment would tend to reduce the supply of savings and investment in general. But a system of differential taxation causes a resource reallocation effect also. A direct tax can also have an indirect effect on resource allocation. Through a shift in income distribution or even otherwise, a direct tax can lead to a shift in demand pattern and cause a reallocation of productive resources.

In addition, diversionary effects of taxes are, however, beneficial and socially very much desirable. In a free economy, very often, undisturbed economic forces may tend to establish a pattern of production which may not be desirable from the social welfare point of view. In such cases, certain forms of taxation may achieve a desirable reallocation of resources, causing improvement in the social benefits. For instance, in a developing economy when luxuries are taxed at a progressive rate, resources will be diverted from such non-essential goods industries to the essential goods industries. Similarly, if harmful goods like tobacco, opium, liquor, etc., are highly taxed so that their consumption is curbed, production of such goods will be reduced and the realized surplus resources would then be made available for better purposes like capital formation, etc. when such allocative effect takes place it is beneficial to the society, which is welfare-oriented, as it implies efficient and optimum use of the scarce resources.

Similarly, concessional taxation on priority industries and heavy taxation on non-priority industries tend to divert the flow of resources (land, labour, capital, etc.) from the latter to the former, which would be a socially desirable channelisation of resources. Likewise, when a protective tariff is raised, it will cause a diversion of the productive resources from non-protected industries to protected industries which might have been assigned a strategic position in the country's economic development. Moreover, a significant diversionary effect of taxation is to shift resources from the present use to future use or sometimes from future use to present use.

Apart from a change in the use of resources, taxes may lead to a shift in resources from one region or place to another. In fact, the main object of a modern public policy is to promote a balanced regional growth, which calls for re-allocation of resources from advanced regions to economically backward regions. This can be effected through appropriate adjustments in the tax structure and tax rates in the different regions. Since the resources have a natural tendency to move from a high-taxed region to a low taxed region, it follows that the Government has to tax the developed regions more heavily than the backward regions, in order to bring about a desired transfer in the interest of balanced growth. Otherwise, if the differential rates are adopted at random by the states in a federation, a lopsided development may result. Thus, the overall effect of the tax policy on allocation of resources should not be judged in isolation because a well-devised system of public expenditure may more than compensate any adverse effect of taxation of production. The basic thing, however, is that the revenue obtained through taxation must be wisely spent, which would help in increasing economic and social welfare in the community.

Public expenditure can help the economy in numerous ways in attaining higher levels of production and growth. The ways in which such effects might be brought about are obviously inter-related. The analysis of these effects can be taken up separately in the context of developed and underdeveloped economies. Developed market economy has enough of flexibility but may be suffering from a deficiency of effective demand. Public expenditure can add to the effective demand directly and thus, generate conditions favourable for the market forces to push up production. Such public investment need not be productive in the sense of adding to the supply side of the market also. This public investment can just be a means of disturbing purchasing power to those who would spend the same and add to the effective demand.

However, the technique of increasing production through increasing demand becomes ineffective once the level of full employment is reached. Money income goes up but real income does not increase correspondingly because real income depends upon the use of real resources. If, therefore, demand is pushed beyond full employment, it will only add to inflationary pressures. Further, public expenditure may not be able to push up production proportionately because of various rigidities from which even a developed economy is likely to suffer. For example, some industries may not have unutilized excess capacity when demand goes up. In some industries monopolistic practices may be in vogue and there can be strong militant trade unions. Under different technical and other types of rigidities the economy may not be able to respond fully to increased demand.

The result is likely to be a partial increase in production when demand increases through the use of public expenditure and the results can be quite inflationary beyond a limit. Once rigidities are recognized from which a developed economy may be suffering and the corresponding lack of complete inter-flow of demand between its various sectors, the co-existence of inflation and unemployment cannot be ruled out. In such a case, the authorities cannot be indifferent as regards the manner in which public expenditure generates additional demand in the economy.

The case is a different one with underdeveloped economies. Such economies are characterized by a low level of saving and investment activity. This deficiency, again, may be remedied by stimulating private saving and investment, or through direct public saving and investment, or both. Thus, in underdeveloped countries, there is a shortage of social overheads, skilled labour, capital equipment and machinery. Public expenditure can be directly used to create and maintain social overheads. It can also be used to create human skills through education and training. In India, good deal of regional disparities is found. Certain districts, or parts thereof, have been enlisted as economically backward. Various tax concessions and credit facilities are being provided for setting up industries in these areas. Public expenditure can be used to provide necessary economic infrastructure for the development of selected economic activities and can be used to give subsidies for increasing their profitability. Thus, the authorities can add to the process of capital accumulation. To the extent this capital formation is financed through foreign aid, the process of economic growth is accelerated.

Public expenditure may also be used to encourage the market sector of an underdeveloped economy for contributing to the process of economic growth. It is not necessary that all the additional investment should be in the form of direct public investment only. Public expenditure can help private investment and production through measures which reduce the cost of production, or push up demand or remove particular shortages and bottle-necks. Creation and maintenance of social overheads lead to an all-round reduction in cost of production and improvement in efficiency. This, therefore, increases profitability and production. Also social overheads bring different regions and sectors of an economy in closer contact, and thereby stimulate the process of economic growth. Also, public investment can go directly into the development of basic and key industries, power, irrigation and mines etc. through these steps, the economy can add to its infrastructure and thus provide a firm basis for growth.

Public expenditure can bring about a better allocation of economic resources as between the present and the future. In a free capitalist society very little provision is made for the future. This is because people prefer the present rather than the future and, therefore, they do not make adequate provision for the future. The state, on the other hand, is the custodian of the interests of the future generations also and, therefore, has to see that adequate provision is made for the future. Thus, certain type of public expenditure such as those on multi-purpose projects, road development, urbanization schemes, etc. do not yield immediate returns but confer social and economic benefits on the future generation. Public expenditure also results in diversion of resources between different regions and thereby reduces regional inequalities.

3.5 Fiscal Policy and Equity

The conception of fiscal equity, that is, equal treatment for equally situated individuals, has been applied to the distribution of taxes, but not to the distribution of expenditure in the same manner. This equity criterion, although motivated on grounds completely divorced from economic efficiency, does carry with it certain implications for efficiency in the structure of private choices. The equal-treatment-for equals principle does not guarantee that private choices are not modified by the fiscal structure, but it does, if fully applied, serve to prevent differential effects on separate groups or individuals.

The meaningfulness of this equity principle depends, however, on the way in which "equals" are defined for purposes of fiscal treatment. Differential taxes could be imposed without violation of the technical version of the equity principle if the group of "equal" is defined sufficiently narrowly. A tax must be applied to rather broad grouping; in other words, "equals" for fiscal purposes must be defined in some reasonable and not wholly arbitrary manner. The general respect for the equity principle in the organization of the fiscal structure has been one factor tending to maintain general neutrality in effects. The deliberate distortion of private choices in a differential way has been prevented, especially in the distribution of taxes. Much of the opposition to the erosion of the income tax base through numerous loopholes, tax shelter, and tax credit schemes stems from the fear that these violate the long-standing principle of horizontal equity.

These devices tend to classify individuals, not in accordance with their ability to pay, but in accordance with the relationship of their private activity to some concept of "private interest". At this point it is suggested merely as one factor which unintentionally, serves to prevent undue distortion of resource allocation mechanism of the private economy by the fiscal structure (Bauchanan, J.M. and Flowers, R.F., 1975). [39]

It is important to distinguish between the static and dynamic effects of fiscal policy on equity. From the vantage point of comparative statistics the key issues are, who bears the tax burden of fiscal policy and who benefits from public expenditure. Of course, even answering these relatively "simple" questions raises knotty theoretical problems. These problems are multiplied when one approaches the issue in a dynamic framework and asks: what has been the effect on, say, the size of distribution of income, over a specified period of time, which can be attributed to fiscal policy? After all, fiscal policy affects growth. And, depending on the structural characteristics of the economy as well as the policy frame, that growth can be associated with more or less equity in the distribution of income or consumption or wealth (Acharya, S., 1988). [40]

The economic structure of underdeveloped countries is characterized by the existence of considerable inequalities in the distribution of income and wealth. A number of studies made in recent years have revealed that these inequalities are much greater in developing countries as compared to those in the advanced capitalist countries of U.S.A. and U.K. The existence of inequality in the distribution of income is held to be conducive to a high rate of capital accumulation; but in the case of the developing countries much of the inequality is of non-functional character which is not justifiable either from the economic or social stand-point. Besides, concentrations of economic power are not compatible with a process of acceleration development in democratic countries because they lead to social and political discontent which undermines the fabric of the body politic and prevents popular participation in the process of development (Tripathy, R.N.,1970) [41] A welfare state should provide social justice by giving equitable distribution of income and wealth. Fiscal policy can serve as an effective means of achieving this much desired goal of socialism in developed as well as developing countries.

Market mechanism by itself generates ever-widening income inequalities. However, the objective of reducing inequalities is likely to come in conflict with that of increasing production and economic growth. The problem is break-up into two parts, short-term and long-term. In short-run, any income and wealth distribution pattern can go in harmony with the production level. Thus, it may be assumed that the total national product is already there and that now the problem is to determine the individual shares of the members of the society. Definitionally, therefore, this stand makes distribution independent of its effects on production. Such a redistribution of income, therefore, may be brought as close to equality as various tax measures. However, there are following points in this connection.

Firstly, unless there is a total political and economic revolution in a country, a quick redistribution of income and wealth is not a possibility. The process is a time-consuming one if measures like progressive income-tax, wealth tax, gift tax, expenditure tax and the like are to be used. So long as the institutions of private property and inheritance are there, the process towards equality is bound to be a slow one. This implies, therefore, that in reality, a proper degree of redistribution might be expected only in the long-run, and for that reason, it is likely to have its consequences on production also.

Secondly, even if it were possible to reduce the inequalities to a desired extent in the short-run, long-term consequences of this policy cannot be ignored. *Thirdly,* in an underdeveloped country like India, use of taxation for reduction in inequalities of income and wealth has its own limitations. Direct taxation, with all its progressive rates, covers only a fraction of the population. The incidence of tax evasion further aggravates its ineffectiveness. Indirect taxes, on the other hand, cannot be progressive enough in spite of their selective coverage and differential rates. Moreover, indirect taxation is inflationary in character, and adds to inequalities. Possibility of evading excise and sales taxes further strengthens this process.

In the long-run, a reduction in inequalities brought about by taxation might be counterbalanced or more than counterbalanced by increasing inequalities of the pre-taxed incomes. This problem may be solved by very steep taxation so as to practically mop-off the income above a certain height and effective checking of tax evasion. Steps towards reducing inequalities can have alternative effects on production and growth. If the progression of taxes is relatively mild, adequate incentives will be left for everyone to work hard and contribute towards economic growth.

Thus, one acceptable objective before the authorities can be to check and reduce relative inequalities over time. This may be done through various progressive tax measures (and, of course, public expenditure devices also) covering income, wealth, gifts, inheritance, windfalls, capital gains, etc. coupled with adequate incentives of producers in the private sector and public sector profitability and savings on the other. However, taxing gifts, unearned increments and capital gains at even steep rates will not reduce the incentives to work and earn because these taxes touch upon those receipts which are not based upon economic efforts of individuals. Wealth tax and inheritance tax, however, can become a disincentive to save if their rates are too steep.

Thus, if income and wealth inequalities are sought to be reduced through tax measures, there is bound to be a conflict between this objective and that of growth. Either, therefore, the state has to abolish the institutions of private property and inheritance and take over the task of economic growth, or it has to provide enough incentives in the economy. In an underdeveloped country, such a conflict between egalitarian and growth objectives is all the more sharp because there is an immediate need for both. There is abject poverty in the masses which should be reduced to some extent at least. But final solution of it can come only through economic growth, otherwise an equality without adequate production would only amount to distributing poverty. In a developed country, on the other hand, since even the poor are not so poor in absolute term, the objective of equality can possibly be postponed. At the same time, those countries are not faced with an immediate problem of economic growth and so they can afford to go ahead with distribution.

Welfare considerations also favour an equitable distribution of income and wealth. The purpose of an economic policy should be to contribute towards achieving the maximum social benefits. Lerner (1946) [42] has shown that even if we do not know the exact way in which marginal utility of income falls with a rise in income and even if we cannot have inter-personal comparisons of utility, still a shift towards equality would probably add to the aggregate satisfaction of the community. Such a shift towards equality, of course, may be achieved through various forms of public expenditure especially those which are meant to help the poorer sections of the society. A number of welfare measures like free education, health, water and other facilities can be given a top priority.

Numerous social security schemes can be adopted whereby people are entitled to old-age pensions, unemployment relief, sickness allowance and so on. Articles of common consumption like food can be subsidized, and the production of those which are in short supply can be taken up in the public sector. Left to market mechanism, the supply of 'merit goods' is likely to be insufficient. Public expenditure, through direct purchases, public production or subsidies can ensure that their supply is augmented to the desired extent. Similarly public expenditure, through appropriate subsidies and other 'purchase and stores' policy encourage labour-intensive techniques of production which reduce unemployment and improve income distribution.

3.6 Fiscal Policy and Economic Stability

One of the most important objectives of fiscal policy is to control business depressions and business booms and maintain business stability. The problem of stability refers to that of recurring cyclical phases of upward and downward cumulative movement in income, employment, output and prices, etc. in the economy. In an underdeveloped country, such instability is mainly caused through pressures originating from abroad and imported through shifts in imports, exports, and external resource flows. Recognition of a close relationship between price changes and the level of output and employment, particularly in developed market economies, has led some economists to claim that economic stability should be interpreted to mean a steady non-inflationary economic expansion in output and employment coupled with a very mild rise in prices. It is normally found that a very mild inflation enables an economy to achieve a continuous expansion.

In the development context, fiscal policy serves both as an instrument of macroeconomic stabilization and as an instrument to achieve growth and poverty reduction objectives. Correspondingly, growth and poverty reduction objectives were under-emphasized. Although stability is necessary for growth, it is not sufficient. The design of fiscal policy needs to identify and also incorporate the transmission channels through which fiscal policy influences long-term growth. This requires that attention be focused on the likely growth effects of the level, composition and efficiency of public spending and taxation. Fiscal policy that neglects these effects runs the risk of achieving stability while potentially undermining long-term growth and poverty reduction.

The evidence from countries that stabilized their economies by reducing their deficits indicates that countries often did so by cutting public capital formation significantly, despite its potential negative impact on growth and poverty reduction. While in many cases the decision to cut investments reflected a political preference, the absence of domestic fiscal institutions that would have enabled governments to take a medium term perspective may have contributed to such short-sighted decisions. Fiscal policy has been broadly successful in achieving economic stabilization in part through reductions in fiscal deficits.

The fiscal deficit is a useful indicator for purposes of stabilization and for controlling the growth of government liabilities, but it offers little indication of longer term effects on government assets or on economic growth. Conceptually, the long-term impact is better captured by examining the impact of fiscal policy on government net worth. While there are practical challenges to accurately estimating a government's net worth, there is clearly a need for fiscal policy to incorporate, as best as possible, the likely impact of the level and composition of expenditure and taxation on long-term growth while also maintaining a focus on indicators essential for stabilization (Development Committee, D.C., 2006). [43]

The stabilization policy seeks to reduce fluctuations in incomes, output, employment and price level and demand management is one of its principal tools. The maintenance of internal stability, which implies price-stability and high level of employment, postulates an adequate level of aggregate demand, which depends upon the level of expenditure and receipt. Aggregate demand should be adequate to provide the purchasing power for the goods produced by a fully employed economy and should expand with economic growth. If there is excess of aggregate demand there would be inflation; and if there is deficiency in demand, output would be less than the potential with inadequate utilization of capacity. If there is depression or slackness in the economy, the expenditure should be in excess of revenue so that unutilized resources are used and economy expands.

Deficit budgeting may be necessary to increase aggregate demand. The development of the concepts of "multiplier" and "accelerator" and the relationship between the macro-variables like investment, income, consumption, and savings enabled the economists to visualize the mechanics of trade cycles and the role which the fiscal policy could play in an economy. This gave rise to the principals of compensatory finance and functional finance. The modern principle of 'compensatory finance'—essentially applicable to developed economies—is now accepted as being also applicable to developing economies. Actually, certain amounts of deficit financing and moderate inflation are regarded as means of accelerating growth in developing economies.

It was realized that, to a large extent, fiscal policy can be effectively used by the Government to neutralize the destabilizing forces because depression is caused by a deficiency of effective demand and fiscal policy can remedy it. Similarly, during a boom period the need is to control the demand which can be partly done through curtailing public expenditure and partly through curbing the private expenditure. Thus, Keynesian remedial scheme is essentially neutralizing changes in total effective demand by increasing it during a depression and decreasing it during a boom. During a depression, public expenditure should be increased through incurring public investment and enhancing consumption expenditure of the Government. Similarly, subsidies (with or without tax concessions) can be used to encourage private consumption and investment.

Deficit financing is a very potent tool in the hands of the Government for increasing effective demand. This is more so if the deficit is financed through creation of additional currency or borrowings from the central bank of the country. Even when the Government borrows from the market and spends the borrowed sums, the aggregate expenditure is most likely to increase because during depression the investment opportunities in the market are not much and savings of the market get spent through the Government. However, the Government's expenditure policy is more effective when the extra purchasing power goes into the hands of those people who have a high marginal propensity to consume. Various social security measures like unemployment relief, old-age pensions, and so on are, therefore, very helpful in raising the total demand in the market. Productive activity picks up faster and the existing unutilized capacity is put to use if the Government expenditure is directed primarily towards consumption and welfare type disbursements without creating additional productive capacity. In that case, the economy would be able to recover from the depression through the multiplier process.

Taxation is considered an effective tool in encouraging expenditure in the private sector. Ordinarily, a general reduction in tax rates or abolition of various taxes is recommended. This pushes up profits and reduces cost of production and prices. Lower prices are expected to increase demand, production and employment, which in turn add to effective demand, and so on.

A similar action can be taken in the field of customs duties also. Raising import duties diverts the domestic demand from imports to home-produced goods; and reducing or abolishing export duties or giving export subsidies increases the demand for exports and contributes towards recovery from depression. Thus, it would be more helpful to lower tax rates on those goods which have a higher elastic demand. Similarly, demand would receive a greater stimulus if persons with a higher marginal propensity to consume are given a relief in direct taxation. In the same manner, investment may be encouraged by specific tax concessions like tax holidays, greater depreciation allowance etc.

When due to large increases in consumption demand by the households or investment expenditure by the entrepreneurs, or bigger budget deficit caused by too large an increase in Government expenditure, aggregate demand increases beyond what the economy can potentially produce by fully employing its given resources, it gives rise to the situation of excess demand which results in inflationary pressures in the economy. This inflationary situation can also arise if too large an increase in money supply in the economy occurs. In these circumstances, inflationary-gap occurs which tend to bring about rise in prices. If successful steps to check the emergence of excess demand are not taken, the economy will experience a period of inflation. For the last some decades, problem of demand-pull inflation has been faced by both the developed and developing countries of the world. An alternative way of looking at inflation is to view it from the angle of business cycles.

Under such circumstances, anti-cyclical fiscal policy calls for reduction in aggregate demand. Thus, fiscal policy measures to control inflation are reducing Government expenditure and increasing taxes. If in the beginning, the Government is having balanced budget, then increasing taxes while keeping Government expenditure constant will yield budget surplus. The creation of budget surplus will cause downward shift in the aggregate demand curve and will therefore help in easing pressure on prices. If there is a balanced budget to begin with and the Government reduces its expenditure, say on defence, subsidies, transfer payments, while keeping taxes constant, this will create budget surplus and result in removing excess demand in the economy.

Taxes do act to some extent as built in stabilizer. Given the level of Government expenditure, the tax system itself tends to create a budgetary surplus during a boom and a deficit during a depression. (A budgetary surplus would curb expenditure and demand while a budgetary deficit would have the opposite effect and thus an anti-cyclical pressure is generated. This happens because revenue from indirect and direct taxes is dependent upon the level of economic activities. Moreover, direct taxes are usually progressive. With increasing money incomes, the direct taxes bill rises more than proportionately, and during a depression, there is a more than proportionate reduction in it. Therefore, yield from these taxes also moves in line with the level of economic activities.

The result is that during a depression, tax revenue falls, and with given Government expenditure, there is a budgetary deficit, which in turn has an expansionary effect. On the other hand, during boom, larger revenue causes a budgetary surplus which has a contractionary effect. However, it is not enough to rely upon only built-in-stabilizing effect of the tax system. Economic stability requires an all-frontal effort in which variation in tax revenue is only a part. During a boom, the market may develop expectations that prices would rise still further. If that happens, tax measures are not likely to succeed in curbing speculative demand and prices.

Similarly, unless producers expect that their investments would be commercially profitable, they would not invest during a depression even when tax rates are lowered. Market imperfections are on the increase even in developed market economies which has adversely affected their adjustability and responsiveness to tax measures. Such limitations of tax devices become more glaring in underdeveloped countries. These economies are riddled with extra rigidities and they have a limited scope for the use of direct taxes.

Accordingly, in these countries, the authorities have to rely to a larger extent on non-taxation measures like import quotas and price controls. Even within the tax system, reliance has to be had on indirect taxes on a selective basis. It is found that the fiscal policy has far more chances of success during a depression, but much less in an inflationary situation. In either case, it will be better if the fiscal policy is helped with appropriate monetary and other measures.

End Notes

1. Shaw, G.K. (1981), "Leading Issues of Tax Policy in Developing Countries: The Economic Problems", in A. Peacock and F. Forte (eds.), *The Political Economy of Taxation,* Black Well, Oxford, p. 148.
2. Malhotra, R.N. (1991), *Banking, Finance and Development*, Southern Economist, Vol. 29, January 1, p. 7.
3. Hansen, A.H. (1941), *Fiscal Policy and Business Cycles*, Allen and Unwin, London, p. 115.
4. Chelliah, R.J. (1960), *Fiscal Policy in Underdeveloped Countries*, George Allen and Unwin Ltd., p. 45.
5. Keynes, J.M. (1936), *General Theory of Employment, Interest and Money*, Macmillan, London, p. 220.
6. Ibid., p. 379.
7. Ibid., p. 245.
8. Chelliah, R.J., *op.cit.*, p. 45.

9. Tripathi, R.N. (1964), *Public Finance in Underdeveloped Countries*, The World Press, p. 43.
10. Chelliah, R.J., *op. cit.*, p. 46.
11. Harrod, R.F. (1948), *Towards a Dynamic Economics*, Macmillan and Co. Ltd., London, p. 6.
12. Domar, E.D. (1957), *Essays in the Theory of Economic Growth*, Oxford University Press, London, p. 39.
13. Musgrave, R.A. (1959), *The Theory of Public Finance* , McGraw Hill Ltd., Tokyo, p. 483.
14. Ibid, p. 483.
15. Chelliah, R.J. (1969), *Fiscal Policy in Under developed Countries*, George Allen and Unwin (India) Pvt. Ltd., 2nd edition, p. 20.
16. Kothari, S.S (2001), *Reform of Fiscal and Economic Policies for Growth*, Macmillan India Ltd., pp. 82-83.
17. Tripathi, R.N., *op. cit.*, p. 82.
18. Caron, Yvon (2002), *Improving Resource Mobilization and Tax Administration System*, Inaugural speech Conference Proceeding, December 10, organized by Association de Planification Fiscale et Financiere (APFF), Montreal, Canada and UNDESA, p. 1.
19. Rastogi, K.M. (1965), *Fiscal Policy and Taxation in Economic Growth*, in Souvenir, Summer School in Economics, Jiwaji University, p. 60.
20. Shende, S.N. (2002), *Improving Financial Resources Mobilization in Developing Countries and Economies in Transition*, Department of Economic and Social Affairs, United Nation, July, pp. 2-4.
21. Gadgil, D.R. (1969), *Problems of Resource Mobilization in the States,* Inaugural Speech Conference proceedings, April 12, The Indian Institute of Public Administration, New Delhi, p. 5.
22. Singh, Tarlok (1947), *India's Development Experience*, Macmillan India, p. 193.
23. Chelliah, R.J. (1969), *op cit.*, p. 65.
24. Higgins, B. (1959), *Economic Development: Principles, Problems and Policies*, W. Norton and Co., New York, p. 24.
25. Bhargwati, Jagdish (1966), *The Economics of Underdeveloped Countries*, Weidenfeld and Nicolson, California, p. 112.
26. Lewis, W.A. (1960), *The Theory of Economics Growth*, Allen and Unwin, London, p. 376.

27. Tripathi, R.N., *op. cit.*, p. 88.
28. Hicks, U.K. (1961), *Public Finance*, Clarendon Press Oxford, p. 8.
29. Shende, S.N. (2002), *op. cit.*, p. 12.
30. Tripathi, R.N. (1970), *Fiscal Policy and Economic Development in India*, World Press, The University of Michigan, pp. 23-25.
31. United Nation (1966), *World Economic Survey, 1965*, p. 3.
32. Government of India (1927), *Report of the Committee on National Debt and Taxation*, p. 236.
33. Hansen, A. H., *op.cit*, p. 381.
34. Aggarwal, M., Chawla, K.L., Medury, Uma, Mukherjee, Indira, Rao, G.S., Sopory, Aparna (2008), *Deficit Financing*, Indira Gandhi National Open University (IGNOU), pp. 16-17, www.egyankosh.ac.in.
35. Aggarwal, M.,Chawla, K.L., Medury, Uma, Mukherjee, Indira, Rao, G.S., Sopory, Aparna., *op. cit.*, pp. 17-25.
36. Mishra, B. (1978), *Economics of Public Finance*, Macmillan, New York, p. 150.
37. Musgrave, R.A. and Musgrave, P.B (1973), *Public Finance in Theory and Practice*, McGraw Hill, New Zealand.
38. Chelliah, R.J., *op. cit.*, p. 44.
39. Bauchanan, J.M. and Flowers, R.F. (1975), *The Public Finances*, Richard D. Irwin Inc., U.S.A., pp. 75-76.
40. Acharya, S. (1988), "India's Fiscal Policy" in Robert E.B Lucas and Gustav F. Papanek *The Indian Economy-Recent Development and Future Prospects*, Centre for Asian Development Studies, Boston University, p. 295.
41. Tripathi, R.N., *op. cit.*, pp. 17-18.
42. Lerner, A.P. (1946), *The Economics of Control*, Macmillan, New York.
43. World Bank (2006), *Fiscal Policy for Growth and Development: An Interim Report*, Development Committee DC-0003, April 6, Washington, p. 5.

4

Philosophy of Fiscal Reforms in India

4.1 Rationale of Fiscal Reforms

India was a latecomer to economic reforms, embarking on the process in earnest only in 1991, in the wake of an exceptionally severe balance of payments crisis. The need for policy shift had became evident much earlier, as many countries in east Asia achieved high growth and poverty reduction through policies which emphasized greater export orientation and encouragement of the private sector. India took some steps in this direction in the 1980s, but it was not until 1991 that the government signalled a systemic shift to a more open economy with greater reliance upon market forces, a larger role for the private sector including foreign investment, and a restructuring of the role of Government (Ahluwalia, M.S., 2002). [1]

After a period of relatively robust economic performance in the late 1980s, the Indian economy entered into a period of unprecedented liquidity crisis during 1990-91. This crisis was the combined effect of a number of events coinciding. These included collapse of the Soviet Union that had emerged as India's major trading partner. The Gulf War that erupted in January 1991 worsened the balance of payments crisis not only with rising oil prices but also by causing a virtual stop-page of remittances from Indian workers in the Gulf. These events coupled with political uncertainty prevailing in the country led international credit rating agencies to lower India's rating both for short and long-term borrowings. The erosion of international confidence in the Indian economy not only made borrowings in international markets difficult but also led to outflow of deposits of non-resident Indians with Indian banks. These developments together brought the country to the verge of default with respect to external payments liability which could be averted by resorting to borrowings from the IMF under the stand-by arrangements and contingency and compensatory financing (CCF) and by mortgaging gold to the Bank of England. This was complemented by emergency measures to restrict imports (Kumar, Nagesh, 2002). [2]

The origin of the crisis is directly attributable to the cavalier macro management of the economy during the 1980s which led to large and persistent macroeconomic imbalances. The fiscal situation which was under strain throughout the 1980s, reached a critical situation in 1990-91. The unabated growths of non-plan expenditure and poor returns from investments made in the public sector have been the main contributory factors in the fiscal crisis. There has been a steady decline in the share of capital formation in the Central Government expenditure. The gross savings of the Government which turned negative for the first time in 1984-85, continued to remain so. The fiscal imbalance also manifested in a sharp increase in internal debt and resultant increase in interest payment.

These problems, in fact, were very much there for years destroying the capacity of the economy to cope with any internal or external shocks. In the 1970s, the Indian economy was strong enough to bear much larger and more sustained oil shocks. But by 1990, the situation had changed so much that minor oil shock made disproportionately large impact on the economy and a macroeconomic crisis erupted in the form of unsustainable fiscal and current account deficits and accelerating inflation. The year 1991-92 was one of the toughest years for the Indian economy. All the macroeconomic indicators became adverse.

The overall economic growth slumped to a mere 1.1 percent. The gross fiscal deficit stood at 8 percent of the GDP and the revenue deficit on the current account at 3.5 percent in 1990-91. Prices shot up to 17 percent, an all time high level. In the external sector, the balance of payments with as little as

US$ 1.1 billion foreign reserves or barely enough to meet two weeks' import bill became precarious. The shortage of foreign exchanges apart from inducing import squeeze for industrial production led the country by June 1991 to face a hard option of defaulting on international commitments such as debt servicing or accepting IMF structural adjustment and stabilization programme. The government decided to adopt in June 1991 a programme of macroeconomic stabilization to restore viability to fiscal balances and the balance of payments.

At the same time it undertook a far reaching programme of structural reforms involving bold initiatives in external trade, exchange trade, industrial policy and so on, all aiming at moving the country to a higher growth trajectory through infusing efficiency and international competitiveness. It also aimed at integrating the Indian economy with the global system and enhancing its robustness through wider access to better technology and benchmarking with the global performers. The reform process was comprehensive. The initial reforms focused on fiscal reforms, policy paradigm shift from physical control regime to the one relying more on market forces and trade related reforms. Subsequently reforms were extended to cover financial sector and to put in place law and regulatory framework compatible with a market system. The full impact of the reform measures edges into view over a long span of time (Sarma, A. and Gupta, M., 2002). [3]

In India, over the last several years, public debate with respect to fiscal policy reforms has proceeded at three distinct levels: at the *microeconomic level*, where discussion has cantered on the base and structure of tax rates and the distribution of Government expenditures across alternative end uses; at the *administrative level*, where concern has been expressed with respect to the quality of Government expenditures, the delivery of its services and the inefficiencies inherent within its tax collecting bureaucracies; and at the aggregate, *macroeconomic level*, where attention has focused on the size of the Government's fiscal deficits (and its various counterparts) and the implications this carries for real interest rates, inflation, investment and growth (Mishra,V., 2001). [4]

Fiscal reforms were the integral and perhaps the most critical part of the macroeconomic stabilization and reforms initiative taken by the Government after the 1991 economic crisis. The fiscal consolidation measures taken immediately after the crisis situation, yielded significant positive results in terms of reduction in fiscal deficit, control in expenditure and marked changes in the fiscal system particularly in the financing pattern of the deficits through reduction in monetization. However, the continued structural imbalances in terms of falling tax buoyancy, nature of fiscal correction in terms of reduction in investment expenditure, increased interest burden owing to borrowing at market related rates, impact of enhanced salary of Government employees, compulsions of increased defence expenditure etc. were some of the major factors which reversed the situation such that at the end of the decade the combine fiscal deficit of Centre and States was almost at the same level as was at the beginning of the reform measures.

The emerging situation has led economist to suggest that the second generation of reforms should constitute a program of action aimed at preventing another major economic crisis and should stimulate rapid economic growth in the country during the new century. In fact, in the strategy outlined by the Finance Minister in his budget speech in February, 2000, declaring the next 10 years as 'India's decade of development' one of the elements is to establish a credible framework of fiscal discipline. Many economists in their surveys have even warned that unless substantial fiscal consolidation is achieved continued fiscal deficits pose India's greatest risk to future destabilization (Deshmukh, H., Chaudhari, K., Powar, Y., Parhar, A. and Shejwal, A., 2006). [5]

The primary objective of the fiscal reforms as announced in the Union Budget 1991-92, was essentially to achieve a reduction in the size of deficit and debt in relation to GDP. It was envisaged that this would be achieved through revenue enhancement and curtailment in current expenditure growth while enlarging spending on investments and infrastructure so as to provide momentum to the growth process. These measures were also intended to curb the pre-emption of institutional resources by the Government and simultaneously to provide a level-playing field to the private investors. Accordingly, fiscal reforms in India were initiated in three distinct but interrelated areas:

1. Restoration of fiscal balance;
2. Restructuring of public sector; and
3. Strengthening of the fiscal-monetary coordination.

The strategy for restoring fiscal balance comprised tax and non-tax reforms, expenditure management and institutional reforms. Public sector restructuring mainly involved disinvestment of Government ownership. Contemporaneously, the steps towards improving fiscal-monetary coordination encompassed deregulation of financial system, elimination of automatic monetization, and reduction in pre-emption of institutional resources by the Government. At the sub-national level, fiscal adjustments began as a consequence of the deterioration in State's finances also.

4.2 What Triggered Fiscal Reforms?

Any review or assessment of fiscal sector reforms should perhaps be seen in the backdrop of certain operational features of the Indian fiscal system which have resulted in a slow and less satisfactory outcome. The complexity of the fiscal issues interlinked with all other macro-variables, deeply entrenched systemic elements of administration, historically strengthened rigidities of expenditure pattern, democratic constraints on unpopular fiscal and tax measures, and above all political uncertainties made fiscal reforms, the most challenging task for all shades (different political parties) of Governments notwithstanding a near consensus on the need of such reform. There are following reasons of fiscal reforms:

1. The growth of the economy slowed down substantially in 1991-92, partly because of a slowdown in agriculture and partly because of a deceleration in industrial growth.
2. Balance of payment, which emerged in 1990-91, had reached crisis proportions by June 1991. The first sign of the current payments crisis became evident in the second half of 1990-91, when the gulf war led to a sharp increase in oil prices.
3. Inflation, which had began to accelerate in 1990-91, reached a peak level of 16.7 percent in August 1991.
4. Fiscal imbalances were reflected in growing budget deficits mainly because of escalating non-plan expenditure in the face of sluggish revenue growth. Increasing budget deficit on the revenue account indicated danger signal.
5. Primary deficits accumulate into debt, unless offset by an excess of growth over interest rate. The ratio of revenue deficit to fiscal deficit indicates the extent to which borrowing is used for current expenditures.

Fiscal profligacy was seen to have caused the balance of payments crisis in 1991 and reduction in the fiscal deficit was therefore an urgent priority at the start of the reforms. The need for comprehensive fiscal reforms in India was apparent during the late 1980s, as there was rapid deterioration in Government finances. During this period, the expenditure of the Central Government rose much faster than its revenue leading to a steep rise in the Centre's fiscal deficit to GDP ratio. A closer analysis of the Central Government finances reveals that a widening of about two percentage points of GDP in gross fiscal deficit (GFD) emanated from the revenue deficit which widened from 1.4 percent of GDP in 1980-81 to 3.3 percent in 1990-91.

The key factor behind the worsening of revenue and fiscal deficit was increase in interest payments which registered a rise of almost two percentage points of GDP over the same period. This reflected a vicious cycle of widening deficit, larger borrowings, increasing debt stocks, higher interest payments and further widening of deficit. The debt stock of the Central Government over the eighties increased by around 14 percentage points of GDP to reach 55.3 percent of GDP in 1990-91. In respect of State Governments, though the revenue deficit widened by almost two percentage points of GDP, the rise in fiscal deficit could be contained at below one percentage point of GDP mainly due to compression in capital expenditure. The main factor behind the widening of revenue deficit of the States was the increase in non-interest revenue expenditure.

The rise in interest payments was, however, of a lower order as they had limited and restricted access to borrowed resources. The sharp increase in revenue deficit of the Central Government and the emergence of such deficits in State finances were the most worrisome developments in the fiscal scenario during the 1980s. Reflecting these developments, there was a sharp increase in the outstanding liabilities of both Central and State Governments as ratio to GDP from 41.6 percent and 16.7 percent respectively in 1980-81 to 55.3 percent and 19.4 percent respectively in 1990-91. The growing size of liabilities eventually generated a considerable debt-service burden, with interest payments as ratio to GDP rising from 1.8 percent to 3.8 percent in case of the Centre and from 0.9 percent to 1.5 percent in case of State during the same period.

The underdeveloped nature of the Government securities market and the heavy dependence of small saving collections on the level of income resulted in an implicit upper ceiling on Government's access to the market resources. This necessitated a large order of monetary accommodation from Reserve Bank of India with its attendant monetary implications. The outstanding net Reserve Bank credit to the Government as ratio to GDP rose from 11.4 percent as at end-March 1981 to 15.6 percent as at end-March 1991. In order to partially abate the inflationary pressure emanating from growing monetization of fiscal deficit, discrete upward changes in cash reserve ratio (CRR) were necessitated.

A large and growing fiscal deficit of the Government had macroeconomic implications in terms of sustainability of growth process. The mounting fiscal deficit in the eighties was increasingly financed by the draft of financial surpluses of the households through statutory pre-emptions of resources from the financial sector at sub-market clearing rates. The statutory liquidity ratio (SLR), which represents statutory investments by banks in Government securities, was raised to its peak level of 38.5 percent by 1990. Furthermore, the tendency of automatic monetization of fiscal deficit compromised effectiveness of monetary policy and fuelled inflation. With both CRR and SLR approaching their statutory upper limits at the time of the onset of unprecedented macroeconomic crisis of 1991, and given the deleterious macroeconomic consequences of high fiscal deficit, the only option available was to adopt a quick fiscal restructuring programme along with other macroeconomic and institutional reforms (Kapila, U., 2004). [6]

Deterioration of the fiscal situation and increased dissaving of Government administration by the latter half of the 1990s renewed the urgency for improving public finances at both Centre and State levels, particularly, in view of the need to benchmark Indian codes and practices to international standards in the aftermath of its membership to G-20 groups of the countries. The strategy of fiscal consolidation initiated in the early nineties was a mix of measures towards revenue augmentation through tax reforms and expenditure compression (Mohan, R., 2008). [7] The need for "fiscal adjustment now"(Pinto, Brian and Zahir, Farah, 2004) [8] arises not because a crisis is imminent but because postponing reform is likely to result in an unmanageable debt and interest burden by the end of the Tenth Plan period notwithstanding the current low interest rates and burgeoning reserves.

In contrast, a phased adjustment beginning now and focusing on a relatively small set of reforms is likely to yield substantial, positive benefits over the same horizon and be more conducive to long-run growth and poverty reduction. By "adjustment" is not meant an immediate, drastic cut in the fiscal deficit. The only way to do so given the extraordinary high level of interest payments would be to cut capital expenditure even more, which would be undesirable. Instead, the advocated focus is on revenue mobilization and in directing "non-merit subsidies" towards capital and development expenditure. A key factor in the fiscal deterioration during the Ninth Plan period has been the significant reform induced losses in revenue (both indirect tax revenue and financial repression revenue), and also the Government inability to adjust public spending (as interest payments take up to increasing share of the budget).

Debt dynamics worsened over 2002-03 despite the record low interest rates. The reason for this and the inadvisability of gambling on the persistence of low interest rates are spelled over. Second, it demonstrates that Government debt dynamics are showing signs of being unsustainable. The primary deficit (non-interest fiscal deficit) is large and real interest rates have converged to growth rates. Third, the Reserve Bank of India's policy of building up reserves and sterilizing them(to cushion against external shocks and keep inflation low, respectively), coupled with constraints on Government spending(because of fiscal deficits and public debt) has resulted in low public and private investment, putting long-run growth in jeopardy relative to the levels needed for rapid poverty alleviation. Moreover, while higher reserves sheet of the Government and the RBI has weakened. Fourth, projections show that postponing fiscal adjustment will push the debt burden to unmanageable levels by the end of the Tenth Plan period; but a phased adjustment that begins immediately will lower deficits and greatly improve spending composition.

4.3 Objectives of Fiscal Reforms

Indian economy needed substantial reforms to overcome

the crises. To implement a programme of macro-economic stabilization, number of structural reforms of trade, industry and public sector were initiated. Structural reforms were necessary to reverse various unhealthy economic trends and tendencies. Without such reforms, Indian economy could not have been brought back on the track of growth and development. The reforms have embraced almost all aspect of the country's economy. These reforms fall under two basic categories:

1. Liberalization measures.
2. Macro-economic reforms and structural adjustments.

Various measures taken together aim at modernizing the country's industrial system, removing unproductive controls, encouraging private investment including foreign investment and integrating India's economy with global economy. All round opening up of the country's economy has been the aim of the various reforms, which were initiated (Mahajan, V. and Mahajan, M., 2003) [9] Governments all over the world have been using fiscal measures to regulate their economic and business activities in order to achieve their objectives.

Following were the main objectives of fiscal sector reforms to enhance the stability and efficiency of the economy:

1. The immediate aim of fiscal policy reforms was to improve the fiscal balance in order to eliminate the inflationary pressure emanating from the budget deficit;
2. To stop further accumulation of public debt;
3. To reduce the level of subsidies in the economy and eliminate open-ended cross-subsidization;
4. To direct Government expenditure towards providing essential public services of a high quality, and finally to restore the Government's capacity to make strategic investments in infrastructure and human resources, and look after the weak and the less privileged (Prasad, C.S., 2005). [10]
5. A key objective of the reform process was the augmentation of non-tax revenue by way of enhancement

of user charges and returns on Government investments through restructuring of public sector undertakings (PSUs). The intention of restructuring PSUs was to improve their efficiency and thereby enhance the capacity to generate returns on Government investments.

4.4 RBI's Perspectives on Fiscal Reforms

RBI's approach to fiscal reforms is that while RBI agrees on the need to eliminate the revenue deficit, and agrees on a nominal limit for fiscal deficit, what is even more important is the mode of financing the fiscal deficit and the use that the resources so raised are put to. In addition, RBI focuses on fiscal empowerment which was clearly articulated around 2000 in the Annual Report of the Board of Directors of the RBI. Exclusive focus on fiscal deficit may tend to reduce the role of the Government, and consequently, it will not be in position to aid the process of growth, in particular, inclusive growth. Re-prioritization of expenditure may be achieved through reduction or elimination of subsidies and deployment of resources thus released to the more needy sectors.

Higher level of resources may also be available through reduction in tax exemption. Indian economy requires structural transformation and investment in social and financial infrastructure, RBI should strive for an appropriate level of fiscal activity particularly because public goods have to be provided and that would enable RBI to maintain fiscal discipline and macro-stability rather than aim for a mechanical reduction in fiscal and revenue deficits at a lower level of fiscal activity. In the light of financial turbulence across the world in the recent period, the relevance of the fisc in the management of the macro economy has become even more important. When RBI have not seen such financial turbulence in our country, it is important to remember that when all else fails, it is only the fiscal that has to take the hit and come to the rescue. One of the rating agencies says "India's monetary management is conservative and prudent, together with its low external debt position and relative ease in local currency funding, this helps alleviate its fiscal weakness". The important point here is if RBI's policy is helping to alleviate fiscal weakness, how can it be conservative? It perhaps needs to be described as "appropriate" (Reddy, Y.V., 2008). [11]

4.5 Quality of Fiscal Reforms

In recent years, we have become progressively more aware of the fact that a given reduction in the fiscal deficit may be genuine and of good quality or of a largely cosmetic kind and of poor quality. The economic effects of the two are likely to be widely divergent. Unfortunately, cosmetic changes are often easier and politically less costly to make. This fact, coupled with the realization that the time horizon that is most important to policy makers often leads to a preference for cosmetic over genuine adjustment. Policy makers tend to follow the line of least resistance.

A reduction of certain magnitude in the fiscal deficit is in most cases, not the result of a single policy decision as would be, say, a devaluation or an increase in interest rates but the summation of many specific policy decisions, both on the revenue side and on the expenditure side (Vito, Tanzi, 1993). [12] A high quality fiscal stabilization must be associated with measures that individually are efficient, durable, and equitable. In other words, these measures must not introduce avoidable distortions; they must not self-destruct in the near future; and they must not eliminate expenditures that are important for economic or social reasons when alternatives are available. The public spending to be reduced must be the one that contributes the least to the efficiency and fairness of the economic system.

On the revenue side, and broadly in order of preference but not in order of facility of introduction, the following measures could be chosen: First, the broadening or the introduction of a general consumption tax, possibly one with characteristics of a value-added tax. Value-added taxes are now important sources of revenue in a relatively efficient way and with relatively short lags. Second, the Government should fully explore the revenue possibility of excise taxes. These excises should be imposed on commodities with inelastic demand, or on those whose consumption generates substantial negative externalities. Third, important changes can be introduced to the personal income tax. Personal income taxes contribute still very little to total revenue in developing countries.

If basic changes are made, the threshold of the tax can remain generous, and high marginal tax rates can be cut, without much revenue loss and with potential gains in work effort and tax payers' compliance. For taxes on corporations, similar considerations apply. Corporate income taxes are often eroded by excessive incentives and complex laws. In particular circumstances, and especially when the rate of inflation is high, alternative forms of taxing corporations may need to be introduced. The next measures, which especially in the short-run can be very important from a revenue point of view, is the rising of public utility prices and the introduction of user charges for particular services provided by the public sector, such as higher education and health.

The real prices at which electricity, water, telephone, transportation and other public sector services are sold normally fall, at times quite drastically, during inflationary periods. This fall increases the demand for these services. Because of losses experienced by the public enterprises, it becomes difficult to expand capacity. Enterprises have also difficulties in providing the funds necessary for operation and maintenance, especially in view of the more intensive utilization of their plants. Thus, capacity will decline and the quality of the service will deteriorate. The greater is the fall in the real tariffs charged by the public enterprises, and the greater is the demand response to that fall, the greater will appear to be the need to expand investment in those activities. Thus, an artificial justification for capacity expansion will be created especially at a time when the resources to satisfy that expansion are sharply reduced (Ibid) [13]. A correction of these prices will thus:

1. Generate more revenue.
2. Reduce the need for additional investment to expand capacity by lowering demand.
3. By reducing overuse, it will reduce maintenance costs.

Finally, imports can be made to generate larger revenues either by dismantling quotas and other quantitative restrictions and replacing them by import duties or by removing the excessive erosion of the import tax base created by incentives and special exemptions, and by introducing a minimum tax on all imports. In both cases, the additional revenue would be accompanied by improved efficiency.

On the expenditure side, a variety of step can be taken: First, and most importantly, unproductive investment projects must be eliminated. The argument often heard that investment must be protected during adjustment is simply misguided. While productive investment is an important source of growth and must be protected, unproductive investment especially if associated with imported machinery and capital equipment is a major burden on the economy. In most developing countries the investment budget is padded with many politically motivated and unproductive investments which can, and should be eliminated.

Unlike consumption expenditure, it may contribute little to the welfare of the country's citizen (Ibid). [14] Furthermore, if it is obtained with foreign credit, it becomes a long-term drag on the economy. Hence, unproductive investment must be the first area where cuts should be made. Some of the savings from this source could be allocated to operations and maintenance expenditure, which would increase the efficiency of the existing capital structure and would permit that structure to support a higher level of income.

A second area where reductions could be made is in the wage bill of the public sector. During stabilization many countries have in fact, attempted to reduce the wage bill of the public sector. However, policy makers have generally preferred to reduce real wages rather than public employment. There is evidence, from some countries, that cuts in real wages have been accompanied by expansions in public sector employment. Since the marginal cost of hiring extra workers falls with the fall in real wages and since adjustment often increases unemployment in the short run pressure is put on the government to be the employment of last resort.

Such a policy does not have much chance for success in reducing the wage bill over the long run and it is likely to increase the inefficiency of public sector employees, especially at a time when the public sector is expected to play a larger role in restructuring the economy. The cut in real wages, unless they were high to start with, almost guarantees that the efficiency of the public sector will fall. Furthermore, a drastic fall in real wages guarantees that they will bounce back as soon as the Government is no longer be able to withstand the pressure of public sector unions (Ibid). [15]

In other words, excessive reduction in real wages will increase fiscal tension. The reduction in real wages, at a time of high unemployment, will generate pressures on the Government to increase its unemployment. In many developing countries the public sector is clearly overstaffed. Therefore, fiscal stabilization that hopes to reduce the wage bill permanently must reduce in some cases quite considerably, the number of public employees. This may require privatizing some activities.

The third important area for reduction, although a politically difficult one, is defence expenditure. Defence expenditure remains excessive in developing countries. Unfortunately, this spending has been able so far to withstand the downward pressures in public expenditure that accompany stabilization programmes (Desai, P. and H. Lorie, 1989) [16] Fourth, many countries engage in various forms of unproductive expenditure, from the building of monuments to the subsidization of unnecessary activities. In many developing countries, for example, a large number of public cars (often expensive ones) are purchased.

In many of these countries the enforcement of useless regulations also requires substantial public sector spending. In conclusion, in most countries there is scope for pruning the budget of many of these activities. Subsidies must be closely scrutinized. Those which are essential, because of social objectives, or because of significant externalities, should be protected. But generalized subsidies, provided through the artificial reduction in the prices of products of general country, should be eliminated. Many subsidies, even when defended on the grounds that they protect the poor, just subsidies the middle classes.

4.6 Sequencing of Fiscal Reforms

A fundamental and common conflict that arises in adjustment programmes is the one between the need to achieve quick results and the time necessary to develop, legislate, and implement sound policies. The need for quick results is often promoted by: (a) the precariousness of the economic situation; (b) the fear that if changes are not made immediately, they will not be made; and (c) by arrangements with international institutions which are often time constrained.

While changes in interest rates, in exchange rates, and in other areas of economic policy can be made relatively quickly and often do not require legislative approval, fiscal reforms, that include tax reform, public sector reorganizations including privatization, reform of public expenditure programmes, and so forth, require time and, in many countries, must be legislated. As a consequence, countries have often gone for 'quick fixes' that is for fiscal reforms that reduce the fiscal deficit in the period immediately ahead with policy changes that are neither durable nor efficient. Common elements of these 'quick fix' solutions have been:

1. Sharp reductions in public sector real wages to levels below their likely long run equilibrium.

2. Sharp and indiscriminate cuts in investment expenditure without much assurance that the projects that are eliminated are least productive.
3. Sharp cuts in expenditures on operation and maintenance leading to a faster deterioration of the existing capital infrastructure and to reduce capacity utilization.
4. Emergency tax legislation, including the temporary introduction of very distortionary taxes such as those on exports and financial instruments, and of temporary surtaxes on import duties, income taxes, and others.
5. Excessive increase in some excises.
6. Anticipation of tax payments, sometimes by providing discounts for anticipated payments to tax payers, thus reducing further tax collection.
7. Tax amnesties.
8. Quick sales of some assets.
9. Delay in making payments.
10. Various imaginative manoeuvres aimed at 'parking' the deficit in part of the public sector not covered by the programme.

Most of the above measures are either self-destructuring, or of questionable quality, or both. They are not the kind of measures that will result in durable stabilization. They will cause a rise in fiscal tension, increasing uncertainty and sending negative signals to investors, thus discouraging capital repatriation, or encouraging capital flight. Given the measured fiscal deficit, the expected rate of return on private investment is likely to be negatively related to the degree of fiscal tension while private investment is positively related to the expected rate of return.

Therefore, a deficit reduction achieved through these means should not be expected to bring about an improvement in economic conditions. Such a reduction can only be justified if it is clearly announced and believed to be a transitory step towards a more durable and higher quality package. Unfortunately, these measures often exhaust the political will of the Government to make the more basic reforms or are seen as the only way to reduce the fiscal deficit. Sustainable fiscal policy requires, almost by definition measures that will not put additional impediments on the efficient allocation of resources. It must involve good macroeconomists working in close cooperation with public finance specialists experienced in both policy and administration.

End Notes

1. Ahluwalia, M.S. (2002), "Economic Reforms in India since 1991: Has Gradualism Worked?" *Economic Perspectives Journal*, Summer 2002, pp. 1-2.
2. Kumar, Nagesh (2002), "Economic Reforms and Their Macroeconomic Impact" in Raj Kapila and Uma Kapila (ed.) *A Decade of Economic Reforms in India*, Academic Foundation Publication, New Delhi, p. 126.
3. Sarma, A. and Gupta, M. (2002), "A Decade of Fiscal Reforms in India", *International Studies Program, Working Paper 02-04,* Georgia State University, Andrew Young School of Policy Studies, U.S.A.
4. Mishra, V. (2001), "Fiscal Deficit and Fiscal Responsibility Act", *Economic and Political Weekly*, February 24, Mumbai, p. 609.
5. Deshmukh, H., Chaudhari, K. and Powar, Y., Parhar, A. and Shejwal, A. (2006), *Fiscal Consolidation in India*, www.it.iitb.ac.in.
6. Kapila, U. (2004), "Fiscal Reforms in India: Policy Measures and Developments" in Uma Kapila (ed.) *Indian Economy since Independence*, Academic Foundation, New Delhi, pp. 114-120.
7. Mohan, R. (2008), *The Role of Fiscal and Monetary Policies in Sustaining Growth with Stability in India,* RBI Monthly Bulletin, December, Mumbai, pp. 2087-2088.
8. Pinto, Brian and Zahir, Farah (2004), "India: Why Fiscal Adjustment Now", *World Bank Policy Research*, Working Paper 3230, March, Washington D.C., p. 3.
9. Mahajan, V. and Mahajan, M. (2003),"Fiscal Discipline: A Key to Success of Fiscal Reform" in P. P. Arya and B. B. Tondon (eds.) *Economic Reforms in India- From First to Second Generation and Beyond*, Deep and Deep Publication Pvt. Ltd.,

New Delhi, p. 210.
10. Prasad, C.S. (2005), "1991-92: Deepening of Economic Crisis" in C.S. Prasad (ed.) *India: Economic Policies and Performance: 1947-48 to 2004-05*, New Century Publications, New Delhi, p. 383.
11. Reddy, Y.V. (2008), "Fiscal Policy and Economic Reforms", *BIS Review 81/2008, National Institute of Public Finance and Policy (NIPF)*, New Delhi, 26 May.
12. Vito, Tanzi (1993), "Fiscal Issues in Adjustment Programs" in Faini, R. and J. de Melo (eds.) *Fiscal Issues in Adjustment in Developing Countries*, St. Martin's Press, New York, pp. 27-28.
13. Ibid, p. 29.
14. Ibid, pp. 29-30.
15. Ibid, pp. 29-30.
16. DeMsai, P. and H. Lorie (1989), *How Resilentare Military Expenditures in the Context of Fund-Supported Programs?*, Staff Papers, IMF, Washington, D.C., 36, pp. 130-165.

5

Fiscal Reform Measures in India

While a move towards fiscal adjustment was discernible in the pronouncements made as a part of long-term fiscal policy announced in the mid-1980s, a comprehensive fiscal reform programme at the Central Government level was initiated only at the beginning of the 1990s as part of the economic adjustment programme initiated in 1991-92. Fiscal reforms at the Centre covered:

1. Tax reforms.
2. Expenditure reforms.
3. Restructuring of public sector.
4. Fiscal-monetary coordination.
5. Institutional measures.

5.1 Tax Reforms

There have been major changes in tax systems of countries with a wide variety of economic systems and levels of development during the last two decades. The motivation for these reforms has varied from one country to another and the thrust of reforms has differed from time to time depending on the development strategy and philosophy of the times. In many developing countries, the immediate reason for tax reforms has been the need to enhance revenues to meet impending fiscal crises. Such reforms, however, are often ad hoc and are done to meet immediate exigencies of revenue. In most cases, such reforms are not in the nature of systemic improvements to enhance the long run productivity of the tax system.

One of the most important reasons for recent tax reforms in many developing and transitional economies has been to evolve a tax system to meet the requirements of international competition. The transition from a predominantly centrally planned development strategy to market based resource allocation has changed the perspective of the role of the state in development. The transition from a public sector based, heavy industry dominated, import substituting industrialization strategy to one of allocating resources according to market signals has necessitated systemic changes in the tax system. In an export-led open economy, the tax system should not only raise the necessary revenues to provide the social and physical infrastructure but also minimize distortions. Thus, the tax system has to meet the requirements of a market economy to ensure international competitiveness (Rao, G.M. and Rao, K.R., 2006). [1]

Tax reforms are needed to promote efficient growth. A transparent and simple tax regime contributes to improving the business and investment climate that is so essential for the private sector to expand employment opportunities. Improving tax collection is an essential element for financing prioritized public investment and public expenditure. Deepening of tax reforms will not only strengthen public governance, it will lead to increasing revenue collection. Increase in revenue collection are necessary for India to be able to finance those programs that are crucial to broadening inclusiveness, including social spending for health, education, sanitation and strengthening social safety nets. Moreover, increasing tax collection will be instrumental towards effectively strengthening the budget as the Government's principal policy instrument to effectively pursue its policy objectives including meeting the Millennium Development Goals (Schaefer, Ursula, 2007). [2]

5.1.1 Raja J. Chelliah Committee: The Government of India constituted a Committee of experts under the chairmanship of Raja J. Chelliah to examine the structure of direct and indirect taxes through its Resolution dated August 29, 1991. The terms of reference of the Committee were to examine and make recommendations on the following matters:

1. Ways of improving the elasticity of tax revenues, both direct and indirect, and increasing the share of direct taxes

as a proportion of total tax revenues and of GDP.

2. Making the tax system fairer and broad-based, with necessary rate adjustments, particularly with regard to commodity taxation and personal taxation.
3. Rationalization of the system of direct taxes with view to removing anomalies, improving equity and sustaining economic incentives.
4. Identifying new areas for taxation.
5. Ways of improving compliance of direct taxes and strengthening enforcement.
6. Simplification and rationalization of customs tariffs with a view to reducing the multiplicity and dispersion of rates and to eliminate exemptions which have become unnecessary.
7. Reducing the level of tariff rates, keeping in view the need for mobilizing resources to facilitate fiscal adjustment and the objective of promoting international competitiveness.
8. Simplification and rationalization of the structure of excise duties for better tax compliance and administration.
9. The scope of extending the MODVAT Scheme.
10. Any other matter related to the above points or incidental thereto.

The Committee submitted its Report in three instalments.

- An Interim Report in December 1991;
- Final Report Part-I in August 1992; and
- Final Report Part-II in January 1993.

These Reports contained recommendations for restructuring and rationalization of personal income tax, corporate income tax, wealth tax, excise duties, import tariff, tax administration and enforcement machinery. Based on the overall direction prescribed by the Tax Reforms Committee (TRC), tax reforms introduced by the Government since mid-1991 are geared to build a structure which is simple, relies on moderated tax rates but with a wider base and better enforcement. Historically, rates of income tax in India have been quite high, almost punitive. For example, in 1973-74, the maximum marginal rate of individual income tax was as high as 97.7 percent.

When high rates proved counter-productive from revenue angle, the Government initiated a series of rate reductions with the result that the top rate declined to 54 percent (including surcharge of 8 percent) in 1990-91. Consequent upon the recommendations of the TRC, the number of income tax rates was reduced and the rates themselves were scaled down. The 1992-93 Budget fixed the maximum marginal rate at 44.8 percent (including surcharge of 12). The 1994-95 Budget abolished the surcharge of 12 percent and therefore the maximum marginal rate of tax became 40 percent on incomes over ₹ 1,20,000. The maximum marginal rate of personal income tax was further reduced from 40 percent to 30 percent in the 1997-98 Budget.

In another significant move, it was made applicable to incomes above ₹ 1,50,000. The 1994-95 Budget abolished the distinction between widely-held domestic companies and closely-held domestic companies and introduce a single tax rate of 40 percent for all types of domestic companies. In the same Budget, the taxes on corporate income were unified at 46 percent for widely held companies and 55 percent for branches of foreign banks. It is noteworthy that no surcharge is applicable on the income of foreign companies. A major reform of excises was implemented to make it more closely resemble a value-added tax and address its major problems. Meanwhile, the manufacturing sector thus far excluded, and, for the first time, some services. Of particular importance also were the decisions to:

- Shift most excise rates from specific to ad-valorem to increase buoyancy;
- Reduce the number of rates; and
- Simplify the system by relying on invoices for value determination.

These reforms considerably simplified and modernized India's tax system and made it possible for the Central

Government to begin to focus its effort on improving tax administration.

The 1995-96 Budget further reduced peak excise duties. It did not reduce corporate tax rates further but it continued the emphasis on simplification, lower rates and greater buoyancy. To strengthen compliance, the authorities proposed tax deduction at source for fees for professionals, technical services and service contracts, and interest income on time deposits. Further, significant tax reforms were introduced in the 1996-97 Budget. Several tax measures have been taken to continue to broaden the tax base, reduce rates, and improve tax administration. This has been particularly important in the case of excise and corporate taxation. Regarding excise taxes, the Finance Minister emphasized the need to move to a more transparent and simple four-rate excise tax structure-zero, a lower rate of excise duty on goods of mass consumption, a single normal rate on all other goods, and a higher rate on luxury items in year or two.

In the meantime, the MODVAT has been extended to the textile fabrics sector with a special tax incentives package (excise and customs duties have been reduced on important inputs) to boost the sector. A mandatory penalty for evasion of excise duty or misuse of MODVAT credit scheme on account of fraud, collusion etc., was also introduced. Excise duties were raised on several items, including all petroleum products except on LPG and Kerosene. On the import duty side, the basic duty rate on a number of items was reduced to 30 or 40 percent. Progress was also made in unifying import duty rates on similar items, in order to avoid disputes arising out of mis-classification and multiplicity of rates.

5.1.2 Minimum Alternative Tax (MAT): The noteworthy development for company income tax was the reduction of a surcharge on corporate tax from 15 percent to 7.5 percent and the introduction of a "Minimum Alternative Tax" (MAT) on companies' book profits to bring into the tax net some 1,000 companies currently under the zero-tax bracket or benefiting from excessive exemptions. Finally, the tax on long-term capital gains for domestic companies has been reduced from 30 percent to 20 percent to bring it in line with that for foreign companies. The scope of the long term capital gains tax exemption was widened to include investment in shares issued by public companies in specified sectors. Regarding personal income tax, the Budget has reduced the income-tax rate for the first bracket from 20 percent to 15 percent. Allowances were also granted for various deductions (interest payments on owner-occupier mortgages, health insurance, and fiscal incentives for saving schemes).

The 1997-98 Budget introduced sharp cuts in income tax rates with a view to stimulate saving and investment and encourage higher tax compliance. Personal and corporate tax rates were reduced and rationalized to bring them to internationally comparable levels. The top marginal personal income tax rate was cut from 40 to 30 percent. The surcharge on companies was completely abolished and the tax rate for domestic companies was reduced from 40 percent to 35 percent. The tax rate on foreign companies was scaled down from 55 to 48 percent. The 1999-2000 Budget undertook a major overhaul of indirect taxes by reducing the multiplicity of rates, rationalizing the rate structure. In a landmark move, the Finance Minister announced in his 1999-2000 Budget a triple rate excise structure.

In other words, the excise duty reform involved reduction of 11 major ad valorem duty rates to 3, viz. a central rate of 16 percent, a merit rate of 8 percent and a demerit rate of 24 percent. The initiative of the Finance Minister to rationalize the rate structure of excise system was widely appreciated. Reduction of the peak protective customs duty resumed after a hiatus of the two years, with a reduction of the peak tariff from 45 percent to 40 percent. The seven major ad valorem rates of basic customs duty were winnowed to five (5 percent, 15 percent, 25 percent, 35 percent, and 40 percent). To reduce dispersion, a basic duty of 5 percent was imposed on a number of commodities (including project imports) which earlier enjoyed duty exemption (but were exempted from the 4 percent special additional duty). This provided some minimal protection to these items.

The basic principles guiding the tax proposals in the Union Budget 2001-02 were the need for revenue buoyancy, further simplification of the tax regime and more effective tax compliance. In the area of direct taxes, the emphasis was on retention of stability in tax rates, widening of the tax base and rationalization and simplification of the tax structure. All surcharges were abolished except the Gujarat earthquake surcharge of 2 percent imposed on all non-corporate and corporate assesses except foreign companies. The ongoing process of reducing rates, rationalizing the tax regime, and simplifying procedures, was carried forward in the sphere of indirect taxes also. The important initiatives adopted during the year were the following:

1. Peak level of customs duty reduced from 38.5 percent to 35 percent with abolition of surcharge on customs duty. Customs duty reduced on specified textile machines, information technology, telecommunications and entertainment industry.
2. Excise duty structure rationalized to a single rate of 16 percent CENVAT (Central Value Added Tax) in 2000-01. The Budget for 2001-02 replaced earlier three special rates of 8 percent, 16 percent, and 24 percent by a single rate of 16 percent.

5.1.3 Task Force on Direct Taxes: The Task Force on Direct Taxes presented its consultation paper to the Government on November 2, 2002. The discussion paper on indirect taxes was presented on November 25, 2002. The consultation papers were made public to facilitate an informed discussion on tax policy. After taking into account the response on the discussion papers, the Task Forces submitted their final reports to the Government in December 2002. The Task Forces made important recommendations on toning up tax administration to put in place a system that is simple, effective and at par with international standards.

The main recommendations on direct taxes related to raising of exemption limit of personal income tax, rationalization of exemptions, abolition of concessional treatment to long-term capital gains, and abolition of wealth tax. In respect of indirect taxes, the main recommendations related to widening of the tax base, removal of exemptions, expansion in the coverage of service tax etc. Accordingly, the tax rates were significantly rationalized and progressively brought down to the levels comparable to some of the developed economies. The key tax reforms have been:

1. Lowering of the maximum marginal personal income tax rate from 60 percent in 1980-81 to the present level of 33 percent (inclusive of 10 percent surcharge on annual income of above ₹ 8.5 lakh, announced in the Union Budget 2003-04);
2. Widening of the tax base by way of a series of steps including introduction of presumptive taxes, adoption of a set of six economic criteria for identification of potential tax payers in urban areas and taxation of services;
3. Reducing the corporate tax rate on both domestic and foreign companies to the current level of 35 percent and 40 percent, respectively, from a level of 65 percent and 70 percent in 1980-81;
4. Unification of tax rates on closely held as well as widely held domestic companies;
5. Rationalization of capital gains tax and dividend tax;
6. Progressive reduction in the peak rate of customs duty on non-agricultural products from a level of more than 300 percent during the period just prior to reforms to the level of 25 percent as announced in the Union Budget 2003-04; and
7. Reduction of 11 major ad-valorem excise duties to three viz., central rate of 16 percent, merit rate of 8 percent and demerit rate of 24 percent in year 1999-2000, introduction

of a uniform 16 percent CENVAT effective from 2000-01, while retaining special excise duties on specified goods and in Union Budget 2003-04 rationalization of excise rate structure by proposing a 3-tier structure of 8 percent, 16 percent and 24 percent which are, however. not applicable to goods attracting specific duty rates.

In the area of direct taxes, the Budget for 2005-06 carried forward the process initiated in the previous Budget. In personal income tax, the tax rates were revised for various tax brackets conferring gain to all taxpayers through higher exemption limits and scaling up, even as standard deduction was withdrawn. In another significant move, neutrality of taxes between various forms of savings was achieved through a general rebate on savings in any approved instrument up to ₹ 1 lakh. Budget of 2005-06 introduced two new taxes: a fringe benefit tax targeted at those benefits enjoyed collectively by the employees and not attributable to individual employees, which were to be taxed in the hands of employer; and a tax on banking cash transactions (withdrawals) over a certain threshold in a single day.

Taking a leaf out of the international best practices, corporate income tax was reduced to 30 percent, albeit with a higher surcharge of 10 percent and reduced depreciation allowance that was a better approximation to the replacement life-value. Further, the withholding tax on technical services was reduced from 20 percent to 10 percent. To facilitate large taxpayers, new large taxpayer units (LTUs), providing single window service, were proposed to be estimated. Adhering to the pre-announced commitment to align customs duties to ASEAN levels, Budget of 2005-06 reduced peak customs duty on non-agricultural products to 15 percent with steeper reductions for capital goods and raw materials and corrections for inverted duty structures.

The Union Budget of 2006-07 kept the tax rates moderate and stable, and no change in the rates of personal income tax or corporate income tax was proposed. Similarly, no new taxes were imposed. There were, however, some marginal revisions in certain tax rates. The rate under minimum alternate tax (MAT) was increased from 7.5 percent of book profits to 10 percent. Long-term capital gains arising out of securities and subject to securities transaction tax (STT) were also included in calculating book profits. MAT-paying companies were allowed the credit for MAT over seven years instead of the five years allowed earlier. Adjustment of MAT credit was also allowed while calculating interest liability. As regards indirect taxes, the objective of bringing about a moderate, rational and simplified tax structure and to align it with ASEAN levels was further by reducing the peak rate of customs duty on non-agricultural products from 15 percent to 12.5 percent with a few exceptions.

In the Budget of 2007-08, the peak rate of custom duty on non-agricultural product was reduced from 12.5 percent to 10 percent, with few exceptions. In the case of excise duties, the following important changes were announced:

1. To improve competitiveness of the small scale sector, the exemption limit for SSI sector was raised from ₹ 1 crore to ₹ 1.5 crore; and
2. Ad valorem component of excise duty on petrol and high speed diesel was reduced from 8 percent to 6 percent.

The number of services liable for taxation was raised from 3 in 1994-95 to 6 in 1996-97, and then gradually to 100 in 2007-08. In the 2007-08 Budget, certain services were specified as taxable services, scope of some of the specified taxable services was changed, threshold limit for small service providers was increased and certain exemptions were announced. Continuing the policy of lower import tariff, the Finance Minister in his 2008-09 Budget speech announced reduction in import duty on project import from 7.5 percent to 5 percent. After successive downward revisions, the peak rate of import duty on non-agricultural products stood at 10 percent. Domestic companies and firms pay 30 percent and foreign companies, 40 percent tax on their profits.

5.1.4 Advisory Group on Tax Policy and Tax Administration: Tax reforms are generally supposed to raise the tax revenue to GDP ratio across countries. Normally, tax revenue is expected to rise in response to a reduction of tax rate from some higher level. The concern with tax rationalization has been reflected in the appointment of a number of committees to review the tax system in the last few years. The Advisory Group on Tax Policy and Tax Administration for the Tenth Plan, 2001 recommended deletion of a number of exemptions and deductions which have become redundant and are not in harmony with a modern tax regime. Similarly, the Expert Committee to Review the System of Administrative Interest Rates and Other Related Issues, 2001 recommended the withdrawal of tax concessions available on small savings. Furthermore, the Task Force on Direct Taxes and Indirect Taxes, 2002 has reiterated the need to withdraw exemptions and concessions to widen the tax base. An assessment of tax reform measures in India has shown significant improvement (compared to pre-reform status) in tax structure in terms of 'economic neutrality', equity, revenue predictability, administrative effectiveness etc. but deterioration in revenue adequacy (tax buoyancy) and revenue stability.

5.2 Expenditure Reforms

Fiscal policy sets growth, stability and equity as the goals where public expenditure management is one of the main operating instruments in pursuing these goals. In this pursuit, public expenditure management plans to achieve intermediate targets set for overall expenditure control, strategic resource allocation as per the policy priorities and efficient, effective and responsive operational management of expenditure. It is the expenditure policy which, in the ultimate sense is responsible for the success or failure of the whole fiscal policy stance. Expenditure management through appropriate prioritization and control is important for any government. The tension between containing the deficit and providing adequate outlays for the relevant heads makes expenditure prioritization an even more important issue in India than what it is in many other countries. There is need for more schools, hospitals, roads, hydroelectric and multipurpose irrigation projects, etc, on the other hand, and sticking to fiscal prudence on the other.

During recent years, there has been a growing recognition of the roles of expenditures and expenditure management in fiscal adjustment and in the pursuit fiscal policies over the medium term. There is also recognition that a prerequisite to the pursuit of sustainable fiscal policies, the quality of expenditure needs to be improved (EPW Research Foundation, 2001). [3] Expenditure management, in its broad perspective includes three major elements:

1. Resource allocation;
2. Resource utilization; and
3. Resource utilizing accounting.

Expenditure policy is a by product both in intent and outcome, of the working of these three inter-related phases. Expenditure policies aim at dealing both with the above mentioned structural issues, as well as with the immediate concerns that are addressed as a part of the overall annual budgetary policy (Mathur, B.P., 1999). [4] Some of the major expenditure reduction/management policies undertaken during the 1990s after the initiation of the economic reform by the Central Government were in the following manner. Immediately after the balance of payments crises, the stabilization package was adopted in 1991 to restore fiscal discipline. The successful reduction in fiscal deficit as a percentage of GDP during 1991-92 could be attributable to:

1. The decision to abolish the export subsidies;
2. To increase the fertilizer prices ; and
3. Steps taken to keep non-plan expenditure (including defence expenditure) in check.

The expenditure reforms to be as important as tax reforms though—the focus of expenditure reform was rather limited. It remained confined to "a continuous monitoring of performance" of welfare expenditures administered by states with the objective of bringing about significant improvements in cost-effectiveness. During 1992-93 several other measures were also adopted. They are as follows:

1. The budgetary support of the central plan was maintained at the nominal level of the previous year budget estimate;
2. Non-plan revenue expenditures were controlled;
3. The decontrol of phosphatic and potassic fertilizers checked the expenditure on fertilizer subsidies;
4. As a part of expenditure control strategy and in order to regulate the level of borrowing from RBI, fiscal deficit, ceiling were prescribed for the quarters ending June, September, and December 1992; and
5. The existing expenditure control mechanisms were strengthened.

During 1994-95, steps were also taken to control the growth of expenditure. They were as follows:

1. Reduction of posts at various levels; and
2. Cut in the overall expenditure on consumption of petrol/diesel, on telephone, restricting the purchase of vehicles.

It was recognized that further steps needed to be taken for more effective financing through user charges. The first major discussion on expenditure reduction and its management began in 1997-98 with the release of a Discussion Paper on Subsidies by the Government of India entitled "Government Subsidies in India" to generate debate and initiate a more open approach to subsidies. Another important step towards fiscal discipline was taken when the financing of the budgetary deficit through the ad-hoc treasury bills was discontinued.

The Union Budget for 1999-2000 recognized the importance of adoption of a medium term fiscal correction target of eliminating revenue deficit and bringing down fiscal deficit to 2 percent of GDP in four years. It was announced that an Expenditure Reform Commission was to be set up to examine the entire gamut of expenditure in an unbiased way, free of any departmental interests. To promote transparency and curb the growth of contingent liabilities, the Budget constituted Guarantee Redemption Fund, with an initial corpus of ₹ 50 crore and later the State Governments were also encouraged to set up similar funds. The Union Budget for 2000-01 proposed a number of a policy measures with the objective of checking the momentum of built in expenditure growth owing to the large proportion of pre-committed expenditure in total expenditure:

1. Subjecting all norms for creation of post and fresh recruitment in Government budgeting;
2. Redeployment of surplus staff and making voluntary retirement scheme (VRS) more effective;
3. All subsidies to be reviewed in line with the cost-based user charges wherever feasible; and
4. Budgetary support to autonomous institutions and encouragement to PSUs would be reviewed and they will be encouraged to generate internal resources.

During the course of the year, the Government took a series of measures for controlling growth in non-plan non-developmental expenditure. Expenditure management, broadly speaking, featured as one of the major objectives of the Government in the Union Budget 2001-02. The objectives as stated in the Budget speech, mainly referred to three aspects-stringent expenditure control of non-productive expenditure, rationalization of subsidies and improvement in the quality of the expenditure. Further, as an institutional arrangement, the Government constituted an Expenditure Reform Commission (ERC) to look into various areas of expenditure correction.

Areas identified by the ERC include, inter alia, creation of a national food security buffer stock and minimization of cost of buffer stock operations and rationalization of fertilizer subsidies through dismantling of controls in a phased manner. It also included optimizing Government staff strength by a ban on the creation of new posts for two years, introduction of voluntary retirement scheme (VRS) and redeployment of surplus staff in various Government departments and autonomous institutions, to which the Government provides budgetary support through grants. With a view to promoting transparency and curbing the growth of contingent Government liabilities, a Guarantee Redemption Fund was set up as a part of expenditure management strategy. Steps undertaken in the light of above proposals included:

1. Dismantling of the administered price mechanism (APM) in the petroleum sector and the Oil Pool Account effective from April 2002;
2. Restriction on fresh recruitments to 1 percent of the total civilian staff strength over the 4 years beginning fiscal 2002-03; and
3. Introduction of a new pension scheme of defined contribution for new recruits in the Budget of 2003-04.

To carry the process of reducing the growth in non-developmental expenditure, the Government set up an Expenditure Reforms Commission in February, 2000. The main terms of reference for the Commission were as follows:

1. To suggest a road map for reducing the functions, activities and administrative structure of the Central Government;
2. To review the framework of all subsidies, both explicit and implicit, examine the economic rationale for their continuance and make recommendations for making subsidies transparent and suggest measures for maximizing their impact on the target population and minimize cost;
3. To review the framework for determination of user charges of departmental and commercial activities: suggest an effective strategy for cost recovery;
4. To review the adequacy of staffing under Central Government Ministries, attached offices etc;
5. To review the procedure for setting up of Government funded autonomous institutions and their pattern of

funding and suggest measures for effecting improvement and reducing budgetary support to their activities; and
6. To consider any other relevant issue concerning expenditure management in government and make suitable recommendation.

Expenditure reforms in the context of liberalization have two aspects:

1. Consideration so as to reduce the quantum of expenditure; and
2. Restructuring with a view to changing the composition of Government expenditure, i.e. shift towards growth-inducing expenditure on infrastructure and human resource development and reduction in unwarranted subsidies (Prasad, C.S., 2007). [5]

5.3 Restructuring of Public Sector Undertakings

The state dominated heavy industries based on Nehru-Mahalanobis strategy of projected industrialization which India has pursued since the mid-fifties, required not only a high rate of domestic savings and investment but also a large share for the public sector in total investment. However, the public sector's own savings performance has been quite disappointing. Though public sector savings have been less than public investment throughout the planning period, this gap widened considerably during the 1980s. The share of public sector in gross domestic savings declined from over 20 percent at the beginning of the decade to only 8 percent by 1989-90.

In plan financing, while the Sixth Plan (1980-81 to 1984-85) envisaged that over 46 percent of the public sector plan outlay would be financed by own resources of the public sector, the actual contribution turned out to be only 37 percent. Similarly, during the Seventh Plan (1985-86 to 1989-90) only 27 percent of the public sector plan outlay was financed from own resources as against a target of over 41 percent. There were 246 Central Government public enterprises as on March

31, 1991, out of which 236 enterprises were in operation. These 236 enterprises yielded a net profit of ₹ 2,368 crore in 1990-91, implying a rate of return of only 2.3 percent on ₹ 1,01,797 crore capital employed. Of this, only ₹ 69 crore came from all the non-oil public enterprises put together.

The record of the State level enterprises is worse. The departmental commercial undertakings of all States and Union Territories together reported a net loss of ₹ 1,885 crore in 1990-91. Of the two major types of non-departmental undertakings, the State Electricity Boards reported a combined loss of ₹ 4,169 crore while the State Road Transport Corporation reported a loss of ₹ 470 crore. Thus, instead of generating a surplus, all public enterprises put together generated a net loss of some ₹ 4,176 crore. Pervasive inefficiencies and poor financial performance in PSEs have remained a major obstacle to industrial development and international competitiveness. Inefficiency and lack of dynamism have resulted from cost-plus pricing and distribution controls.

Many public sector enterprises have been de facto monopolies, protected from competition. A soft budget constraint-easy access to budget funds and/or credit from the financial sector- has allowed sick PSEs to survive. Ambiguous relationships with Government supervisory authorities were not conducive to efficiency. These enterprises have also been constrained by multiple objectives, lack of managerial autonomy and overstaffing pressures in relation to operational needs. They have constituted a serious drain on Government resources. Reformists argue for a far more concrete exit policy and for reforms to be undertaken at the State level where public enterprises are even less efficient and less profitable than at the national level, and where the effect on limited resources is more serious.

The reforms aim to increase efficiency and reduce the losses that so many public enterprises impose on the Government budget. It is recognized that the budget should not support sick enterprises but it should not even provide the funds for their expansion. Rather, these should come from their own funds or from the capital market.

The 20th December 1991 speech by the Prime Minister elaborated policy on the public sector following the July 1991 new industrial policy. The demand for reform of public sector enterprises seems to be more on pragmatic than ideological grounds. As the economic environment is being made more conducive to cost and quality considerations and attempts are being made to foster competition, pressures on performance orientation in the public sector are also mounting. The policy response in the form of public sector reforms by the Central Government, however, has been slow. Under structural reforms, the Government has decided to give greater managerial autonomy to public enterprises to enable them to work efficiently. In addition to this, two other key elements of the Government's strategy for public enterprise reform are the promotion of increased private sector competition in areas where social considerations are not paramount and partial disinvestment of equity in selected enterprises.

During the reforms period, there has been a distinct change in the public perception in favour of reducing the size of public sector and improving private participation. With these underlying objectives, a two-pronged strategy was adopted by the Central Government- reduction in budgetary support to the PSUs, and privatization of existing PSUs. Public sector restructuring had two-fold objectives—to provide fiscal support to the Government in terms of additional resources and to improve the efficiency of these enterprises.

Given the need to expand activities such as educational, health and medicine, it was envisaged that substantial additional resources could be generated through a programmed disinvestment of some PSUs. With disinvestment, private shareholders are expected to enhance discipline by their monitoring. Managers, who act as agent of the shareholders, are forced to act in their interests by increasing the value of the firm. This would transform the PSUs on more efficient lines. The strategy towards public sector enterprises reform encompasses a judicious mix of strengthening strategic units, privatizing non-strategic ones through gradual disinvestment or strategic sale and devising viable rehabilitation strategies for weak units. The latest policy announced in the budget speech 2000-01 by the Finance Minister had the following as main elements:

1. Restructure and revive potentially viable PSUs;
2. Close down PSUs which cannot be revived; and
3. Bring down Government equity in all non-strategic PSUs to 26 percent or lower, if necessary; and fully protect the interest of workers.

During the last two years, financial restructuring of 20 PSUs has been approved by the Government. As a result, many PSUs have been able to restructure their operations, improve productivity and achieve a turnaround in performance. Even so, a large number of procedural as well as policy issues continue to constrain the progress on disinvestment process. In the area of PSEs following steps were taken by the Government:

1. The system of monitoring has been strengthened with Memorandum of Undertakings (MOUs). The MOUs are being claimed in official circles as major instruments of the rollback of State involvement in the running of the public enterprises by citing statistic such as the following: During 1990-91, 23 public enterprises signed MOUs with their administrative ministries, of which 14 were evaluated as excellent, 8 as good and 1 as poor. In 1991-92, 71 enterprises signed MOUs while in 1992-93, 120 enterprises were identified for this purpose (Mookherji, Dilip, 1993). [6] A major objective assessment of the situation, therefore, calls for a cleaner break with the old traditional culture of running the PSEs through back seat driving. The experience with the MOUs in the past has not been very positive. A change of attitude in the new era of

liberalization may lead to some improvement in the results in the years to come, but much more is needed than MOUs to distance the Government from the actual running of the PSEs.

2. Moving from sale of equity to the surpluses and deficits of PSEs, according to the economic survey, 2000, the ratio of pre-tax profit to capital employed of central public sector undertakings rose from an average of 3.5 percent during 1990-93 to 8.0 percent during 1995-98. This aggregate profitability measures is misleading, since the enterprises whose profits are aggregated included State oil and petroleum monopolies. In addition, at least for those enterprises that are competing with private enterprises, their post-tax return has to be compared with similar returns for their private counterparts. Be that as it may, if we measure PSE performance by the deficit in their plan expenditure (mainly on investment) relative to their net internal resources, the deficit of the Central Government PSEs (CPSEs) as a ratio of GDP has halved from 3.0 percent in 1990-91 to a budget estimate of 1.5 percent in 1999-2000. The factors contributing to the decline are the fall in PSEs investment from 4.8 percent of GDP in 1990-91 to 3.4 percent in 1999-2000 and the growing importance of petroleum and telecom enterprises, which now account for nearly half the investment and generate more than two-thirds of the net internal resources of CPSEs. In other words, government support (through loans and financing of losses) of CPSE has declined sharply as a proportion of GDP.
3. The programme of divestment in PSUs had slippages due to pricing problems and sluggishness of the capital market in the late 1990s. Targets set for divestments could not be achieved in most of the years (barring 1991-92, 1994-95 and 1998-99) during the decade of the 1990s. Since 1991-92, Government equity has been divested in 48 units and strategies sale was undertaken in another 16 units. Of the

total amount of ₹ 78,300 crore could targeted be mobilized through divestments/strategies sale, ₹ 30,917 crore could be realized up to March 31, 2002. Initially, the Government (with the exception of Modern Foods) sold only minority stakes in different PSUs. However, since 2000, the Government began strategies sales as these were judged to be revenue enhancing and signalled commitment to enhanced efficiency that transfer of management could bring about. To establish a systematic policy approach to disinvestments and privatization and give fresh impetus to strategies sale of identified PSUs, the Government has established a new department for disinvestment. During its existence, the disinvestment commission issued eleven reports containing recommendations on fifty-eight of the sixty-four PSEs referred to it. The recommendations in only thirteen cases were or are being implemented. The "Disinvestment Fund", set up in 1996 on the advice of the commission to use the sale of proceeds for restructuring PSEs and to finance voluntary retirements of excess staff, is not yet operational.

4. Some steps have been taken towards the marketisation of the PSEs. An important aspect of marketisation is corporatization. A major example of corporatization can be seen in the telecommunications sector. A beginning was made in the 1986 by setting up a new corporate entity, i.e. the Mahanagar Telephone Nigam Ltd. (MTNL). The company made a profit of ₹ 1.4 billion in the very first year of its operation. This has now raised expectation.

The loss making sick PSEs have been brought under the ambit of Board for Industrial and Financial Restructuring (BIFR) which was already with the sick private sector units. The economic survey of 1998-99 reported that between its inception in May 1987 and the end of November 1998, BIFR received 3441 references, of which 2404 were registered and 452 were dismissed as non-maintainable under the Sick Industries Company Act of 1985. It recommended winding up of 606 and rehabilitating another 637 and declared 214 as no longer sick. Out of the 225 PSEs that were referred, it registered 157, recommended closing down 29 and rehabilitating 50, and declared 6 to be no longer sick.

The Government policy of marginal disinvestment of the equity of public sector enterprises has been dominantly governed by the compulsions of financing the fiscal deficits. The whole disinvestment approach is so incremental and so thinly spread that it fails to address the basic issue of how to improve the very low returns on the capital invested in the public sector. Not much has been done to bring about effective changes in the functioning of these enterprises. The approach of disinvestment is based on the assumption that the induction of private shareholders will alter the corporate culture in these enterprises and provide them a stronger commercial orientation in response to normal shareholder expectations. This is a tall assumption indeed.

The 1991-92 Budget earmarked US$ 67 million for the National Renewal Fund (NRF). The International Development Agency promised over US$ 166 million during 1992-93 and the same amount in 1993-94. The NRF is expected to provide assistance to firm's undertakings modernization and technological upgrading of existing capacities to cover the costs of retraining and redeployment of employees. The fund would also provide compensation to employees affected by restructuring or closure of industrial units in both the private and public sectors. A social safety net would be provided for workers through allocating funds to finance employment generation schemes in the organized and unorganized sectors. The willingness of the Government to form strategic alliances has been demonstrated in the case of Maruti Udyog Ltd. an automobile joint venture with Suzuki Motor Corporation of Japan. This unit was originally set up in the early 1980s with Suzuki having a 40 percent stake and the Government of India the remaining 60 percent. Later, as part of the policy of encouraging foreign investors to increase their shareholding, Suzuki was allowed to increase its share holding to 50 percent by purchase of fresh equity and also to acquire greater management control.

5. The disinvestment programme made some progress during 2001-02 with the strategic sale process of some public sector undertakings gaining momentum; nevertheless the actual proceeds were lower than the targeted amount. In 2002-03, the disinvestment process remained below expectations. A major challenge facing the programme of public sector restructuring has been the closing down of persistently loss making and non-viable public sector undertakings (PSUs) so that the profitability of the other public enterprises could be a major source of resources generation to provide budgetary support. The stage is set for reforms in the PSUs by restructuring of potentially viable PSUs and improving the profitability and efficiency of the viable units. Priorities in reforms include raising return on investments in PSUs and infusing professionalisation in management.

On the whole the reforms of PSUs including privatization and phasing out of unviable units have not gathered as much momentum as had been hoped for. Disinvestment has been piecemeal and the funds so raised are being used to reduce budget deficits, rather than strengthening the PSUs. As Bimal Jalan points out: 'the sale of public sector enterprises would be of little help unless macroeconomic environment is improved and it is quite probable that if macroeconomic stabilization is successful, disinvestment of equity in public sector enterprises may not be necessary'(Jalan, Bimal,1991). [7]

5.4 Fiscal-Monetary Coordination

Fiscal policy and monetary policy are the two arms of macroeconomic policy, aimed at growth, equity and macroeconomic stability. While fiscal and monetary policies have common objectives, the instruments used differ. Fiscal policy resets upon instruments such as government expenditure, taxes and borrowing. Monetary policy influences the level of economic activity through actions that impinge on the cost of funds and the availability of overall liquidity in the system. Effective macroeconomic management presupposes a well-knit and coordinated fiscal and monetary policy environment, since fiscal policy continues to have a close bearing on the conduct of monetary policy. A high fiscal deficit impedes the effective use of monetary policy instruments.

The growing fiscal deficit during the pre-reform period was increasingly financed through the pre-emption of institutional resources at sub-market rates by progressive increase in SLR and monetization by the Reserve Bank. These developments eventually resulted in crowding out of private investment, growing financial repression and imposed constraints on the conduct of monetary policy. Thus, the efforts towards better monetary-fiscal coordination were aimed at elimination of automatic monetization by the Reserve Bank and movement away from financial repression through the reduction in statutory pre-emption of banks and long-term resources to allow a level-playing field to private investors.

During the 1990s, the Reserve Bank undertook a series of steps towards deepening and widening the Government securities market. Some of the major steps in this direction included aligning of coupon rates on Government securities with market interest rates, introduction of an auction system, introduction of primary dealers and setting up of Delivery versus Payment (DvP) system. Furthermore, following the 'Supplemental Agreement' between the Government of India and Reserve Bank in September 1994, the abolition of ad hoc treasury bills was made effective from April 1997, thereby replacing the automatic monetization of deficit by a system of ways and means advances (WMA) to meet only the temporary mismatches in cash flows of the Central Government. Concomitant to these measures, statutory liquidity ratio (SLR) was reduced to 25 percent by 1997 and cash reserve ratio

(CRR) was reduced in phases to 4.75 percent by November 2002.

These measures resulted in the emergence of an active, wide and deep Government securities market and paved the way for complete elimination of automatic monetization and substantial lowering of statutory pre-emption of institutional resources by the Government. These developments were also reflected in the structural changes in the financing pattern of fiscal deficit during the reform period-with a marked shift towards market borrowings. Accordingly, the share of market borrowings, which constituted 26.9 percent of gross fiscal deficit (GFD) in the 1980s rose sharply to 59.1 percent in the latter half of the 1990s and financed about 70 percent of the GFD by 2001-02. On the other hand, ad hoc treasury bills which financed a sizeable proportion of GFD, both in the 1980s and in the 1990s up to 1996-97, no longer exist as a financing item with their replacement by WMA in 1997-98.

Similarly, the share of external finance which was around 10 percent in the 1980s also came down sharply to an average of 2.9 percent during 1997-98 to 2001-02. The share of other liabilities has been relatively stable and averaged around 40.0 percent, both, in the 1980s as well as in the 1990s. In case of State Governments, the fiscal gap is financed by way of loans from the Centre, small savings and market borrowings. Like the Central Government, the share of market borrowings in financing GFD of States has steadily increased. The financing pattern of the GFD indicates that, on an average, the share of loans from the Centre and small savings declined from 51.9 percent and 37.1 percent, respectively, in the 1980s to 47.5 percent and 36.6 percent, respectively, during the 1990s. The share of market borrowings arose from 11.0 percent to 15.8 percent between these two periods.

The growing reliance on market borrowing for financing the fiscal deficit has been accompanied by restraint to reserve money growth and moderation of inflationary pressure. This has also had the effect of raising interest payments. In order for the strategy to finance fiscal deficit through borrowings at market related rates to have a favourable macroeconomic impact, some discipline on growth of the fiscal deficit is necessary. In addition to borrowings to finance fiscal deficit, Governments, both at the Centre and State levels, also avail WMA from the Reserve Bank to bridge short-term mismatches in revenue and expenditure.

5.5 Institutional Measures

As an institutional mechanism to promote the conduct of prudent and accountable fiscal policy, the Central Government introduced in the Lok Sabha in December 2000 the Fiscal Responsibility and Budget Management Bill (FRBM), 2000. Emphasizing the importance of the Bill, the *Economic Survey*, 2000-01 observed, "The introduction of FRBM, 2000 in Lok Sabha in December, 2000 is a historic step in our fiscal history. It shifts the emphasis of fiscal management from a purely short term perspective to a longer time horizon for conduct of prudent and accountable fiscal policy. Introduction of rule based budget management practices will also enable the economic agents and the community at large to take informed decisions. Besides, its enactment is likely to be seen as a demonstration of our country's resolve to maintaining macro-economic stability. Placing limits on the Central Government borrowings, debt and deficits and emphasizing greater transparency in fiscal operations would also greatly facilitate effective conduct of monetary policy". The Bill provided for a legal and institutional framework to:

1. Eliminate revenue deficit.
2. Bring down fiscal deficit.
3. Contain the growth of public debt.
4. Stabilize debt as a proportion of GDP within time frame.

The Bill, covering only the finances of the Central Government, defined the principles of fiscal responsibility in terms of budgetary deficit, Government borrowings and public debt. The Bill stresses on inter-generational equity in fiscal management and long-term macroeconomic stability. The original Bill introduced in the Parliament (17th December, 2000) had envisaged a complete elimination of revenue deficit and reduction of the fiscal deficit-GDP ratio to 2 percent by the Central Government by end-March 2006. The Bill also envisaged a reduction in total liabilities of the Centre to not more than 50 percent of GDP by March, 2011.

Under borrowing-related norms, the Bill proposed to prohibit certain types of borrowings from RBI. Similarly, under debt-related norms, it proposed to prescribe a limit on the debt stock. Thus, the Bill envisaged that within a period of 10 financial years, the total liabilities (including external debt at current exchange rate) would not exceed 50 percent of the estimated GDP. The Bill was referred to Parliament's Standing Committee on Finance (November 2001) which watered down the proposals of the original Bill and suggested doing away with numerical ceilings and a time frame for achieving the targets of revenue and fiscal deficit. Based on the Parliamentary Committee's recommendations, a Fiscal Responsibility and Budget Management Act was passed in August 2003.

The Act stipulates that, 'Government shall take appropriate measures to reduce fiscal deficit and revenue deficit so as to eliminate revenue deficit by 31 March 2008,' and, 'Government shall by rules specify, annual targets for reduction of fiscal and revenue deficit.' Subsequently, through an amendment the target date for elimination of revenue deficit has been shifted to 2008-09. At the time of the presentation of the Budget for 2004-05 in the Parliament, the Finance Minister laid down the targets for the reduction of revenue deficit, fiscal deficit and outstanding liabilities for three years. Statements as required under FRBM Act presented with the Budget of 2005-06 shows that none of the targets for 2004-05 have been met. While the target for 2004-05 for revenue deficit as percentage of GDP was 2.5 percent and fiscal deficit was 4.4 percent, it ended up with 2.7 percent and 4.5 percent respectively.

For 2005-06, the targets of revenue deficit of 1.8 percent and fiscal deficit of 4 percent have been scaled up to 2.7 percent and 4.3 percent respectively. The Finance Minister has advanced the argument that the Twelfth Finance Commission award has been largely responsible for not meeting the deficit reduction targets. It appears that the objective of fiscal prudence as envisaged in the FRBM Act is not going to be met. Highlighting the importance of FRBMA, the *Economic Survey*, 2006-07 noted, "FRBMA is an important institutional expression to ensure fiscal prudence and support for macroeconomic balance. With the enactment of the FRBMA, the traditional annual budgeting moved to a more meaningful medium-term fiscal planning framework.

According to the rules, revenue deficit is to be reduced by an amount equivalent to half percent or more of the estimated GDP at the end of each financial year and eliminated by March 31, 2009. Fiscal deficit is to be reduced by an amount equivalent to 0.3 percent or more of the estimated GDP at the end of more financial year and reduced to no more than 3 percent of the estimated GDP by the financial year ending on March 31, 2009". The Indian Government's lackadaisical approach to the FRBM Act, enacted after great dithering, typically reflects characteristics of a soft as described by Gunnar Myrdal (1968). The Government needs to take hard decision in the interest of the long-term fiscal health of the economy. One time tested rule of fiscal finance is that no borrowing should be resorted to for current consumption and all borrowings should be for investment and capital projects only. The Parliament should legislate to this effect to keep a check on an extravagant Executive (Mathur, B. P., 2005). [8]

End Notes

1. Rao, G.M. and Rao, K.R. (2006), "Trends and Issues in Tax Policy and Reforms in India", *National Institute of Public Finance and Policy (NIPFP)*, New Delhi, p. 59.
2. Schaefer, Ursula (2007), "Tax Reform in India-Achievement and Challenges", *ADB, At the International Tax Conference*, 2

July, New Delhi.

3. EPW Research Foundation (2001), "Finances of Government of India", *Economic and Political Weekly*, April 14, Mumbai.
4. Mathur, B.P. (ed.) (1999), "Budgetary Reforms and Expenditure Management in Government", *National Institute of Financial Management*, Faridabad, New Delhi.
5. Prasad, C.S. (2007), "India's Fiscal Policy: From Fiscal Adjustments to Fiscal Accounting" in C.S. Prasad (ed.) *Economic Survey 1947-48 to 2008-09*, New Century Publications, New Delhi, pp. 268-270.
6. Mookherji, Dilip (1993), "New Economic Policies", *Working Paper, NIPFP*, New Delhi, p. 36.
7. Jalan, Bimal (1991), *India's Economic Crisis: The Way Ahead*, Oxford University Press, Delhi, p. 76.
8. Mathur, B.P. (2005), "Budgetary Reform and Expenditure Management" in *Alternative Economic Survey (AES), India 2004-05: Disequalising Growth*, Dhruva Narayan Publication, Mumbai, pp. 165-166.

6

Tax Reforms in India

The primary objective of tax policy in developing countries is to mobilize resources for the public sector to finance welfare and developmental plans. The extent to which tax policy is used for this purpose is a matter of interest for national policy makers and foreign aid donors. Foreign governments and international organizations usually assess the efforts made by receipt countries to raise resources domestically. Level of taxation in a country is traditionally judged in terms of the ratio which taxes bear to some measure of national income. This ratio is called tax-GDP ratio and change in it is determined by variations in both the numerator (total tax revenue) and the denominator (National income). Trends in taxation in a country or a group of countries are analyzed mainly in terms of this ratio, and the composition of tax revenues. The latter may change owing to variations in tax-GDP ratio. In a situation where huge investments are required for building social and economic infrastructure, we need to raise the tax-GDP ratio. The Central Government has not been able to achieve this objective of tax reforms.

6.1 Evolution of Indian Tax System

Tax policy in India has evolved as an important component of fiscal policy that played a central role in the planned development strategy. In particular, tax policy was the principal instrument for transferring private savings to public consumption and investment (Bagchi and Stern, 1994). [1] Tax policy was also used to encourage savings and investments, reduced inequalities of income and wealth, foster balanced regional development, encourage small-scale industries on the assumption that they are employment intensive, and influence the volume and direction of economic activities in the country.

The evolution of tax policy within the framework of an industrialization strategy based on the public sector, heavy industry, and import substitution has had several implications. First, tax policy was directed to raise resources for the large and increasing requirements of public consumption and investment irrespective of the efficiency implications it entailed. Second, the objective of achieving a socialistic pattern of society, combined with the large oligopolistic rents generated by the system of licences, quotas, and restrictions, necessitated steeply progressive tax structure in both direct and indirect taxes. Third, the pursuit of a multiplicity of objectives enormously complicated the tax system with adverse consequences on efficiency and horizontal equity.

It also opened-up large avenues for evasion and avoidance of taxes. The disregard for efficiency considerations was a part of the import substituting industrialization strategy. Fourth, not only did all of this require differentiation in tax rates based on arbitrary criteria, but plan priorities also legitimized selectivity and discretion in tax policy and administration. Once selectivity and discretion were accepted as legitimate, it mattered little whether these were exercised as intended. This provided enough scope for the special interest groups to influence tax policy and administration. Fifth, the influence of special interest groups, changing priorities, and the lack of an information system and scientific analysis led to ad hoc and often, inconsistent calibration of policies. Finally, the poor information system was the cause of selective application of the tax system as well as its effect (Rao, M.G. and Rao, R.K., 2006). [2]

Taxation in the developing countries traditionally has two objectives. The first aim provides the tax concessions and incentives to stimulate private enterprises. The second purpose is the mobilization of resources to finance public expenditure. The political and economic ideology of the developing countries and its socio-economic progress depends largely on its government's ability to generate sufficient revenues to spend on essential and basic public services health, education, transportation, communication and components of the economic and social infrastructure. Most of the governments in the developing countries are directly involved in economic activities through their ownership, control of public corporations and state trading corporations.

Tax levies on public corporations and private individuals to enable the Government to finance the capital and recurrent expenditure. In recent years the problems of fiscal deficit and public expenditure are rising greatly in excess of public revenue, resulting from a development programmes, external shocks, debt burdens, falling inflation, growing trade balance and declining investment rate. Consequently, cutting Government expenditure mostly on social services and raising revenue through efficient tax collection for developmental activities of the nation. Development of social services is also important to achieve higher productivity.

Reforming the tax system is critical to achieve fiscal consolidation, minimize distortions in the economy and to create stable and predictable market environment for the markets to function. Not surprisingly, the wave of tax reforms across the world that began in the mid 1980s accelerated in the 1990s motivated by a number of factors. Tax reforms and movements in tax rates in India validate the Laffer curve relationship between tax rate and tax collections particularly in the current decade. The tax structure evolved in the event of large resource requirement during the initial decades after independence was characterized by multiplicity of tax rates which were increased to very high levels across all the taxes. Analysts viewed such a tax structure as a hindrance in achieving the full potential of the economy. The need for large scale tax reforms became increasingly imperative during the 1980s which is considered to be the decade of tax reforms.

Indian tax reforms have passed through five phases since Independence:

1. *First Phase*: The first phase witnessed tax reforms based on the recommendations of the Taxation Enquiry Commission 1954.
2. *Second Phase*: The second phase was guided by the Nicholas Kaldor's recommendations of 1957.
3. *Third Phase*: The third phase was ushered in by the recommendations of the Direct Taxes Enquiry Committee of 1971, (Wanchoo Committee).
4. *Fourth Phase*: The fourth phase started with the new economic policy of V.P. Singh through the Union Budget for 1985-86.
5. *Fifth Phase*: The most important phase of tax reforms was introduced during the 1990s based on the recommendations of the Tax Reforms Committee, 1991-93 (Chelliah Committee) (Thimmaiah, G., 2002). [3]

Tax reforms are undertaken by governments to mobilize more revenue in the long run. Even in the short run, governments expect revenue neutrality from tax reforms. Indian tax reforms were mainly guided by these revenue considerations all through the five phases of tax reforms. But during the first two phases though the Government of India experienced a sudden increase in the revenue from both direct and indirect taxes, after a few years the revenue yield from direct taxes started losing its buoyancy. So the third phase of tax reforms was intended to increase the revenue buoyancy by reducing the marginal tax-rates of direct taxes. This started showing positive results. The fourth phase continued the tax rate cut measures which did not show consistently positive results. Even the fifth phase of tax reforms is not showing consistently encouraging results in terms of their revenue impact.

If the mid-1980s saw the launch of modern tax reform in India, the 1990s witnessed its fruition. Shortly after coming to power in mid-1991, the Narasimha Rao/Manmohan Singh Congress Government made comprehensive tax reforms as one of its main reform planks. The Tax Reforms Committee

(TRC), chaired by the country's leading public finance authority, Raja. J. Chelliah, was swiftly established and it quickly gave an Interim Report (December 1991), followed by a two-part Final Report (August 1992 and January 1993). Taken together, these three volumes of the Chelliah Committee Report constitute the finest treatment of tax policy and reform issues in India in the past thirty years.

The Report provided an excellent combination of lucid, theoretical analysis, empirical supporting evidence and practical policy recommendations. The broad approach of the Committee in formulating its recommendations relating to tax reforms was that the rates of tax should be moderate and the tax base should be widened so that the tax reform measures were not only revenue neutral in the short-run but would also be elastic in the long run. The most important recommendations of the Committee may be grouped under the following measures:

1. Tax-rate cut measures encompassing almost all taxes;
2. Measures for widening the tax base, particularly the tax base of personal income tax (PIT);
3. Modernization of indirect taxes by gradually replacing both central excise and states' sales tax by a two-tier VAT; and
4. Simplifying assessment and compliance procedures so as to reduce the cost of compliance.

The Chelliah Committee recommended tax rate cuts to promote tax honesty and corporate savings. At the same time the Committee recommended measures to widen the tax base such as imposition of presumptive tax and introduction of tax on estimated income. The presumptive tax on hard-to-tax income groups was introduced in 1993. But the revenue yield has been unimpressive. Tax on estimated income has also been introduced in the form of tax on the value of services such as on contractors, transport operators etc., with some success. The recent one-in-six criteria approach seems to be bringing in a number of income earners into the tax net.

No doubt, as a consequence of all these measures the number of income tax payers has increased to 23 million and the revenue from direct taxes has increased at a much faster than that of indirect taxes to constitute a larger proportion of total tax revenue. But the annual rates of growth of revenue from major direct taxes of the Central Government have been fluctuating from year to year.

The Central Government levies four main taxes viz., personal income tax, corporation tax, custom duties and Union excise duties. These taxes account for almost total tax proceeds of the Central Government. Custom duties had remained the major source of the revenues of the Central Government for a long time. During the early 1970s the Union excise duties had become the major source of Central Government revenue. In fact, from the time the Government decided to give protection to industries during the fourth decade of the 20th century, the importance of custom duties as a source of revenue started declining during World War-II and the post-War period, restrictions were imposed on imports of various consumer goods. This policy made it difficult to collect large proceeds from customs duties. When the process of economic planning begins, imports increased, but their heavy taxation was ruled out due to their strategic importance in the country's development.

In the whole of the planning period capital equipment, necessary raw materials, food grains and petroleum constituted more than 90 percent of the country's imports and the Government could not impose heavy duties on them. With some progress in the industrial sector, the Central Government attempted to expand the base of excise duties, and as a consequence some time back it became the major source of its revenue. However, with time the relative position of these taxes changed considerably.

6.2 Direct Tax Reforms

The direct tax structure of 1973-74 was the product of two

decades of tax policy changes to bring about 'a socialistic pattern of society' and raise tax revenues to finance a public investment led strategy of planned economic development. The Taxation Enquiry Commission Report of 1954 (GOI, 1954) [4] emphasized the need to raise more revenues through higher taxes, including through greater progressivity of direct taxes. Its recommendations were largely implemented. This approach gained further impetus from Kaldor's (1956) prescriptions, which ushered in a set of 'integrated direct taxes' including an expenditure tax, a wealth tax and gift tax in addition to the already present taxes on income, capital gains and estates (Acharya, Shankar, 2005). [5]

In ensuring years the scope of these taxes was expanded and the rates were inexorably raised. One gets a flavour of the prevailing tax ideology of the times from perusing the budget speeches of those years. Thus, Indira Gandhi, presenting the Budget for 1970-71, stated, "Taxation is also a major instrument in all modern societies to achieve greater equality of incomes and wealth. It is, therefore, proposed to make our direct tax system serve this purpose by increasing income taxation at higher levels as well as by substantially enhancing the present rates of taxation on wealth and gift".

6.2.1 Personal Income Tax: In the Budget for 1974-75 the Finance Minister Y.B. Chavan reversed his earlier stance and implemented the recommendation by reducing the top marginal income tax rate to 70 percent and surcharge to 10 percent. Simultaneously, however, the wealth tax rates were increased. In 1976-77, the marginal rate was further reduced to 66 percent, and the wealth tax rate was reduced from 5 percent to 2.5 percent. In 1979-80, the income tax surcharge was increased, and the wealth tax rate returned to a maximum of 5 percent. A major simplification and rationalization initiative, however, came in 1985-86, when the number of tax brackets was reduced from 8 to 4, the highest marginal tax rate was brought down to 50 percent, and wealth tax rates came down to 2.5 percent.

The last wave of reforms in personal income tax was initiated on the basis of the recommendations of the Tax Reforms Committee (TRC). Under the reforms, there were only three tax brackets of 20, 30, and 40 percent, starting in 1992-93. Financial assets were excluded from the wealth tax, and the maximum marginal rate was reduced to 1 percent. Further reductions came in 1997-98, when the three rates were brought down further to 10, 20, and 30 percent. In subsequent years, the need for revenue has increased to a general surcharge and additional surcharge of 2 percent dedicated to primary education, the latter applicable on all taxes.

A major problem that has haunted the tax system and reduced the tax base is the generous tax preferences. The Advisory Group on Tax Policy and Tax Administration in its Report listed the personal income tax preferences, and the Task Force on Tax Policy and Tax Administration also made a detailed list of these concessions (GoI, 2001a). [6] The tax preferences included the incentives and concessions for savings, housing, retirement benefits, investment in and return from certain types of financial assets, investments in retirement schemes, and income of charitable trusts. These preferences have not only distorted the after-tax rates of return on various types of investments in unintended ways but have also significantly eroded the tax base.

The process of moderation of personal income tax was continued the Budget of 1994-95. The personal tax exemption limit was raised from ₹ 30,000 to ₹ 35,000. Besides, the surcharge of 12 percent on non-corporate incomes was withdrawn. Personal tax rates were not changed, but there was a widening of tax slab. The personal income tax rates were not altered in the Budget for 1995-96 so that the full effect of earlier rate reductions into higher revenue realizations. The exemption limit was, however, raised from ₹ 35,000 to ₹ 40,000. The 1997-98 Budget introduced sharp cuts in income tax rates at 10, 20, and 30 percent and have remained stable since 1997-98, with some changes in the associated tax brackets.

A surcharge of 5 percent of the income tax payable was imposed in 2002-03 in the wake of the Kargil war and was discontinued the following year. It was replaced, however, with a separate 10 percent surcharge imposed on all taxpayers with taxable incomes above ₹ 8,50,000; the level was raised to ₹ 10,00,000 in the 2005-06 Budget.

Further, all taxes are topped up by a 2 percent education cess a surcharge dedicated to an education fund from 2004-05 onward. Although the income exemption limit has remained at ₹ 50,000 since 1998-99, the generous standard deduction and the exemptions on dividends and interest on government securities up to specified limits have effectively increased the threshold substantially.

The 2004-05 Budget did not raise the exemption limit but provided that those with incomes under ₹ 1,00,000 need not pay the tax. The Budget still retained the existing tax brackets, however, which gave rise to a peculiar problem those with taxable incomes above ₹ 1,00,000 were left with lower after-tax incomes than those with incomes marginally lower than ₹ 1,00,000, requiring an ad hoc correction.

The Budget for 2005-06 raised the exemption limit itself to ₹ 1,00,000, abolished the standard deduction, and made marginal changes in the tax brackets. The exemption limit was increased to ₹ 1,35,000 for women and to ₹ 1,85,000 for senior citizens.

Savings in variety of instruments including pension funds up to Rs.100, 000 were made deductible from taxable income. The Budget for 2012-13 buoyed by enhanced income tax collections and better tax compliance by individuals allowed the Government to raise the basic exemption limit for all assesses from ₹ 1,80,000 to ₹ 2,00,000.

The Income Tax Act has a provision to assess the value of identifiable perquisites provided by companies to their employees and to include the same in the taxable income of the individual. The Budget for 2005-06 went a step further and classifies a range of other expenses by the company, which provide indirect perquisites to the entire group of employees but are not directly assignable to any single employee. A specified proportion of each of these benefits is to be taxed at a rate of 30 percent through a fringe benefits tax, to be paid by the employer.

6.2.2 Corporation Tax: Following the recommendations of the TRC, the distinction between closely held and widely held companies was done away with and the tax rates were unified at 40 percent in 1993-94. In 1997-98, the corporate rate was further reduced to 35 percent, and the 10 percent tax on dividends was shifted from individuals to companies. Since then the measures adopted have lacked direction. The dividends tax rate was increased to 20 percent in 2000-01, then reduced again to 10 percent in 2001-02 and levied on shareholders rather than the company. The policy was reversed once again in 2003-04, with the dividend tax imposed on the company.

The major corporate tax preferences are investment and depreciation allowances. Tax incentives were also provided for businesses locating in underdeveloped areas. As a result, some companies planned their activities to take full advantage of the generous concessions and fully avoid the tax. This form of tax avoidance by "zero-tax" companies was minimized by the introduction of a minimum alternative tax (MAT) in 1996-97. Even as companies can take advantage of the tax preferences, they are required to pay a tax on 30 percent of their book profits. In subsequent years, a provision was incorporated allowing these companies paying a MAT to take a partial credit against income tax liabilities in the following years. Since the MAT meant that a lot of the other preferences accorded in the tax statute like accelerated depreciation were not available to business units, the partial credit mechanism sought to dilute the impact of the MAT on business units that were liable for the MAT only sporadically.

While tax reforms were calibrated on the basis of a

consistent theoretical framework until the mid-1990s, some of the subsequent changes were ad hoc. The prime example is the decision to introduce the MAT instead of phasing out tax preferences. Setting the tax rate on corporate profits higher than the highest marginal rate on personal income is another example. Similarly, to improve tax compliance and create an audit trail, a securities transactions tax was introduced in April 2004 and tax of 0.1 percent on all cash withdrawals above ₹ 25,000 from current accounts of commercial banks was introduced in April 2005. These measures, however, are retrograde. The former hinder the development of stock market and discriminates against investments in shares. The latter penalizes small and medium-size firms, which have to withdraw large amounts of cash just to pay the salaries of their employees (Arbalaez, Burman and Zuluaga, 2002). [7]

The structure of corporate incomes tax has remained stable since 1997-98, when the rate was reduced to 35 percent. In 2005-06, the corporate income tax was reduced to 30 percent on domestic companies. The rate remains unchanged in Budget 2012-2013. The Union Budget 2011-2012, however, reduced the surcharge of 7.5 percent on domestic companies to 5 percent. Simultaneously, the rate of Minimum Alternate Tax (MAT) was increased from the 18 percent to 18.5 percent of book profits to keep the effective rate of the MAT at the same level.

6.3 Indirect Tax Reforms

The principal indirect taxes levied in India are custom duties, excise duties, service tax and sales tax or VAT. Now the excise duties have emerged as the biggest source of revenue. Under the Constitution, the Central Government has exclusive power to levy customs duties and excise duties on commodities other than alcoholic liquors and narcotics. From a modest beginning in 1994-95, service tax grown into a significant source of revenue. The States have been allocated exclusive jurisdiction over the excise on alcoholic liquors and taxes or sale or purchase of goods, except newspapers.

6.3.1 Union Excise Duties: After Independence, excise duties were levied on selected goods to raise revenue. Over the years, as the revenue requirement increased, the list of commodities subject to tax was expanded. In the initial years, for reasons of administrative convenience, the taxed commodities tended to be raw materials and intermediate goods rather than final consumer goods (GoI, 1977). [8] As pressure to raise revenue increased, final consumer goods were included. In 1975-76, the tax was extended to all manufactured goods.

By this time the structure of excise duties was complex and highly distortionary. Some commodities were subject to specific duties and others to ad valorem taxes; on the latter alone there were twenty-four different rates ranging from 2 to 100 percent (tobacco and petroleum products were taxed at even higher rates). The process of converting specific duties to ad valorem rates was more or less completed by 1993-94. The number of rates did not decrease, however, which led to several classification disputes. In effect, the excise duty became a manufacturers' sales tax administered on the basis of goods cleared from the warehouse. "Cascading" from the tax resulted not merely from its pre-retail nature but also because it was levied not only on final consumer goods but also on inputs and capital goods. The tax system was complex and opaque, and a detailed analysis showed significant variation in the effective rates (Ahmad and Stern, 1983). [9]

Although the Indirect Tax Enquiry Report issued in 1977 provided a detailed analysis of the allocative and distributional consequences of the Union excise duties, its recommendations were not implemented for almost a decade. The recommendations included converting specific duties into ad valorem taxes, unifying rates, and introducing an input tax credit to convert the cascading manufacturers' sales tax into a manufacturing stage value-added tax (MANVAT). The interesting part of the reform was that there was virtually no preparation and the introduction of modified value-added tax

(MODVAT) was a process of "learning by doing". This was a strange combination of taxation based on physical verification of goods with provision of an input tax credit. The coverage of the credit mechanism also evolved over time.

It began with selected items, with credit based on a one-to-one correspondence between inputs and outputs. It was only by 1996-97, that it covered a majority of commodities in the excise tariff and incorporated comprehensive credit. Nowhere else in the world can one find VAT introduction so complicated in its structure, so difficult in its operations, and so incomplete in its coverage. In fact, the revenue from the tax as a ratio of GDP declined after the introduction of MODVAT. The Tax Reform Committee, 1991 identified many items which were outside the excise could be considered for levying excise duty. Some of the identified items included: butter and cheese, skimmed milk powder, spices, fertilizers, feature films, wood pulp, umbrellas, bicycles, toys and sports goods, buttons, vacuum flasks.

The declining ratio of the Union excise duties to GDP since reforms were introduced is truly a matter of concern as the loss of revenue has been a constraint in further reducing import duties. Although the ratio has been stagnant at 3.3 percent for several years, that is significantly lower than the ratio in 1991-92 (4.1 percent). Union excise duty collections by commodity, highlights some interesting features with implications for both efficiency and equity of the tax system. One of the most important features is the commodity concentration. Three-fourth of all Union excise duties are paid by just five groups of commodities petroleum products, chemicals, basic metals, transport vehicles, and electrical and electronic goods.

One would normally except this concentration to decrease as manufacturing diversified. This increased concentration imposes a disproportionate tax burden on different sector of the economy. Moreover, this type of commodity concentration does not allow objective calibration of policies regarding excise duties as the Finance Ministry would not like to lose revenue from this lucrative source. Another important feature of the pattern of excise revenue collections is that the overwhelming proportion is paid by commodity groups that are in the nature of intermediate products used in the production of goods or services that are not subject to excise. A striking feature of excise duty collections is that, as in the case of corporate income taxes, a predominant proportion is paid by public sector enterprises.

In 1997-98 Budget the excise duty changes were aimed at reducing dispersion in rates. The scheme of excise duty concession for the small scale units was simplified. Further reforms of the excise duties came with the implementation of the recommendations of the TRC. The measures included gradual unification of rates and greater reliance on account-based administration. In 1999-2000, eleven tax rates were merged into three, with a handful of "luxury" items subject to an additional non-rebatable tax (6 and 16 percent). The three rates were merged into a single rate in 2000-01 to be called a central VAT (CENVAT), along with three special additional excises of 8, 16, and 24 percent for a few commodities. Further, the tax base was widened; some exemptions were replaced by a tax at 8 percent. Some simplification of the tax on the small-scale sector was also attempted. Small businesses could either take an exemption or pay tax at a concessional rate of 60 percent of tax due, with access to the tax credit mechanism. This option, however, was withdrawn from the Budget of 2005-06.

6.3.2 Customs Duties: Contrary to the general patterns seen in low-income countries, where an overwhelming proportion of revenues is raised from international trade taxes, revenue from this source was not very large in the initial years of independent India, largely because imports were restricted (Chelliah,1986). [10] In addition, high and differentiated tariffs, with rates varying with the stage of production (lower rates on inputs and higher rates on finished goods) and income elasticity of demand (lower rates on necessities and higher rates on luxury items) not only resulted in high and widely varying effective rates of protection, but provided large premiums for inefficiency and caused unintended distortions in the allocation of resources.

By the mid-1980s, the tariff rates were very high and the structure was quite complex. The Government's Long-Term Fiscal Policy (LTFP) presented in the Parliament in 1985-86 emphasized the need to reduce tariffs, apply fewer and more uniform rates, and reduce and eventually eliminate quantitative restrictions on imports. The reforms undertaken, however, were not comprehensive. Rationalization in the rates was attempted for specific industries such as capital goods, drug intermediates, and electronic goods. In fact, contrary to the LTFP recommendations, the tariffs were raised for revenue reasons, and the weighted average rate increased from 38 percent in 1980-81 to 87 percent in 1989-90 (GoI, 1991). [11]. Thus, by 1990-91, the tariff structure ranged from 0 to 400 percent. More than 10 percent of imports were subjected to tariffs of 120 percent or more. Wide-ranging exemptions, reflecting the influence of various special interest groups on tax policy, often granted outside the budgetary process, further complicated the system and made it ad hoc.

The reform of import duties in earnest began in 1991-92 when all duties on non-agricultural goods above 150 percent were reduced to this level. This 'peak' rate was lowered over the next four years to 50 percent, and then to 40 percent in 1997-98, 30 percent in 2002-03, 25 percent in 2003-04 to 15 percent in 2005-06. The peak rate of custom duty on non-agricultural products was reduced from 12.5 percent in 2006-07 to 10 percent in 2007-08. It remains the same in Budget 2012-2013. Along with relaxation of quantitative restrictions on imports and exchange rate depreciation, the change in the tariffs constituted a major change in the foreign trade regime.

The number of major duty rates was reduced from twenty-two in 1990-91 to four in 2003-04. Of course, some items are outside these four rates, but 90 percent of the customs is collected from items under the four rates. At the same time, a special additional duty was imposed on goods imported into the country on the rationale that if the commodity was domestically produced and sold interstate, it would have attracted the tax rate of 4 percent. This duty was abolished in January 2004, only to be reintroduced in 2005-06. Thus, the direction of reforms was not always consistent, but overall the thrust has been to reduce the rates and reduce their dispersion. However, tariff rates still vary with the stage of processing, and this practice has caused very high effective rates of protection on assembly of consumer durables and luxury consumption items.

6.3.3 Service Tax: An interesting aspect of the tax system in India is that except for a few specified services assigned to the States such as the entertainment tax, passengers and goods tax, and the electricity duty, the services were not specifically assigned to either the Centre or the States. This omission violated the principle of neutrality in consumption as it discriminated against the goods component of consumption. Because services are relatively more income elastic, the tax system is rendered less progressive when these are not taxed. An even more important argument for taxing services is to enable a coordinated calibration of a consumption tax system on goods and services because services enter into goods production and vice versa.

Although there was no specific authority to tax services, the Central Government levied taxes on three services in 1994-95: insurance other than life insurance, stock brokerages, and telecommunications. The list was expanded in succeeding years and now includes more than eighty services. The initial 5 percent tax rate was increased to 8 percent in 2003-04 and to 10 percent in 2004-05 and 2005-06. At present (2012-2013), service tax rate is 12 percent. The Expert Group on Taxation of Services recommended extending the tax to all services, providing an input tax credit for both goods and services, and eventually integrating the services tax with the CENVAT (GoI, 2001b). [12] With these reforms, the tax system can effectively be called a manufacturing-stage VAT. The exceptions were to be two small lists—one, a list of exempt services, and the other, a negative list of services, where the tax credit mechanism would not cover taxes paid on these services. The recommendation on the levy of general taxation of services has not been implemented, and the tax continues to be levied on selective services. However, the recommendation pertaining to the extension of input tax credit for goods entering into services and vice versa has been implemented.

The main reasons for the imposition of the service tax have been as follows:

- The growth in the service sector during the period of last one decade or so has been spectacular. Now services account for more than 55 percent of GDP. At the same time, their contribution to the Government exchequer has not all been commensurate. In 2006-07, revenue from service tax accounted for only 8 percent of the Union tax revenue and contributed 0.9 percent of GDP.
- Considerations of efficiency and equity also strongly govern the inclusion of services under taxation. With discriminatory taxation of goods and services, efficiency in resource allocation is bound to suffer. This is because resources move from taxed to non-taxed sectors. In the absence of service taxation equity suffers since services are consumed more by the high income households.
- If services are not taxed, traders cannot claim VAT on their service input. This is likely to cause cascading, distort choice and encourage business to develop in house services.

While the direct taxes showed, even with the lower rates, a rising tax-GDP ratio, this ratio for the indirect taxes kept sliding down. The indirect taxes had a larger share in the total tax revenues of the Centre and the fall in the indirect tax to GDP ratio could not be compensated by a rise in the direct taxes. As a result, the overall Central tax-GDP ratio fell" (TFC, 2004). [13] Of late, however, recovery is noticeable in the tax-GDP ratio at the level of Central Government.

Unlike direct taxes, rate cuts have been important factors in reducing the indirect tax collection, as there was no commensurate gain in terms of base expansion or better compliance. It was expected that the sharp cut in custom duties from peak rate of more than 300 percent in the period just prior to reforms to about 30 percent in 2002-03 would lead to a net fall in custom duty collections. Fall in excise duty collections, however, came as a surprise as the rate cuts were expected to boost growth in industrial output.

6.4 Various Tax Reforms Committees

6.4.1 Taxation Enquiry Commission (TEC): Immediately after independence, the Government of India opted for Government sponsored economic planning for increasing the pace of socio-economic development. This called for mobilization of huge financial resources for investment in the public sector. Accordingly the Government of India appointed the Taxation Enquiry Commission (TEC), in 1953, to suggest tax reform measures to raise more revenue. The TEC was guided by the need to promote the old philosophy of justice in taxation. The TEC recommended to increase the degree of progressivity of direct taxes, supplemented by measures to ensure effective enforcement of collection to reduce inequality of income.

The TEC emphasized the need for raising more resources through taxation for investment in the public sector with minimum disincentive for the private sector. The TEC tried to achieve this objective by recommending taxation of consumption of all classes to divert increased income from going to conspicuous consumption to public saving. The TEC assigned greater role to indirect taxes to achieve this objective. Even in the sphere of direct taxes, the TEC recommended for the reduction of exemption limit from ₹ 4,200 to ₹ 3,000;

clubbing of incomes of husband and wife with family allowance and enlarging the number of income brackets to inject graduate progressivity.

The TEC did not forget the need for tax incentives for new enterprises and recommended tax holiday as an effective means of encouraging private investment. These recommendations including those related to State Governments' taxes were implemented by the Government of India and the State Governments.

6.4.2 Nicholas Kaldor Report: But the Government of India was not satisfied with these recommendations. They needed much more radical tax measures to achieve the goal of 'socialistic pattern of society'. So the Government invited Nicholas Kaldor (1956) [14] to recommend further tax reforms. On his advice the Government introduced a set of 'integrated direct taxes' which included expenditure tax, wealth tax and gifts tax in addition to the already existing income tax, capital-gains tax and estate duty. The Government tried to convince the masses that the rich people were bearing a very high tax burden and therefore, the masses should also contribute to whatever extent possible through indirect taxes for the development efforts of the country. This philosophy led to frequent revision of rates and coverage of indirect taxes.

Such unprecedented increase in indirect taxation also gave a lever to the private sector, which was protected from foreign competition, to use it as an excuse for increasing the profit margin by pushing up prices. While the Government was lulled into complacency on the assumption that increased indirect taxation would reduce the consumption and bring down the price level and also that the system of integrated direct taxes would prevent evasion of direct taxes and reduce inequalities of income and wealth, in actual practice prices went on rising as and when the rates of indirect taxes were increased and the really rich and self-employed income earners and wealth-owners went on evading direct taxes.

The system of direct taxes introduced on the advice of

Kaldor encouraged the emergence of the black money phenomenon in India. These were the consequences of high rates of direct taxes with innumerable tax incentives and a complex system of indirect taxes levied by the Central and the State Governments on the same base thereby creating a cascading effect on the prices.

6.4.3 Direct Taxes Enquiry Committee: By 1970, the Government of India realized the futility of levying very high rates of direct taxes and appointed the Direct Taxes Enquiry Committee (DTEC) under the chairmanship of K.N. Wanchoo. The DTEC considered, inter alia, the problem of tax evasion and established the income on which tax was evaded for 1968-69 at a figure of ₹ 1,400 crore. The amount of tax evasion for the same year was put at ₹ 470 crore. The Committee suggested various measures to fight the evil of tax evasion. Some of the measures suggested were as follows: reduction in tax rates, minimization of controls and licences, regulation of donations to political parties, creating confidence among small tax payers, substitution of sales tax by excise duty, vigorous prosecution policy and compulsory maintenance of accounts.

The Report of DTEC was milestone in the area of income tax rates. The Committee made a number of far-reaching suggestions for unearthing black money, preventing evasion and avoidance of taxes, and reducing arrears. One important recommendation of the Committee related to reduction in the rates of direct taxes which in its view were mainly responsible for tax evasion because they made tax evasion profitable and attractive. The rates of individual income tax were quite high till the year 1973-74. However, pursuant to the recommendations of the DTEC, the Government initiated a series of rate reductions in individual income tax. The marginal rate of tax was reduced from 97.7 percent in 1973-74 to 77 percent in 1974-75 and further down to 66 percent in 1976-75. It is noteworthy that DTEC had recommended a maximum marginal rate of 75 percent.

Thus, the tax reform measures introduced in 1953 and

1956 failed to achieve the intended objectives mainly because they were based on wrong assumptions, namely, that high nominal tax rates would reduce inequalities of income and wealth and all forms of direct taxes levied simultaneously would reduce tax evasion.

It may be observed that while the yield from indirect taxes showed buoyancy, the yield from direct taxes became unimpressive. Considering the tall objectives assigned to the direct taxes during 1956 and 1970 of tax reforms, they ended in failure. Realizing this failure, high marginal rates were brought down during the mid-1970s. The tax reforms which were initiated in the mid-1970s started yielding positive results. Even then they did not form part of a comprehensive package of economic reforms. They were ad hoc in nature and the policy-makers assumed that except high rates of taxes all other economic policies were appropriate and were working well. These assumptions were shattered by the unimpressive performance of the Indian economy under the Five Year Plan regime. Hence, in 1985, Rajiv Gandhi's Government attempted to introduce a set of new economic policy reforms in which tax reforms were a part.

6.4.4 Long Term Fiscal Policy: The tax reform measures introduced in 1985-86 by the Union Finance Minister, V.P. Singh, included raising of exemption limit for personal income tax, reducing the number of slabs from 6 to 4, reducing marginal rate of income tax, abolishing compulsory deposit scheme and surcharge on income tax. Besides these, there were many other tax-relief measures such as removing the 20 percent ceiling on business expenditure incurred on sales promotion. He also announced a Long Term Fiscal Policy (LTFP) for the first time a long-term perspective for fiscal policy in which the Central Government recognized the deteriorating fiscal position as the most important challenge of the 1980s and set out specific targets and policies for achieving fiscal turnaround.

It indicated a direction of change in tax policy required to promote growth, increase built-in elasticity of the tax system, secure better tax compliance and move towards a more equitable distribution of the burden of financing the plan. LTFP outlined the possible reduction in corporate tax and rationalization of other axes in the following years. Subsequently, the recommendations of the Indirect Taxation Enquiry Committee of 1977 (Jha Committee), was accepted and reduced the rates of the Central excise duties and introduced modified value added tax (MODVAT), in place of Central excise duties on some selected commodities. There were very bold measures considering the anti-reform lobby which was operating in the country. But the LTFP measures could not be implemented because of the political developments which pushed all economic reforms to the background. These political developments proved that political stability is an important prerequisite for implementing any meaningful tax reforms in a democracy.

6.4.5 Tax Reforms Committee: The foreign exchange crisis of 1991 paved the way for comprehensive economic reforms. Manmohan Singh, who became the Union Finance Minister, continued the tax rate reduction policy and subsequently accepted and implemented the comprehensive tax reform measures recommended by the Tax Reforms Committee of 1991-93 (Chelliah Committee). The Committee identified its approach in the following words: "As is well known, our general approach is that the best results, in terms of compliance, (and therefore, revenue), efficiency and equity are obtained through a system incorporating moderate rates on a broad base" (GoI, 1992b). [15]

The broad approach of the Committee in formulating its recommendations relating to tax reforms was that the rates of tax should be moderate and the tax base should be widened so that the tax reform measures were not only revenue neutral in the short-run but would also be elastic in the long-run. The most important recommendations of the Committee may be grouped under the following measures:

1. Tax-rate cut measures encompassing almost all taxes.
2. Measures for widening the tax base, particularly the tax base of PIT.
3. Modernization of indirect taxes by gradually replacing both Central excise and States sales tax by a two-tier VAT; and simplifying assessment and compliance procedures so as to reduce the cost of compliance.

The Chelliah Committee has been able to influence the Central Government to modernize the tax structure by replacing Union excise duties by MODVAT and eventually CENVAT. It has recommended to the Central Government to take necessary initiative to persuade the State Governments to modernize their tax structures by replacing the sales tax by VAT. The Chelliah Committee has globalized the Indian tax system which will facilitate reaping of benefits under WTO. Its recommendations have introduced an element of transparency into the operation of Indian tax system.

Within the country, the Committee has created awareness among tax administers, tax policy-makers and economists that we should aim at realizing the dream of the framers of the Constitution to create one national common market by removing inter-state trade barriers and by harmonizing tax rates across the States. These are all intangible benefits which will be reaped by the country only in the long-run. Thus the long-run benefits of the Chelliah Committee recommendations are positive though the short-run revenue implications are not so impressive (Thimmaiah, G., 2002). [16]

6.4.6 Task Force on Direct Taxes: At the time of presenting the first batch of supplementary demands for grants to Parliament in July 2002, the Finance Minister had proposed setting up of two task forces to recommend measures for simplification and rationalization of direct and indirect taxes. Accordingly, two task forces were set up in September 2002 under the chairmanship of Vijay Kelkar, Adviser to Ministry of Finance and Company Affairs. The Task Force on Direct Taxes presented its consultation paper to the Government on

November 2, 2002. The discussion paper on indirect taxes was presented on November 25, 2002. These consultation papers were made public to facilitate an informed discussion on tax policy. After taking into account the response on the discussion papers, the Task Forces submitted their final Reports to the Government in December 2002. These Task Forces made important recommendations on toning up tax administration to put in place a system that is simple, effective and at par with international standards.

The main recommendations on direct taxes related to raising of exemption limit of personal income tax, rationalization of exemptions, abolition of concessional treatment to long-term capital gains, and abolition of wealth tax. In respect of indirect taxes, the main recommendations related to widening of the tax base, removal of exemptions, and expansion in the coverage of service tax.

In the last few years, various study groups and task forces have focused on the tax reforms in the tax system at the Central level. The Advisory Group on the Tax Policy and Administration for the Tenth Plan and the Kelkar Task Force (KTF) reports on direct and indirect taxes and more recently the KTF on the implementation of the FRBM Act have comprehensively examined the tax system and made important recommendations for reform (GoI, 2001a, 2002a, 2002b, 2004b). [17] All these are in conformity with the direction set by the TRC in 1991 and 1993, which called for broadening the tax base, reducing the rates, minimizing rate differentiation, and simplifying the tax systems. While there are differences on specific recommendations, these newer force reports share broad agreement on the direction and thrust of reforms and on the need to reform tax administration and the tax information system (TIN).

Tax reform in India has made enormous progress in the last thirty years. The tax structure today bears little resemblance to that prevailing in the mid-1970s. Almost all the change has been for the better, judged by the usual standards of economic efficiency, equity, built-in-revenue elasticity and transparency. But the work of tax reform is never finished (Achariya, Shankar, 2005). [18]

6.5 National Level Goods and Services Tax (GST)

In his Budget speech while presenting the Union Budget for the year 2006-2007 to Parliament, Minister of Finance Shri P. Chidambaram proposed that India should move towards a national level Goods and Services Tax (GST) that should be shared between the Centre and the States. He proposed to set April 1, 2010 as the date for introducing GST.

Thus, GST is a part of the proposed tax reforms to evolve an efficient and harmonized consumption tax system in the country. Presently, there are parallel systems of indirect taxation at the central and state levels. Each of the systems needs to be reformed to eventually harmonize them.

GST is proposed to be a comprehensive indirect tax levy on manufacture, sale and consumption of goods as well as services at the national level. GST would give India a world class tax system and improve tax collections. It would end the long standing distortions of differential treatment of manufacturing and service sector. The introduction of GST will lead to the abolition of various central and state indirect taxes and eliminate the cascading effects of multiple layers of taxation. It is claimed that GST will facilitate seamless credit across the entire supply chain and across all states under a common tax base.

The changeover to GST will be a game-changing tax reform measure which will significantly contribute to the buoyancy of tax revenues, acceleration of growth, and generation of many positive externalities.

In his speech while presenting the Budget for 2010-11 to the Parliament on February 26, 2010, Shri Pranab Mukherjee, Minister of Finance, rescheduled the time limit for the implementation of GST and expressed the hope that GST, along with the Direct Tax Code (DTC), would be introduced from April 1, 2011.

While declaring its intention to introduce GST from April 1, 2010, the Central Government had indicated that the Empowered Committee of State Finance Ministers would work with the Central Government to prepare a road map for introduction of GST. The Empowered Committee of State Finance Ministers prepared a report on a model and road map for GST.

In November 2007, a Joint Working Group consisting of representatives of the Empowered Committee and the Government of India prepared a report on the changeover to GST. This report was discussed by the Empowered Committee, which then prepared *A Model and Road Map for Goods and Service Tax in India* (April 2008). The model and roadmap, while recommending that a dual GST be put in place, also provided preliminary views on the central and state taxes to be subsumed within the GST.

The model detailed the operational issues which needed to be addressed, including the number of rates, exemptions and exclusions from GST, as well as the treatment of inter-state transactions.

The roadmap outlined the legal and administrative steps which needed to be taken in order to comply with the April 2010 time line.

The comments of Government of India on the proposed design of GST were sent to the Empowered Committee in January 2010. A joint group of officers has been constituted to prepare draft Constitutional Bill, Central GST legislation, model State GST legislation and rules required to introduce GST.

6.6 Direct Taxes Code (DTC)

In the Central Government Budget for 2009-10, the importance of continuing the process of structural changes in direct taxes was reiterated and a comprehensive code to this effect was envisaged. A Discussion Paper along with a draft

Direct Taxes Code was put in the public domain on August 12, 2009. The Code seeks to consolidate and amend the law relating to all direct taxes, namely income tax, dividend distribution tax and wealth tax so as to establish an economically efficient, effective and equitable direct tax system which will facilitate voluntary compliance and help increase the tax-GDP ratio.

All the direct taxes have been brought under a single code and compliance procedures unified, which will eventually pave the way for a single unified taxpayer reporting system. The need for the Code arose from concerns about the complex structure of half a century old Income Tax Act, 1961, which has been amended a large number of times, making it incomprehensible to the average tax payer. The Discussion Paper states that marginal tax rates have been steadily lowered and the rate structure rationalized to reflect best international practices and any further rationalization of the tax rates may not be feasible without corresponding increase in the tax base to enhance revenue productivity of the tax system and improve its horizontal equity.

A three-fold strategy for broadening the base has been articulated in the Code.

The first element of the strategy is to minimize exemptions that have eroded the tax base. The removal of these exemptions would: (a) increase tax-GDP ratio, (b) enhance GDP growth, (c) improve equity (both horizontal and vertical), (d) reduce compliance costs, (e) lower administrative burdens, and (f) discourage corruption.

The second element of the strategy seeks to address the problem of ambiguity in the law which facilitates tax avoidance.

The third element of the strategy relates to checking of erosion of the tax base through tax evasion.

Following are the salient features of the Direct Taxes Code.

1. The Discussion Paper discusses the principles of

residence-based taxation of income and source-based taxation of income in terms of international best practices that are mixes of the two. Under the Code, residence-based taxation is applied to residents and source-based to non-residents. A resident of India will be liable to tax in India on his worldwide income. However, a non-resident will be liable to tax in India only in respect of accruals and receipts in India (including deemed accruals and receipts).

2. The draft Code simplifies the dualistic concepts of *previous year* and *assessment year* used in the Act and replaces them with the unified concept of *financial year* and decrees that all rights and obligations of the taxpayer and the tax administration will be made with reference to the *financial year*.
3. The Discussion Paper argues for special treatment of capital gains under an income tax regime for two reasons. Firstly, taxing gains each year, as they accrue, would strain the finances of an individual who is yet to receive these gains in hand. Secondly, the capital gain realized when a capital asset is sold is usually the accumulated appreciation in the value of the asset over a number of years. The *bunching* of such appreciation in the year in which the asset is sold pushes the seller into a higher marginal tax bracket, if the value of the asset is sufficiently high. As such, if no special treatment is accorded to capital gains, a progressive income tax would discriminate against those whose income from capital assets is in the form of capital gains as compared to those whose income is derived from interest or dividends. The Code also seeks to eliminate the present distinction between short-term investment asset and long-term investment asset on the basis of the length of holding period of the asset.
4. On tax incentives, the Discussion Paper argues that they are inefficient, distorting, iniquitous, impose greater compliance burden on the taxpayer and on the administration, result in loss of revenue, create special

interest groups, add to the complexity of the tax laws, and encourage tax avoidance and rent-seeking behaviour. Based on a comprehensive review, the Code proposes that profit- linked tax deductions will be replaced by investment-linked deductions in areas of positive externality.

5. The draft Code argues against area-based exemptions which allocate/divert resources to areas where there is no comparative advantage. Such exemptions also lead to tax evasion and avoidance. It proposes that area-based exemptions that are available under the Income Tax Act, 1961 will be grandfathered.
6. The draft Code proposes to rationalise the tax incentives for savings through the introduction of the Exempt-Exempt-Taxation (EET) method of taxation of savings. Under this method, the contributions are exempt from tax (this represents the first E under the EET method), the accumulations/accretions are exempt (free from any tax incidence) till such time as they remain invested (this represents the second E) and all withdrawals at any time would be subject to tax at the applicable personal marginal rate of tax (this represents the T under the EET method).

Direct Taxes Code Bill was introduced in Parliament in August 2010. The Code was proposed to be introduced from April 1, 2012.

To sum up, tax reforms introduced by the Government since mid-1991 have helped to build a structure which is simple, relies on moderate tax rates but with a wider base and better enforcement. Historically, rates of income tax in India have been quite high, almost punitive. For example, in 1973-74, the maximum marginal rate of individual income tax was as high as 97.7 percent. When high rates proved counter-productive from revenue angle, the Government initiated a series of rate reductions with the result that the top rate for individual taxpayers declined to 30 percent (financial year 2011-12).

Multiple rates of commodity taxes have long been considered a weakness of the indirect tax system of India. Thus, in a landmark move, the Finance Minister announced in his 1999-2000 Budget a triple rate excise structure. In other words, the then existing 11 major *ad valorem* rates were reduced to 3, viz. a central rate of 16 percent, a merit rate of 8 percent and a demerit rate of 24 percent. The initiative of the Finance Minister to rationalise the rate structure of excise system was widely appreciated.

Tax reforms since June 1991 have helped in correcting structural imbalances in the tax system. They are *soft* on industry with a view to create new investment climate and make India internationally competitive. By lowering the tax rates, the Government expects speedy industrial development and hence buoyancy in tax revenues.

The country is keenly awaiting implementation of the Goods and Services Tax (GST) and the Direct Tax Code (DTC). GST is India's most ambitious indirect tax reform. Lack of political consensus is holding up progress and the Government has already missed the April 1, 2012 deadline of implementing GST.

End Notes

1. Bagchi, Amaresh and Nicholas, Stern (1994), *Tax Policy and Planning in Developing Countries,* Oxford University Press, New Delhi.
2. Rao, M.G. and Rao, R.K. (2006), "Trends and Issues in Tax Policy and Reform in India", *National Institute of Public Finance and Policy (NIPFP),* pp. 64-65.
3. Thimmaiah, G. (2002), "Evaluation of Tax Reforms in India", in M. Govinda Rao (ed.), *Development, Poverty and Fiscal Policy,* Oxford University Press, New Delhi, p. 129.
4. Government of India (1954), *Report of the Taxation Enquiry Commission*, Ministry of Finance, New Delhi.
5. Acharya, Shankar (2005), "Thirty Years of Tax Reform in India", *Economic and Political Weekly*, May 14, p. 2063.
6. Government of India (2001a), *Report of the Advisory Group on Tax Policy and Tax Administration for the Tenth Plan,* Planning

Commission, New Delhi. (Planning Commission.nic.in/aboutus/committee/wrkgrp/tptarpt.pdf.)

7. Arbalaez, M.A., Burman, L.E and Zuluaga, S.C (2002), "The Bank Debit Tax in Columbia", *Documentos de trabajo, FEDESAROLLO 000828.* (ftp://ftp.fedesarrollo.org.co/pub/documentos/wp.
8. Government of India (1977), *Report of the Indirect Taxation Enquiry Committee*, Ministry of Finance, New Delhi.
9. Ahmad, Ehtisham and Nicholas, Stern (1983), "Effective Taxes and Tax Reform in India", *Discussion Paper 25, Development Economics Research Centre*, University of Warwick.
10. Chelliah, R.J. (1986), "Change in the Tax Structure: A Case Study of India", *Paper Presented at the 42nd Congress of the International Institute of Public Finance.* Athens, Greece.
11. Government of India, (1991), *Tax Reforms Committee Interim Report*, Ministry of Finance, New Delhi.
12. —(2000b), *Report of the Expert Group on Taxation of Services*, Ministry of Finance, New Delhi.
13. Government of India (2004) *Report of the Twelfth Finance Commission (2005-10)*, Ministry of Finance, November, p. 31.
14. Kaldor, N., (1956), *Indian Tax Reform: Report of a Survey*, Ministry of Finance, Government of India, New Delhi
15. Government of India, (1992b), *Tax Reforms Committee*, Part I, Ministry of Finance, New Delhi, p. 11.
16. Thimmaiah, G. (2002), *op.cit.* pp. 129-138.
17. Government of India (2001a, 2002a, 2002b, 2004b).
18. Acharya, Shankar (2005), *op. cit.*, p. 2068.

7

Public Expenditure Reforms in India

Central and State Governments in India spend massive amounts on developmental, welfare and administrative activities. Public expenditure at the Central as well as at the level of State Governments has registered sharp rise since Independence. The reasons for increase in public activities and hence public expenditure are many and of diverse nature.

7.1 Role of Public Expenditure

Before independence, the amount and pattern of public expenditure in this country were determined by the colonial policy of the British rulers. Changes in the expenditure policy of the Government, however, became inevitable after India got Independence and the process of planning began. The nationalist Government laid down its own priorities and the volume and pattern of expenditure were determined accordingly. Both intensive and extensive expansion in the activities of the Government during the planning period has resulted in a spectacular rise in the public expenditure.

The role of public expenditure in the fiscal policy goals of growth, equity and stability, has varied across different phases of economic development in India. Public expenditure in India assumed significance in the context of mixed economy model adopted after independence in India whereby the Government assumed the primary responsibility of building the capital and infrastructure base to promote economic growth. The concerns regarding equity and poverty alleviation after two decades of independence i.e. 1970s, added another important dimension to public expenditure in terms of redistribution of resources. The inadequate returns on capital outlays and the macroeconomic crisis of early 1990s arising out of high fiscal deficit shifted the focus of public expenditure to efficiency in its management for facilitating adequate returns and restoring macroeconomic stability.

While the fiscal policy goal of stability could be achieved, the *modus operandi* of public expenditure management through curtailing capital expenditure raised concerns about infrastructure investment and its impact on the long-term growth potential. The upward movement in Government's revenue expenditure was partly responsible for fiscal deterioration which set in during the latter half of 1990s. With a renewed commitment towards fiscal consolidation since 2003-04, re-prioritization of expenditure and emphasis of outcomes rather than outlays are the guiding principles of public expenditure management. A series of expenditure management measures to check the built-in growth of expenditures as well as to bring about a structural change in the expenditure composition were announced in successive budgets of the Central Government since the early 1990s.

7.2 Need for Prudent Expenditure Management in India

Although sharp cuts in expenditure were effected as part of the stabilization package in 1991, attempts to curb expenditure growth in successive Central Government budgets in the 1990s were found to be mostly 'sporadic and arbitrary in nature' (Premchand, A. and Chattopadhyay, S., 2002). [1] It is only in the second generation of economic reforms that expenditure reform has become an integral part of the overall fiscal reform. Expenditure Reforms Commission set up by the Government suggested a host of measures to curb built-in-growth in expenditure and to bring about structural changes in the composition of expenditure. Some of these measures have been implemented by the Government. These included:

1. Subjecting all ongoing schemes to zero-based budgeting;
2. Assessment of manpower requirements of Government departments through reviewing norms for creation of posts and introduction of voluntary retirement schemes (VRS)

and redeployment of surplus staff;

3. Review of all subsidies with a view to introducing cost-based user charges wherever feasible; and
4. Review of budgetary support to autonomous institutions, and encouragement to PSUs to maximize generation of internal resources.

Notwithstanding the wide range of measures, the expenditure compression was mainly effected in the capital expenditure. Notably, the capital outlay of the Centre declined from 3.0 percent of GDP in 1986-87 to 2.1 percent in 1990-91 and further to 1.0 percent in 1996-97. Since then, there has been a significant reversal of the trend with a renewed focus of expenditure management.

A major initiative towards institutionalizing an expenditure management system was through constitution of Expenditure Reforms Commission (ERC) to look into various areas of expenditure correction. These included creation of national food stock along with cost minimization of buffer stock operations, rationalization of fertilizer subsidies through phased dismantling of controls, imposing a ceiling on Government staff strength through a two-year ban on new recruitment. Endeavour was also made to promote transparency and curb growth in contingent liabilities by setting up the Guarantee Redemption Fund. As a part of these efforts, some major expenditure management policies initiated by the Government during the current decade include:

1. Administered Price Mechanism (APM) in the petroleum sector was dismantled from April 2002;
2. Restriction on fresh recruitment to 1 percent of the total civilian staff strength over the 4 years beginning fiscal 2002-03;
3. Introduction of a new pension scheme of defined contribution for new recruits since January 2004 and introduction of an outcome budget in 2005-06 to evaluate the quality of expenditure; and
4. Avoiding rush of expenditure through releases in a time-

sliced manner and simplification of procedures (Pattnaik, R.K., Raj, D.S. and Chander, Jai, 2009). [2]

Performance audit by the Comptroller and Auditor General of India (CAG) of selected programmes continued to throw up important lessons for expenditure management. Further, the CAG has recently framed and notified Regulations of Audit and Account for the Government departments and other bodies and authorities under their control. Notification of the Regulations has brought transparency in Government audit and accounting process of CAG (Kapila, Uma, 2008). [3]

Given consumption and investment spending constitute an important part of aggregate demand in the economy. It influences growth through several channels. An increase in public spending on physical capital could positively influence the long-term growth. The impact of such spending in human capital formation could be larger but benefits require longer gestation period. So is the case with Government spending on research and development (R&D).

As such, any programme of stabilization-cum adjustment, has to be given considerable attention to the expenditure side of fiscal restructuring. It is important to plan expenditure reduction while improving quality of public spending to aim simultaneously at supporting growth with equity and improving fiscal balances.

In India, expenditure/GDP ratio of the Centre had risen from about 12.3 percent in 1970-71 to around 20 percent in the latter half of the 1980s. This had placed a difficult burden on budgetary balances. With a view to narrowing down the fiscal gap, particularly by bridging the revenue deficit, a cut in current expenditure was considered essential (Kapila, Uma, 2003). [4]

7.3 Classification of Public Expenditure

Public expenditure in India has various classifications which are important because they: (a) explain the interrelationship between the government sector and the rest of the economy, and (b) reveal the relative size of different governmental activities in the economy.

While certain classifications are the outcome of constitutional requirements, others are meant to facilitate understanding of the significance of governmental transactions. Thus, under Articles 112 and 202 of the Constitution, Central and State Governments are required respectively to present their expenditure estimates under the categories of revenue expenditure and capital expenditure.

To this classification is added a further classification, viz. Plan and non-Plan expenditure. Plan expenditure by tradition includes only new expenditure (both capital and revenue) on Plan projects undertaken during a Plan period. Furthermore, convention has it that new expenditure only under developmental heads can be included in the Plan. Thus, construction of a new jail house, though capital expenditure, does not qualify to be Plan expenditure.

7.3.1 Structure of Revenue Expenditure: Revenue expenditure (Table 7.1) relates to the normal expenditure required for running of Government departments and various services, interest charges on debt incurred by the Government, and grants given to State Governments and other parties. Broadly speaking, all those expenditure of the Government which does not result in the creation of physical or financial assets may be treated as revenue expenditure.

Budget documents classify revenue expenditure into plan and non-plan revenue expenditure. Plan revenue expenditure pertains to Central plan and Central assistance for State and Union Territory plans. However, the more important non-plan expenditure covers a wide variety of general, social and economic services of the Government. The three major items of non-plan revenue expenditures are: (a) interest payments, (b) defence, and (c) subsidies (Sury, M.M., 2007). [5]

A. Interest Payments: Interest payments constitute the single largest component of revenue non-Plan expenditure. It is in the nature of committed expenditure arising out of past profligacy. The high level of interest payments is directly linked to high reliance on borrowings.

Table 7.1: Composition of Central Government Total Expenditure, 2012-13

(₹ crore)

I. Total Revenue Expenditure (A+B)	**12,86,109**
A. Revenue Non-Plan expenditure, of which	8,65,596
1. Interest payment	3,19,759
2. Defence	1,13,829
3. Major subsidies	1,90,015
B. Revenue Plan expenditure, of which	4,20,513
1. Central Plan	3,03,528
2. Central assistance for State and U.T. Plans	1,16,985
II. Total Capital Expenditure (A+B)	**1,50,025**
A. Capital non-Plan expenditure, of which	1,04,304
1. Defence	79,579
2. Loans to public enterprises	465
B. Capital Plan expenditure, of which	1,00,512
1. Central Plan	87,499
2. Central assistance for State Plans	13,013
III. Total Expenditure (I + II)	**14,36,134**

Source: Government of India, Ministry of Finance, Budget Papers (March 2012), *Budget at a Glance.*

The increased reliance on borrowings has directly multiplied the debt servicing liabilities of the Government. Fiscal experts have warned against an internal debt trap, a situation in which borrowings have to be resorted to just to keep up with debt servicing.

Reduction in interest rates is one alternative to arrest the rising debt servicing obligations of the Government.

However, cuts in interest rates will provide only short-lived relief.

For a long-term solution of the problem, the borrowed funds must be used for productive purposes and for projects which ensure reasonable rates of return. This is also the underlying philosophy of public debt.

B. Defence Expenditure: Defence expenditure, chiefly determined by geo-political situation, is almost a committed expenditure. Defence expenditure is a sacred cow in India and any suggestion to control or reduce it is construed as almost unpatriotic. However, restraining defence expenditure should not be understood in terms of weakening defence preparedness. It simply means exploring the possibilities of achieving the existing level of defence preparedness at reduced costs. As a result of the implementation of the recommendations of various pay commissions, the wage component of the defence budget has increased disproportionately (Sury, M.M., 2003). [6]

C. Subsidies: See section 7.7 ahead.

7.3.2 Structure of Capital Expenditure: Those expenditure of the Government which leads to the creation of physical or financial assets or reduction in recurring financial liabilities fall under the category of capital expenditure (Table 7.1). Such expenditures pertain to payments on acquisition of assets like land, buildings, machinery, equipment, as also investments in shares, and loans and advances given to State Governments, public sector enterprises and other parties. Capital disbursements are of two kinds: those spent directly (capital outlays) and those spent indirectly by extending loans and advances (Sury, M.M., 2003). [7]

7.4 Public Expenditure Policy

Expenditure reforms in the context of liberalisation have two aspects: (a) consolidation so as to reduce the quantum of expenditure, and (b) restructuring with a view to changing the composition of government expenditure, i.e. shift towards growth-inducing expenditure on infrastructure and human resource development and reduction in unwarranted subsidies.

Government has taken various initiatives in recent years to streamline public expenditure management. The focus has shifted from financial outlays to outcomes for ensuring that the budgetary provisions are not merely spent within the financial year but have resulted in intended outcomes. The quarterly exchequer control based cash and expenditure management system which, *inter alia,* involves preparing a Monthly Expenditure Plan (MEP) is followed in select Demands for Grants. At the same time, steps have also been taken in the form of austerity instructions to reduce expenditure in non-priority areas without compromising on operational efficiency.

Initiatives have been taken to evenly pace plan expenditure during the year and also to avoid rush of expenditure at the year end which results in poor quality of expenditure. The practice of restricting the expenditure in the month of March to 15 percent of budget allocation within the fourth quarter ceiling of 33 percent is being enforced religiously.

7.5 Restructuring of Government Expenditure Suggested by the Eleventh Finance Commission

The Eleventh Finance Commission examined at length the pattern of public expenditure at the level of Central and State Governments and made a number of suggestions to rationalise it in order to control budgetary deficits. It observed, "Alongside revenue augmentation, restructuring of public finances will require structural changes on the expenditure side as well. While the thrust should be on compression, the composition of expenditure would need to be restructured in favour of priority sectors like elementary education, primary health care, water supply, sanitation, roads and bridges and other infrastructure. Items that would require a tight rein are salary and pensions, interest payments and subsidies. There has to be a radical change in the method of financing the plan expenditure as well.

Salaries: Wages and salaries have been growing primarily because of periodic revisions carried out on the recommendations of the Pay Commissions of the Centre, and the States falling in line, without due regard to the capacity of individual States to pay. The burden of pay revision is compounded by releases of DA twice a year by the Centre which has an effect on the States too. While it is the prerogative of the States to decide the size of their government, the total wage bill cannot be allowed to rise beyond a certain proportion of revenue receipts which represent the capacity to pay. In this background, we recommend the following:

- As full neutralisation for the increase in the prices has been given to all categories of employees there is no need to appoint any new Pay Commission as a matter of routine and at intervals of ten years. A new Pay Commission should be appointed only when warranted by special circumstances.
- As the recommendations of the Central Pay Commission have an impact on the States, the terms of reference of the Pay Commission should be settled in consultation with the States. Similarly, the decision on the recommendations of the Pay Commission should be taken in consultation with the States.
- It is noticed that the size of establishment is disproportionately large in relation to the requirements of administration in several States. In implementing the Pay Commission recommendations the Central Government has been in some respects more generous than what the recommendations of the Pay Commission implied. Some States have gone even beyond those levels resulting in the rise of emoluments of the employees beyond what is warranted by their capacity to pay.
- Salaries and other allowances should bear a relationship with the revenue expenditure of the Central and the States and the ratio should be such so as to leave adequate funds for maintenance and development expenditure. It is suggested that an Expert Committee may be appointed to determine the present relationship between salaries and other allowances with the revenue expenditure of the Centre and the States to suggest the relationship which would be attempted.

- The capacity of the Centre/States to pay salaries from their own resources should be one of the main criteria for determining the pay and allowances of the employees.

Pensions: Pensions have been the fastest growing item of the States' budgets in recent years. At the rate at which pensions are growing, liability for pension payments is going to cast a very heavy burden on the budgets in the coming years. Several factors have contributed to the growth of pensions. One has been the generous rise in the pensions recommended by the Fifth Pay Commission and, two the recent judicial pronouncement directing that no distinction should be made between people retiring at different points of time and all pensioners should be treated alike in the matter of their pension rights. Another factor has been the addition of the liability on account of pensions payable to retired employees of aided institutions and local bodies to the government's pension bill. The increasing longevity of people, though welcome, has also meant growing pension liability of governments. What causes concern is the fact that pensions are paid by governments on pay as you go basis i.e. there is no corpus or fund which could take care of the pension liabilities. Consideration needs to be given to evolving a system under which pensions do not become an unsustainable burden on the State exchequer. A large amount of pension burden is on account of retired defence employees. A suitable scheme to absorb the retirees from the armed forces in other government departments can help to contain the growth of defence pensions.

Interest Payment: Interest as a proportion of the revenue receipts of the States has increased sharply over the years, particularly during the last 10 years. The scheme of deficit reduction outlined in our restructuring plan, should help to check the debt growth of the States and thereby the growth of interest payments. From the supplementary memorandum on small savings received from the Ministry of Finance, it appears that the Centre may offer the State governments an option of pre-payment or rescheduling of past loans attributable to small savings. The guiding principle would be incentive based maturity reduction. Thus a loan of 25 years' duration could be rescheduled to 15 years' loan with lower interest rates.

Subsidies: Subsidies are provided by governments implicitly as well as explicitly. While the Centre's budget provides estimates of explicit subsidies in the State budgets, the outgo on account of subsidies is scattered under several heads. Subsidies, no doubt, have their uses as these help to alleviate the poverty of the low income segments of the population by providing access to essential goods and services free or at affordable prices. However, subsidies are apt to be misused and often go to the benefit of the non-poor." [8]

7.6 Restructuring of Government Expenditure Suggested by the Twelfth Finance Commission

After examining in detail the structure of expenditure at the levels of Central and State Governments, the Twelfth Finance Commission recommended its restructuring on the following lines, "In restructuring expenditures, there is need to make reference to the basic objectives of government intervention in economic activities, as also to the basic objectives for assignment of responsibilities as between central and sub-national governments. It is also important to relate government expenditures to outcomes in terms of the quality, reach, and impact of government services. This would be facilitated if governments focus more on their primary responsibilities rather than spreading resources thinly in many areas where the private sector can provide the necessary services.

The primary role of government is to provide public goods like defence, law and order, and general administration. This represents one kind of market failure. The role of governments extends to merit goods and services with large positive externalities like education and health. The services should be assigned to the central government if the scope of public goods is nation-wide like defence. The services get assigned to state governments if the scope of the public good is limited to regions or if externalities are more local in character like the health services.

Admittedly there may be many examples of benefit spillovers, some of which can be internalized to the state level decision makers by a suitable scheme of grants. There is a felt need to examine whether the central government is not partaking in many responsibilities that legitimately belong to the domain of the states. Governments at both levels have also stepped into the provision of many private goods, which adversely affects the quantum and quality of service in regard to public and merit goods. Two key elements of restructuring government expenditures relate to augmentation of capital expenditure relative to GDP, focused on infrastructure and a reduction of central government's expenditures on subjects listed as state responsibilities." [9]

7.7 Controversy about Subsidies

A subsidy is a grant of money from an outside third party to either the buyer or the seller of a commodity. Subsidies allow a buyer to procure a commodity/service at a lower price than would otherwise have been necessary. Similarly, a business firm will not stay in operation unless revenue is sufficient enough to cover cost plus some return on investment. If revenue from buyers is insufficient, a subsidy from an outside agency may keep the firm in operation.

The effect of a subsidy is opposite of the effect of a tax. A cash subsidy is the opposite of a direct tax while a subsidised commodity is the opposite of a taxed commodity. Hence, subsidies are sometimes called negative taxation.

7.7.1 Food Subsidy: Foodgrains occupy an important place in the family budget of a large section of the population in India. Hence, a certain minimum supply of foodgrains at reasonable prices constitutes the rock-bottom of Government's economic policy. To ensure minimum health and efficiency standards, the prices of foodgrains must be held stable at levels within the reach of the poorer sections of the community.

Food Security is one of the major components of social security. It consists of ensuring: (a) that food is available at all times, (b) that all persons have means of and access to it, (c) that it is nutritionally adequate in terms of quantity, quality and variety, and (d) that it is acceptable within the given culture. There are three elements in the above definition: availability, access and suitability.

In recent years, nutrition has been considered as part of food security, and is therefore, referred to as Food and Nutrition Security.

The objectives of a sound agricultural price policy are two-fold: (a) to ensure fair prices for the produce of the farmers, and (b) to ensure adequate and regular supply of agricultural commodities to the consumers at reasonable prices.

Food subsidies in India comprise subsidies to farmers through support prices and purchase operations of the Food Corporation of India (FCI), consumer subsidies through the public distribution system (PDS), and subsidies to FCI to cover all its costs. Food subsidies are mainly on account of paddy and wheat. The rapid increase in food subsidy in recent years is attributable to what is called the 'economic costs' of foodgrains, which include the minimum support prices paid to farmers in the procurement process.

7.7.2 Fertiliser Subsidy: Use of fertilisers is necessary to improve yield of various crops. The objective of providing fertilizers to farmers at affordable prices, while also ensuring adequate return on investment to the producing units, has been the corner stone of the fertilizer pricing policy of the government.

In order to control the fluctuations in fertilizer prices, the Government of India regulates the fertilizer market through the Retention Price Scheme (RPS). The RPS was first introduced for nitrogenous fertilizers in November 1977, and extended to complex fertilizers in February 1979.

The RPS is essentially a cost-plus approach with some norms for capacity utilization and conversion coefficients. The plant specific retention prices (RP) are revised every quarter so that price increases in plant inputs can be taken into account. The retail price of fertilizers is fixed and is uniform throughout the country. The difference between the retention price (adjusted for freight and dealer's margin) and the price at which the fertilizers are provided to the farmer is paid back to the manufacturer as subsidy. Transportation costs are also compensated on the basis of equated freight computed on a normative basis.

Subsidies, on food and fertilisers, are primarily meant to help poor households in urban and rural areas. However, under the present system even the well-off sections of society are also beneficiaries of subsidised items. Application of some economic criterion is necessary to rationalise and regulate the benefits of subsidies without jeopardising the interest of weaker sections.

7.7.3 Petroleum Subsidy: Prior to April 2002, prices of motor spirit, high speed diesel, kerosene for public distribution system (PDS) and domestic liquefied petroleum gas (LPG) were decided by the Government and administered through the Oil Coordination Committee (OCC), and there was an elaborate system of cross-subsidisation of PDS kerosene and domestic LPG through higher prices of motor spirit. The net result from cross-subsidization of products by petroleum companies, predominantly public sector companies both in the upstream and downstream sectors, constituted the so-called oil-pool surplus or deficit. These balances were carried on the books of the state-owned oil companies, and occasionally settled by Government intervention. Thus, subsidisation in the oil sector was in the nature of a quasi-fiscal operation.

In November 1997, Government set a timetable for a phased transition from an administered price regime to a market-determined system with continued subsidization of PDS kerosene and LPG, but on a gradually reducing scale.

Subsidies on kerosene and LPG for household use were to be phased down over time to smaller price subsidies of 33.3 percent and 15 percent, respectively, by end-March 2002. As part of the energy sector reforms, the prices of many petroleum products, for example, naphtha, furnace oil, low-sulphur heavy stock (LSHS), light diesel oil (LDO) and bitumen, have been liberalized since April, 1998. One important achievement was the linking of high speed diesel prices to international prices and an elimination of subsidy since September 1997 for some time. However, LPG and kerosene, consumed mainly by the domestic sector, continue to be heavily subsidized.

The phased reduction in subsidies has fallen behind schedule. In March 2002, Government decided that the subsidy on domestic LPG and PDS kerosene would be provided on a specified flat-rate basis from the Consolidated Fund from April 1, 2002. In this situation, Government reimburses the firms for the cost of the subsidy, which is carried as a line item in the budget and called the petroleum subsidy.

7.7.4 LPG and Kerosene Subsidies: LPG subsidy benefits largely the higher expenditure groups in the urban areas, and may be regressive. With regard to kerosene, on a per capita basis, the urban areas receive a larger subsidy. The limited availability of subsidized kerosene in rural areas biases its use in favour of lighting rather than cooking. Moreover, the kerosene subsidy in rural areas is regressive as higher expenditure groups receive more subsidized kerosene than lower expenditure groups.

Kerosene subsidy is prone to mis-utilisation with about half the subsidized kerosene supplies diverted and never reaching the intended groups. These arguments suggest that the LPG and kerosene subsidies are ineffective in serving the desired objectives. Therefore, the removal of LPG subsidy in a gradual manner, or at least a substantial reduction in the subsidy element, may be recommended. A more cautious approach may be justified in the reduction of kerosene subsidies since about a half of the rural households use kerosene primarily to light their homes.

Generally, it is assumed that clean fuels like kerosene, that are relatively environment-friendly compared to fuel wood, are not used as they are not affordable because of high prices and low purchasing power of the poor households. However, it is not affordability, but non-availability that may be restricting the use of clean fuels by poor rural households. Thus, the approach that may be sustainable in the long run for the purposes of expanding access and improving the quality of service is to create an open and competitive market with clearly defined and well-enforced rules and regulations for all participants.

Cash transfer to the poor to compensate for the reduction or elimination of subsidy does not appear to be a suitable strategy for inducing a shift toward hydrocarbons for use as cooking fuels. The urban poor and all rural households may use more wood with enhanced incomes from a modest cash transfer. An alternate approach may be to channel all sales of kerosene through the retail markets, and encourage small distributors of fuels. Coupons may be issued only to poor ration card holders with entitlement to purchase kerosene from a retailer at the subsidised price. This would discourage direct diversion of subsidised kerosene to other sectors.

To conclude, the domestic LPG and PDS kerosene subsidies seem to be ineffective in serving the desired objectives. Therefore, the domestic LPG subsidy may be gradually reduced or at least substantially restricted to people outside the purview of income tax. However, a more cautious approach is needed as regards reduction of subsidy on kerosene.

7.7.5 Post-liberalisation Thinking on Subsidies: Of late, drastic changes have occurred in Government's policy towards subsidies. The crux of this policy is to roll back subsidies and thus curb the growth of non-Plan expenditure. Another dimension of the present policy is to restrict the availability of subsidised items to vulnerable sections of society.

The economic reforms programme initiated in 1991 aimed at, among other things, reducing fiscal imbalances and improving allocative efficiency by minimizing the distortions in relative prices arising from budgetary and fiscal imprudence. Containing and targeting subsidies constituted an important element of reforms. Containment and targeting of subsidies can serve the following objectives: (a) remove economic distortions, thereby improving economic efficiency and growth, (b) achieve redistributive objective, and (c) reduce budgetary burden and release precious resources.

Government showed its seriousness about targeting subsidies at the poor and the truly needy in the budget speech of the Finance Minister for 2006-07. Extensive discussions with stakeholders on three major subsidies, namely, food, fertilizer and petroleum were held for the purpose.

Views of the general public were also sought. Working groups/committees have gone into the question of fertilizer and petroleum subsidies. Government is trying to evolve a consensus on the issue of subsidies. However the Government has pledged that all subsidies will be targeted sharply at the poor and the truly needy the small and marginal farmers, farm labour and urban poor.

End Notes

1. Premchand, A. and Chattopadhyay, S. (2002), "Fiscal Adjustment and Expenditure Management", *National Institute of Public Finance and Policy, Discussion Paper No.3,* January.
2. Pattnaik, R.K., Raj, D.S. and Chander, Jai (2009), *Data Empirical Fiscal Research in India: A Survey, RBI Staff Studies*, www.rbi.org.in.
3. Kapila, Uma (2008), *IndianEeconomy Since Independence*, 19th edition, Academic Foundation, New Delhi, p. 116.
4. Kapila, Uma (2003), *op. cit*, p. 134.
5. Sury, M. M. (2007), *Fiscal Policy Developments in India, 1947 to 2007*, New Century Publications, New Delhi, p. 378.
6. Sury, M.M. (2003) *India: Central Government Budgets, 1947-48 to 2003-04*, New Century Publications, New Delhi, p. 44.
7. Ibid, p. 48.

8. Report of the Eleventh Finance Commission, June 2000, pp. 29-31.
9. Report of the Twelfth Finance Commission, November 2004, pp. 78-79.

8

Evaluation of Fiscal Reforms in India

8.1 Economic Crisis and Fiscal Reforms

Fiscal reforms have been in the forefront of India's economic reforms programme initiated in 1991. The fiscal situation prevailing at the end of the 1980s was marked by large and persistent deficits in the Government budgets, hence needed strong corrective action was recognized on all hands well before the onset of the balance of payments crisis that compelled the country to seek the assistance of the IMF and the World Bank to keep the economy going.

The Prime Minister's Economic Advisory Council chaired by the late Sukhamoy Chakravarty had in their report of December 1989 drawn pointed attention to the uncertainties posed by the twin imbalances that had been plaguing the Indian economy at the time despite notable acceleration in output growth during the decade, one on the fiscal side and other in external trade (Government of India, 1989). [1]

While the reform launched to combat the crisis that came to a head in 1991 sought to correct the imbalances through measures mounted on several fronts, the focus was on fiscal reform as the key to stabilization and growth on a sustainable basis. The deficits in the Government budget were seen as a prime source of imbalance on the external front too as they were thought to spill into the balance of payments and raise questions about the country's solvency at home and abroad (Bagchi, Amaresh ,1998). [2]

The gross fiscal deficit (GFD) of the Centre witnessed a decline during the first half of the 1990s. Tax revenue as a proportion of GDP fell during this period as a result of restructuring of tax system with focus on simplification and rationalization of both direct and indirect taxes, drawing mainly from the recommendations of the Tax Reforms Committee, 1991. The fiscal correction strategy focused on the expenditure front, whereby corrective measures initiated at the beginning of the 1990s, mostly in the terms of curtailment of expenditure growth, yielded some promising results.

In fact, the reduction in revenue receipts brought about by the decline in tax/GDP ratio was more than offset by the reduction in revenue expenditure, resulting in a marginal reduction in the ratio of revenue deficit to GDP during this period. However, the fiscal consolidation even during the first half of he 1990s was brought about primarily through curtailment in capital outlay and net lending.

8.2 Fiscal Responsibility and Budget Management Act

The key policies that induced these favourable fiscal developments varied across the two Central levels, the enactment of the Fiscal Responsibility and Budget Management (FRBM) Act in 2003-04 capped several years of technocratic and political efforts and gave a significant stimulus to the cause of fiscal consolidation. The FRBM Act targeted elimination of the Centre's revenue deficit by 2008-09 and a reduction of the fiscal deficit to 3 percent of GDP. It also specified minimum improvement towards these targets each year. The fiscal deficit target had been preety much achieved by 2007-08, with relatively modest recourse to creative accounting, such as incurring of off-budget liabilities. (The year 2008-09, will be a wholly different matter, thanks to huge implicit and explicit subsidies for fuel, fertilizers and food as well as the effects of the Sixth Pay Commission and the loan waiver for farmers announced in 2008-09 Budget).

The second major policy initiative at the Central level was a concerted and sustained programme to raise the tax-GDP ratio through better application of information technology and other means to strengthen tax administration (Chakravarty, Shomit, 2004). [3]

8.3 Measurement of Fiscal Gap

The term fiscal gap is normally used to indicate the overall resources gap in countries finances which might include various kinds of deficits including fiscal deficits. But, Mihir Rakshit (2000) [4] used this term to indicate a particular type of deficit. He defined 'Fiscal Gap' as, "is nothing but the Governments incremental financial liability (IFL) less monetized deficit. Fiscal gap thus represents the yearly increase in Government debt to the rest of the economy plus reduction in its financial assets, and hence constitute, better measure than fiscal deficit of the Governments incremental debt burden due to current budgetary measures".

He defines incremental financial liability (IFL) to be equivalent to capital disbursement plus revenue deficit plus non-debt capital receipt (NDCCR). Capital disbursement plus revenue deficit is nothing but fiscal deficit, the additional factor therefore is NDCCR. Rakshit's argument is that NDCCR is significant as different kinds of receipts should be treated separately on the basis of their implications for future earning in terms of which all NDCCR may not be put on the same footing. For example, disinvestment in PSUs cannot be treated on the same footing as the tax collection because although both are non-debt creating receipts, disinvestment proceeds reduce future earnings of the Government by way of interest and dividends. "From view point of budgetary viability there can thus be little doubt that reduction of fiscal deficit through disinvestment cannot but be worse than tax financing"(Rakshit, Mihir, 2000). [5]

Rakshit (2000) [6] is of the view that the fiscal deficit as is commonly defined is not appropriate for judging the sustainability of debt financing or the efficacy of Governments budgetary operations in pursuing the objectives of fiscal policy. But limitations of conventional measures of fiscal deficit are well recognized. "...There is no such thing as the fiscal deficit, but rather a series of alternative measures each with advantages and disadvantages" (Blejer, Mario and

Cheasty, Adrienne, 1993). [7] Thus, there could be number of measures appropriateness of their use depends upon the purpose for which they are being used like which set of macroeconomic consequences of fiscal policy is intended to be assessed. So Rakshits concept of fiscal gap may prove to be useful in evaluating the budgetary policy of the country.

It appears from the discussion on various deficit concepts that fiscal deficit alone may not be of much use if not supported by other informations. Fiscal deficit, as discussed, indicates the public sectors borrowing requirement which may arise on account of Governments spending in excess of its receipts. But overspending itself may not be good or bad for its own sake. Other informations which are required to make use of the concept of fiscal deficit would be whether the overspending is because of Governments capital investment or simply the revenue expenditure, and secondly the rate of return expected on the investment. If the investment is in the form of creating infrastructure which does not add to the Governments revenue directly but it surely increases the Governments tax receipts (as the infrastructure would result in enhanced output). If the increase in Governments receipts in the form of tax or non-tax revenue is of greater magnitude than the cost of borrowings debt financed investment is alright otherwise it would require a review of the investment decision of the Government.

If the said borrowings requirement is on account of financing the consumption expenditure then situation would be termed as alarming. But even then it would be still open to judgement if the revenue deficit is properly measured. It is said there are number of expenditures that, in normal budgetary accounting, have the effects of investments, for example, the expenditure on education since large part of the education goes towards the salaries of the teachers it is put into the category of revenue expenditure in most of the countries including India. But such expenditure is basically an investment in human capital which in the time to come will surely contribute to the productivity enhancement. It can, therefore, be said different types of Government expenditures like public consumption, investment and transfers have different implications for future receipts of the Government. Thus, for examining the sustainability of fiscal stance or evaluating the macroeconomic consequences of it, the composition of Government expenditure, not simply its aggregates, has to be taken into consideration.

Debt crisis in many countries during 1980s had brought the focus on fiscal policy with fiscal deficit as key element. Fiscal imbalances were then considered (and continued to be considered) as the principal cause for various macro-economic problem like inflation, balance of payments disequilibrium, investment crowding-out and as a result slowing down of economic growth. These problems, in turn, were supposed to be responsible for low revenue collection which means further deficit and hence the perpetuity of the crises. The correction of such imbalances began to be accorded top priority among all other measures to bring about macroeconomic corrections.

But the question is, whether such effects of fiscal imbalances are real or illusionary. Another important question that arises, which measure of deficit as fiscal deficit itself can be measured variously; besides, there are other deficit concept also like 'revenue deficit' and monetized deficit etc. which have the potentiality of influencing with varying degree, above mentioned macro variables. Answer to such questions lies on the purpose for which the fiscal deficit is being measured. "Although the deficit measure is relevant primarily as an indicator of the macroeconomic consequences of fiscal policy, the set of consequences that policy makers desire to assess may itself determine the correct deficit measures"(Blejer, Mario and Cheasty, Adreienne 1993). [8]

Since selection of appropriate measure itself is so important for any analytical study of the influence of fiscal policy on macroeconomic variables, measurement of deficit as also its determinants assume significance. Though the discussion is general in nature, references here are mostly cited from the studies on Indian economy. This may not be out of time in view of the following observations. "Although country circumstances vary greatly, fundamental principles of fiscal management apply everywhere" (World Development Report, 1998). [9]

The above mentioned World Development Report was probably the first document that initiated a debate on the measurement aspect of the deficit. There is near unanimity on the point that the deficit per se may not be of any analytical value. To what extent it is distortionary, can be judged from the various items of expenditure and revenue as also from the way it is financed. "Deficits in themselves do not automatically imply macroeconomic problems. If the use of public resources is sufficiently productive, future income can be generated to cover the servicing cost of any debt incurred" (Ibid). [10]

It appears from the above observation that the prime concern about fiscal deficit seems to be for its contribution to public debt and its sustainability. Therefore, the appropriate measures has been found to be the one which measures the public sectors borrowing requirements (PSBR) as it represents the total excess of expenditure over revenue which has to be financed through borrowings. This measure has been termed as 'fiscal deficit' and is considered to be the most appropriate for measuring the net claim on resources by public sector which may turn out to be the explanatory variable for various macro imbalances.

If so defined fiscal deficit is compared with the conventionally measured budgetary deficit in India's context, it is found that later does not completely serve the purpose. The fiscal gap up to the mid-1980s was measured in terms of 'budgetary deficit' which referred mainly to the changes in the amount of ad hoc Treasury Bills and other 91-day Treasury Bills outstanding and the changes in the Central Governments deposit balances with the Reserve Bank and its other cash balances. In fact, until the beginning of the 1990s, there was no unique concept of budget deficit relevant to all purposes and occasions. Depending on the nature of the quest, the relevant budget deficit concept could have seen the Government revenue deficit, the capital deficit, or overall deficit (Gill, K.S., 1991). [11]

While the budget deficit, as was defined at that time, severely understated the monetary impact of fiscal operations since it did not include Reserve Banks investment in dated securities, there was also some over statement of the monetary impact to the extent that the Treasury Bills were held by the banks. Thus, its argument is that 'An unambiguous and economically meaningful measure of the monetary impact of fiscal operations is provided by the change in Reserve Bank credit to Government. In view of this, the Chakravarty Committee emphasized the need to have a measure for the full extent of Governments reliance on Reserve Bank so as to quantify the monetary impact of fiscal operations.

Since a sizeable part of the new issues of Government securities was taken up by the Reserve Bank in the absence of adequate response from the market and subscriptions to dated securities had a much effect on the reserve money growth as purchase of Treasury Bills, the Committee recommended that the net changes in the Reserve Banks holding of dated securities and Treasury Bills after adjusting the Government deposit with the Reserve Bank i.e., the net RBI credit to the Government, may be taken to measure the extent of monetization of Government deficit. The Committee also recommended that the fiscal gap be measured in terms of fiscal deficit which would measure the net borrowing requirement of the Government.

8.4 Measurement of Fiscal Deficit

Though appropriate measure of deficit as has been mentioned earlier would depend upon the purpose for which it is to be used, the measure that gauge the public sectors claim on resources of the economy has been considered to be the best among all and that is 'fiscal deficit'. Since it measures the public sector's borrowing requirement, it is supposed that it reflects the expansionary impact of the budget. However, it remains to be seen as to what extent this perception is correct. The measures based on above requirement are following:

8.4.1 Gross Fiscal Deficit (GFD): (GFD) = (Revenue expenditure + capital expenditure + net domestic lending) – (Revenue receipts + grants)

Shortcomings of the traditional measure of budget deficit are evident when it is compared with GFD. While the gross fiscal deficit captures the entire shortfall in Governments fiscal operations (domestic and foreign) and/or running down on its cash holdings, the traditional measure is confined, besides the depletion of liquidity holdings, only to one particular form of domestic borrowings, i.e., 91-day Treasury bills, thus ignoring other domestic borrowings, i.e., such as current loans, small savings, provident funds, etc., as well as foreign borrowings (Rangarajan, C., 2004). [12]

Since in most of the developing countries Government used to act like financial intermediary by re-lending the borrowed amount to other sectors like State and local Government, public enterprises etc. This means such lending does not result in Government acquiring profitable financial asset. This however is done in order to fulfil the capital requirements of these sectors. But for the purpose of measurement it will be proper that this amount may be netted out from the gross fiscal deficit otherwise figure for the consolidated fiscal deficit will be overstated on account of double counting. Therefore, the net fiscal deficit is more relevant and has following identity.

8.4.2 Net Fiscal Deficit (NFD): (NFD) = Gross fiscal deficit – net domestic lendings = (Revenue expenditure + capital expenditure) – (Revenue receipts + grants)

Traditional budgetary deficit has been found to be inadequate in capturing the full impact of fiscal expansion because they have at least three limitations (Tanzi,Vito, 1993) [13]:

1. Different taxes and expenditure affect demand differently, so that for a given deficit the composition of the budget is important.
2. Tax revenue is not a completely independent policy variable but is subject to feedback from the rest of the economy.
3. Excess demand stemming from the deficit depends not only on the size of the deficit but also on the manner in which it is financed.

Thus, fiscal deficit which measures the public sectors borrowing requirement is considered to be the appropriate measure as it does not go into the details of the causes of this requirement i.e. whether need for borrowing arises on account of deficit in revenue account or capital account. But a careful scrutiny of fiscal deficit suggests that it too is incapable of reflecting monetary expansion accurately because part of deficit is financed by borrowings and part by creating new money. If Government is able to sell its securities to the public independent of its central bank's support, then borrowing represents only the resource transfer.

Secondly, the definition of revenue receipts and revenue expenditure is also important from the view point of the effectiveness of fiscal deficit measure. Normally, all receipts that do not increase the financial liabilities of the Government are included in the revenue receipts whether it is tax receipt or non-tax receipt. But how are we to treat the proceeds from disinvestment or from the sale of assets? Is it revenue receipt or not? This question assumes significance if the appropriateness of fiscal deficit measure is under consideration. It depends upon the purpose for which the deficit measure is to be used. As Chelliah puts it, "If the short-term impact of the budget on aggregate demand through net borrowings is to be judged, the sale proceeds could be netted out against capital formation expenditure" (Chelliah, R.J.,

1996). [14] Thus, it is apparent that fiscal deficit has to be supplemented by some other information in order to make it effective even for the very purpose for which it has been discovered i.e. impact of monetary expansion.

Tanzi (1993) [15] also criticised the current account deficit measure. He finds it useless on account of: (a) the futility of classifying the expenditure into current revenue and investments, and (b) false and arbitrary demarcation between capital and current expenditure. He finds such classification futile because expenditure's short term impact on balance of payments disequilibrium will not only be the same but the investment spending may have larger negative impact and for (b) above, he argues that it is not possible to classify the expenditure into current and investment because there are number of expenditure that can be put in either of the category depending upon the argument.

For example, there is strong case for some current spending on education and health to be placed along investment expenditure because of their long-run effects on growth. Secondly, investment could be bad enough which instead of augmenting future income may just be a source of complete waste. Thus he says "I am skeptical that current account budgetary deficit may tell us much, although investment would certainly be concerned about a country that is running a fiscal deficit even when investment expenditure, however defined, is netted out. For sure the current account deficit will tell us nothing about the impact of fiscal policy on the balance of payments and perhaps not much about the impact of fiscal policy on growth"(Tanzi,Vito,1993). [16]

Thus, Tanzi does not find out utility of revenue deficit. But the counter argument is that perhaps Tanzi has misplaced his focus as impact on balance of payments is not the purpose of revenue deficit measure rather it is used to find whether the expenditure on current consumption is fully met by current revenue because otherwise a country would be working against the well accepted principle of public finance that society as a whole should bear the cost of the goods and services that it collectively consumes regardless of the preference of the individual members of the society. Further, revenue account deficit/surplus is the measure of Governments contribution to dissaving/saving which is very important variable from the view point of economic growth, though savings automatically do not lead to growth.

8.4.3 Revenue Deficit: Revenue Deficit = Total revenue expenditure – Total revenue receipts.

Revenue account balance is also a very useful indicator especially for the economies which are running into huge revenue account deficit. As fiscal deficit only tell us the overall borrowing requirement, it is revenue account that tell us the overall borrowing goes into financing consumption expenditure. Thus, the fact that revenue deficit measure suffers from various limitations does not prove its futility. Revenue deficit measure along with other concept of deficits are employed to gauge the fiscal health of the economy and that all such measures are supplementary rather than substitutes for the fiscal deficit measure because fiscal deficit measure itself is subject to various limitation.

One important limitation of the fiscal deficit is that they do not necessarily reflect the extent to which the current discretionary fiscal actions improve or worsen the Government's net indebtedness. In particular, interest payments in the current period are obligatory, but reflect past budgets. In such situation if interest payments are excluded it yield the figure known as primary deficit. It is primary deficit that determine whether current fiscal measures are improving the situation or worsening it. It is primary deficit that is responsible for the growth of public debt as it has to be financed through borrowings. If borrowing increases faster than GDP, debt-GDP ratio will rise. Thus, primary deficit measure will have to be employed to supplement fiscal deficit in order to gauge the contribution of fiscal deficit to public debt. Corresponding to the two concepts of fiscal deficit, i.e., gross and net, two measures of primary deficit could be constructed thus:

8.4.4 Gross Primary Deficit (GPD): GPD = (Gross fiscal deficit) – (interest payments – interest earnings) = (Revenue expenditure + capital expenditure + net domestic lendings) – (Revenue receipts + grants) – (interest payments – interest earnings) = (Non-interest revenue expenditure + capital expenditure + net domestic lendings) – (Non-interest revenue receipts + grants).

8.4.5 Net Primary Deficit (NPD): NPD = (Non-interest revenue expenditure+ capital expenditure) – (Non- interest revenue receipts + grants).

Primary deficit concepts, thus defined, indicate the precise extent to which current fiscal actions affect the indebtedness of the Central Government and is, therefore, most suitable for the present study (Rangarajan, C., 2004). [17]

Yet another controversial issue that has to be settled is how to treat arrears. Payments of arrears are on account of past commitments therefore to that extent the rise in expenditure may be temporary and may not be reflective of Governments current policy stance. Similarly, some payments that might become due but may be deferred i.e. unpaid interest on debt. This becomes possible if debts are rescheduled which is normal practice in case of external debt. In such situation it has to be specified in a measure of fiscal deficit whether unpaid interest on external debt are being registered or not.

Still another area which has been debated in the literature on fiscal deficit is the receipts acquired through diluting the assets or which the reduction in receipt is on account of tax amnesty, (which may be introduced as once and for all measure) or the freeze in wages below their long-term economic equilibrium. These measures are said to affect the fiscal deficit in the short-run, permanent effect on fiscal deficit may not be expected. Thus, Tanzi remarks "for this reason, (short-term adjustment measures) in some cases it would be desirable to present a measure of the fiscal deficit that would remove the impact of such short term measures. This adjustment would give an underlying or core deficit that would better reflect the fiscal situation of the country over the long run. Such correction would be desirable, although in many cases it might be difficult to do in practice" (Tanzi,Vito,1993). [18]

The inability of fiscal deficit measure and other relevant indicators discussed above to capture the full view of unhealthy trend in Indian economy has been mentioned by Rakshit. He suggested it appears from the usual indicators movements that there is no deterioration in the fiscal health of the economy during 1990s (Rakshit, Mihir, 2000). [19]

Following factor may be mentioned:

1. Public debt-GDP ratio did not show any rising trend, except during the later part of the period.
2. Fiscal deficit as a ratio of GDP also registered a declining trend in the earlier period, but rose in the later period.
3. Growth rate of the economy exceeded the interest rate on Government borrowing (a crucial condition for debt sustainability).

The disturbing trend is the slippage in the later part of the period but that may be attributed to the transitory rise in expenditure on account of the payments of arrears on the award of fifth pay commission. A greater disturbing trend that could not be noticed is the rise in non-RBI held public debt (RBI's holding of public debt is of no significance in Rakshit's Scheme). Therefore, the deteriorating fiscal health cannot be measured through fiscal deficit. It is for this reason that he emphasized the measure he called "fiscal gap" which measures the yearly increase in Government debt to the rest of the economy plus reduction in its financial assets. Fiscal gap can be measured as under;

8.4.6 Fiscal Gap: Fiscal Gap = Incremental financial liability (IFL) – monetized deficit.

(Where IFL is equal to capital disbursement + revenue deficit).

One weakness that appears in this measure is that it presumes the deficit on revenue account. Though identity of IFL appears to be no different from that of fiscal deficit but Rakshit further qualifies it by following statement.

"IFL is nothing but fiscal deficit plus non-debt creating capital receipt". But even this clarification may not be sufficient as foreign grants may not be sufficient as foreign grants may also be non-debt creating capital receipt while Rakshit seeks to include such receipts which are responsible for reduction in further income which basically means receipts through sale of assets.

Thus, it is clear from the above discussions that there is no unique measure of deficit satisfactory to everybody and for every purpose. Each could be justified for some use and none is useful for all uses.

8.5 Fiscal Reforms: An Assessment

Fiscal policy has been playing important role in stimulating the rate of growth of the Indian economy. Clearly, the appropriate design of fiscal policy is important since fiscal policy could act both as a stimulant as well as an obstacle for rapid economic growth. If tax and expenditure policies are geared towards encouraging savings and investment and the efficient use of capital fiscal policy can help stimulate economic growth. However, fiscal policy can hurt prospects for economic growth if, for example, profligate Government machinery runs up successively high budget deficits and crowds out productive private investment (Jha, Raghbendra, 2004). [20]

The rapid deterioration in the Government finances during the late 1980s caused by a faster rise in expenditure growth relative to revenue growth resulted in a steep rise in the Central Government fiscal deficit to GDP ratio which culminated in a balance of payments crisis. The macroeconomic crisis of 1991 created an exigency and led to the chartering of a strong reversal of hitherto followed policies.

The biggest challenge facing the conduct of fiscal policy in India is to continue the accelerated growth process while maintaining price and financial stability. The conduct of fiscal policy since the early 1990s has broadly succeeded in setting the economy on a higher growth path.

Far reaching fiscal reforms have been undertaken during this period, which are finally bearing fruit through increased revenue mobilization, some compression in expenditure, and consequent reduction in the fiscal deficit, leading to the beginning of some reduction in the debt-GDP ratio through revenue enhancement and curtailment in current expenditure growth while enlarging spending on investment and infrastructure so as to provide momentum to the growth process. Measures were undertaken to curb the pre-emption of institutional resources by the Government and simultaneously to provide a level-playing field to the private investors.

The strategy for restoring fiscal balance comprised tax and non-tax reforms, expenditure management and institutional reforms. Restructuring public sector mainly involved divestment of Government ownership which was initiated in 1991-92. Fiscal-monetary coordination was sought to be improved through deregulation of financial system, elimination of automatic monetization to reduce the size of monetized deficit, and reduction in pre-emption of institutional resources by the Government (Pattnaik, R.K., Raj, D.S. and Chander, Jai, 2006). [21]

The fiscal deficit of both the Centre and the State is basically financed through domestic sources over 90 percent of GFD. Within domestic sources, market borrowings have emerged as the most important instrument for the Central Government accounting for about three-fourth of financing with the rest contributed by others, such as small savings, provident funds and reserve funds deposits and advances. This is in contrast to the scenario before 1997-98, when the fiscal deficit was also financed through monetization. This development has contributed to the overall market determination of interest rates in the economy, and hence to the relevance and effectiveness of monetary policy (Mohan, Rakesh, 2008). [22]

A high level of fiscal deficit impacts the practice of monetary policy and trends to have a negative impact on real GDP growth through 'crowding out' effects and/or rise in interest rates in the economy.

The high level of fiscal deficit between 1997-98 and 2002-03 was associated with relatively low GDP growth. The reduction in fiscal deficit since 2003-04 has been associated with a phase of high GDP growth. Thus, fiscal correction and consolidation, which is major ingredient of macroeconomic stability, provide a conducive environment for propelling growth of the economy. Low fiscal deficits also enable more effective monetary policy (Mohan, Rakesh, 2008). [23]

8.6 Problems and Challenges of Fiscal Reforms

The detailed analysis of the fiscal performance during the reform period drew attention to the downward rigidity in current expenditure. In the face of sluggish revenue growth, this results in a persistent increase in revenue deficit. This has been a critical factor in the resurgence of fiscal deficit during the latter half of the 1990s. Although the tax reform measures initiated have imparted rationality to the tax structure, the revenue buoyancy expected through a Laffer-curve effect has not come through. This is because cuts in indirect tax rates were not accompanied by removal of concessions and exemptions. Therefore, there has been neither significant increase in the tax base nor has tax compliance improved. With the result, the improvement in direct tax collection on account of an expansion of tax base and perhaps better compliance was not adequate to compensate the drop in customs and excise duty collections. Eventually, the tax-GDP ratio suffered deterioration during the reform period.

The non-tax revenue of the Centre as a proportion to GDP recorded some rise. Poor cost recovery for the services provided by the Government has been responsible for this trend. Inadequate progress in public sector restructuring specifically reflected in the inability to raise user charges and continued low returns on investments, have also resulted in stagnation in non-tax revenue at Centre Government level. Thus, on the whole, reform did not result in adequate pick up in revenue growth in relation to growing expenditure requirement during the 1990s.

The faster growth in committed expenditure like interest payments, wages and salaries and subsidies has imparted downward inflexibility in revenue expenditure. More importantly, expenditure on interest payments continued to grow unabated, reflecting the impact of sizeable outstanding liabilities contracted at higher interest rates in the first half of the 1990s.

Progress towards better fiscal-monetary coordination during the reform period was an important achievement. The major policy initiative in this direction was the elimination of automatic monetization of the Central Government fiscal deficit. This, together with structural and institutional reforms undertaken by the Reserve Bank in the 1990s, has strengthened the public debt management process enabling wider market participation in the Government securities market and significant reduction in the pre-emption of institutional resources by the Government to finance fiscal gap. The Government borrowings at market related rates have intended to provide level-playing field for the private investor. It was also expected to induce fiscal discipline. The overall reform experience has been that, while the public debt management has been made market-based, fiscal deficits remain unrestrained. Market-based regime with unrestrained fiscal deficit could worsen the fiscal situation. The above development unfolds certain important issues for the Indian fiscal system.

The underlying objective of improving monetary-fiscal co-ordination by eliminating automatic monetization and reducing pre-emption of institutional resources was to contain crowding-out arising from pre-emption of funds by the Government and, thus, allow level-playing field to the private investor. Although the Government at present borrows from the market on equal term with private borrowers, the crowding-out effect of Government borrowings still remains a critical issue in view of the high fiscal deficit (Kapila, Uma, 2003). [24] The moot question, however, is whether more coordination is necessarily better. If the Central bank and the Government agree on what needs to be done, but a coordinated approach cannot be put in effect because of errant behaviour by one of the two authorities, then coordination must improve things whereby the sensible policy maker must dominate the perverse one. In reality, however, fiscal and monetary policies are often poorly coordinated. If both authorities take consistent and credible actions, then the lack of coordination can stem from one of three causes:

1. The fiscal and monetary authorities might have different objectives, i.e., different conceptions of what is best for society;
2. The two authorities might have different opinions about the likely effects of fiscal and/or monetary policy actions on the economy, i.e., they might adhere to different economic theories; and
3. The two authorities might make different forecasts of the likely state of the economy in the absence of policy intervention.

The coordination problem can be solved by vesting the powers of decision making in the hands of the authority with the proper objective or correct theory or accurate forecast, if it is known which of the two authorities is correct. In reality, this is rarely known in advance. The best strategy, therefore, is to give some ability to cancel out the actions of the other, although this may result in a conflict of interest in the worst case or, more often, end in a deadlock. In the context of role of fiscal policy in reinvigorating growth, it needs to be recognized that the fiscal stance affects output itself as well as the variability of output. Imbalances between aggregate demand and aggregate supply feed back into the realized fiscal deficit.

Given this simultaneity, an important question is to examine the design of fiscal policy to see whether fiscal policy automatically smoothens the business cycle or discretionary interventions are required. This aspect is usually examined by looking at built-in automatic stabilizers and by decomposing the actual fiscal deficit into a structural component (unresponsive to cycles in the economy) and a cyclical component (responsive to cycles). Previous research has shown that fiscal deficits in India have been predominantly structural with cyclical component almost negligible. This suggests that discretionary policy had an important role to play in counter-cyclical measures in the Indian context.

The analysis shows that the level of fiscal deficit relative to GDP in India at 2001-02 was higher than not only that of most internationally comparable benchmark levels (e.g. the Maastricht Treaty requires fiscal deficit to be 3.0 percent of GDP) but also the levels recommended by the Eleventh Finance Commission (4.5 percent for Central Government). Further, fiscal deficit in 2001-02 had also exceeded the levels witnessed on the eve of the 1991 crisis. Notwithstanding these developments, most other macroeconomic parameters have been sustainable. As a result, the higher fiscal deficit has not spilled over to the external sector. In this setting, questions have been raised whether the high fiscal deficit should be a matter of much concern.

Another issue which emerges in the context of downward rigidity exhibited by the fiscal deficit is the rise in debt-GDP ratio. It needs to be reviewed whether the fiscal stance and the debt accumulation process is sustainable or not. The progressive lowering of the fiscal deficit has been one of the touchstones for the reform process. When reform began, fiscal policy was conditioned by what might be called 'deficit pessimism', the notion that high levels of fiscal deficits were unsustainable. They would lead to higher interest rates, a worsening balance of payments and a rising public debt to GDP ratio.

On the first two counts, such pessimism has turned out to be unfounded. Interest rates have declined, although rates on commercial loans have not declined as much as those on Government securities. Huge inflows of remittances have negated the malign effects on the balance of payments associated with large deficits. It is the rise in the public debt to GDP ratio since 1997-98, in the earlier post-reform period, that has caused the fiscal deficit ratio to look unsustainable. The key issue, therefore, is whether any worsening of the public debt to GDP ratio can be checked (Mohan, T.T., 2003). [25]

High levels of debt-GDP ratio result in high interest payments relative to revenue receipts. Since interest payments are committed expenditures, revenue deficits are bound to increase when revenue receipts to GDP ratios remain sluggish. This has the effect of lowering the saving rate on the one hand and increasing the fiscal deficit on the other to maintain primary expenditures. Eventually, these changes have the potential of developing into a spiral of rising fiscal deficits, debt, interest payments, revenue deficit and back to a higher fiscal deficit. This gives rise to the issue of sustainability of debt (Srivastava, D.K., 2005). [26]

On the expenditure side, containing the subsidy burden has proved difficult, although its increase as a proportion of GDP has been contained. The current world environment of elevated oil, food and fertilizer prices is not conducive to the expectation of significant reduction in these subsidies in the near future. The prognosis on international prices of energy and food is not encouraging in the medium term as of now. So public policy in these areas has to be taken into account expectations over the medium-term: if elevated prices are deemed to be temporary, smoothening of prices of such important items of common consumption can be justified.

Funding such subsidies over an extended period of time is likely to become unsustainable; hence directly addressing the needs of those less well-off and who are less capable of coping with these price increases may be more desirable, rather than suppressing prices overall.

If the need for these subsidies persists, the recent practice of issuing bonds to fund these subsidies is also not sustainable. The second issue on the expenditure side relates to the funding of public investment, particularly related to infrastructure. Public investment has been reduced over the past decade or so. Whereas private investment has clearly substituted or complemented public investment successfully in areas such as telecom, ports and airports, and particularly in roads and power, total investment in infrastructure is clearly inadequate, in overall economic growth. With increasing urbanization there is need for accelerated public investment in infrastructure. While processes for inducing private investment need continuous improvement, there is need for a reassessment of desirable, expected and feasible public investment requirements, which are likely to be higher than what is currently envisaged. Third, the Government is already engaged in expanding programmes and spending for human development. Funding for these needs will continue to require enhancement (Mohan, Rakesh, 2008). [27]

The issues like rigidities in bringing expenditure to a lower level or in channelising it toward productive lines apart from sustainability of public debt, which continue to pose problems for the on-going process of fiscal consolidation could have been addressed adequately. Fiscal consolidation requires altering the pattern of expenditure. The level of expenditure of the Central Government is heavily loaded in favour of obligatory constituents—interest payments, defence, and statutory grants to States—reducing thereby, strategy of fiscal policy. Capital expenditure, which adds to the productive capacity in the economy, is being progressively pre-empted by growth in revenue expenditure.

Although explicit subsidies provided by the Central Government have declined, there is a wide range of hidden subsidies which need to be contained. Proper targeting of subsidies is needed to reduce leakages and misappropriation. In this regard, the dismantling of the administered price mechanism in the petroleum sector has been a welcome step as it would not only bring transparency to the fiscal operations, but would also improve the productivity, efficiency and international competitiveness of the domestic petroleum industry. In this regard, formulating a long-term energy policy, taking into account the future of public sector oil companies, is necessary to exploit the strong forward and backward linkages of the energy sector with other sector of the economy.

The Government has drawn up plans for undertaking effective and efficient economic and social expenditures, the potential risk to the fiscal stability arise on the likely increase in interest payments due to projected significant rise in its market borrowing programme. This may jeopardize the Governments plans to phase out revenue deficit by 2008-09. The Kelkar Task Force's strategy of reaching this FRBM target is contingent on freezing of stock of debt at the level that existed at the beginning of the FRBM implementation and softer interest rate conditions which would enable the Government to replace old securities as and when they mature with new securities issued al lower interest rates. The substantial increase in market borrowings of the Centre budgeted for the year 2005-06 and firming up of interest rate conditions and consequent possibility of rising Governments interest expenditure would pose a potential source of risk for reaching the FRBM target of phasing out revenue deficits by 2008-09.

If the committed expenses in the form of interest expenditure mount, this would, perforce, make the Government to compromise on other productive expenditures. Specifically, the Kelkar Task Force had projected a growth of 12.8 percent per annum in plan expenditure of the Centre and that capital expenditure at least maintains its ratio to total expenditure at 2003-04 level in the base line scenario (or a steady increase in capital expenditure to reach about 0.5 percent of GDP higher than the baseline projection by 2008-09). Therefore, the Government would be facing a dilemma of whether to stick to its stated outlays so as to pursue its social and economic expenditure goals or compromise so as to be on track of achieving FRBM targets by 2008-09 (Pattnaik, R.K., Bose, D., Bhattacharyya, I. and Chander, Jai, 2005). [28]

In case of direct taxes, personal income tax reform should involve further simplification of the tax system by withdrawing tax exemptions and concessions on income from specified activities. It is also necessary to abolish the surcharge and to further simplify the tax by reducing the number of tax brackets. In fact, there is considerable virtue in having a single tax rate with an exemption limit, as many of the transitional economies have found. Moving towards a single tax rate may not politically feasible at this juncture, however, but it may be possible to reduce the number of tax rates to two, with a small reduction in the marginal tax rate.

On the corporate tax, it is necessary to broaden the tax base by getting rid of the tax concessions and preferences. In particular, the exemption for profits from exports, free trade zones, and Technology Park, as well as exemptions for area-based development and for infrastructure should be phased out. Similarly, the current depreciation allowance, even after the proposed reduction in 2005-06 is quite generous, and there is a case for reducing it to more realistic levels while at the same time reducing the tax rate to align it with the marginal tax rate on personal income tax. It is most important, however, to avoid flip-flop in tax policy.

The other important issue involving the corporate income tax is the differential between the rates applicable to domestic and foreign companies. Part of the rationale for a differential involves the dividend tax, which is payable by domestic companies alone. The rationalization of these two aspects therefore needs to go together.

With regard to import duties, reform should move in the direction of further reduction and unification of the rates. As most non-agricultural tariffs fall between 0 and 15 percent, a uniform tariff of 10 percent would considerably simplify and rationalize the system (Panagariya, Arvind, 2005). [29] Equally important is the need to get rid of an excessive amount of exemptions and concessional treatment for various categories including imports for special projects.

Wide ranging exemptions are also a problem with excise duties. Therefore, one of the most important base-broadening measures should be to reduce the exemptions. The rate structure should be rationalized by converting the remaining items subject to specific duties to ad valorem and by unifying the rates toward a single CENVAT rate.

With the reduction in import duties, almost all imports have been made subject to countervailing duty and the countervailing duty in turn has been made eligible for MODVAT credit like the excise duty. There have also been several improvements and subject to certain limitations the invoice has been made the basis of tax assessment.

Some attempt has also been made to broaden the base through the removal of exemptions, although here the fear of political opposition and the strong pressures exerted by the affected groups have prevented the inclusion of many commodities within the tax net whose exemptions are clearly unjustified. But there is no denying the fact that the excise tax system is a much more rational and simpler system today than it was in 1991.

End Notes

1. Government of India (1989), *Report on the Current Economic Situation and Priority Areas for Action*, Ministry of Finance, New Delhi.
2. Bagchi, Amaresh (1998), *India's Fiscal Reform: Some Signposts*, Vol. 28, No. 1, January-March, Indian Institute of Management, Ahmedabad.

3. Chakravarty, Shomit (2004), "Reform of Tax Administration in India-A Quiet Revolution", in *ADB India Economic Bulletin*, October , New Delhi.
4. Rakshit, Mihir (2000), "On Correcting Fiscal Imbalances in Indian Economy", *ICRA Bulletin*, July-September.
5. Rakshit, Mihir, (2000), *op.cit.*
6. Rakshit, Mihir, (2000), *op.cit.*
7. Blejer, Mario and Cheasty, Adrienn (1993), *How to Measure Fiscal Deficit*, IMF.
8. Blejer, Mario and Cheasty, Adreienne (1993) "Measuring the Fiscal Deficit, Overview of the Issue" in Blejer and Cheasty (eds.) *How to Measure the Fiscal Deficit'*, IMF.
9. World Bank (1988), *World Development Report*, Washington D.C.
10. Ibid.
11. Gill, K.S. (1991), "Budget Deficit of the Central Government", *Economic and Political Weekly,* January, Mumbai.
12. Rangarajan, C. (2004), "Dynamics of Interaction between Government Deficit and Domestic Debt in India", in R. Kannan (ed.) *Select Essays on Indian Economy by C. Rangarajan*', Academic Foundation, New Delhi, p. 19.
13. Tanzi, Vito (1993) "Fiscal Deficit Measurement, Basic Issues" in Blejer percent Cheasty (eds.), *How to Measure Fiscal Deficit*, IMF, Washington D.C.
14. Chelliah, R.J. (1996), *Towards Sustainable Growth, Essays in Fiscal and Financial Sector Reforms in India,* Oxford University Press, Delhi.
15. Tanzi, Vito (1993), *op.cit.*
16. Tanzi, Vito (1993), *op.cit.*
17. Rangarajan, C. (2004), *op.cit*, p.19-20.
18. Tanzi, Vito (1993), *op.cit.*
19. Rakshit, Mihir (2000), "On Correcting Fiscal Imbalance in Indian Economy", *ICRA Bulletin*, July-September 2000.
20. Jha, Raghbendra (2004), *The Challenge of Fiscal Reform in India*, Australia South Asia Research Centre, Australian National University Canberra ACT 0200, Australia, www.r.jha@anu.edu.au
21. Pattnaik, R.K., Raj, D.S and Chander, Jai (2006), *Fiscal Policy Indicators in a Rule-based Framework: An Indian Experience*, RBI Staff Studies, www.rbidocs.rbi.org.in.

22. Mohan, Rakesh (2008), "The Role of Fiscal and Monetary Policies in Sustaining Growth with Stability in India", *RBI Monthly Bulletin*, December, p. 2093.
23. Ibid, p. 2094.
24. Kapila, Uma (2003-04), "Fiscal Reforms in India" in Uma Kapila(ed.) *Indian Economy Since Independence,* Academic Foundation, New Delhi, pp. 144-147.
25. Mohan, T.T. (2003), "A More Relaxed View of Fiscal Consolidation", *EPW*, March 15, p. 1014.
26. Srivastava, D.K. (2005), "Indian Public Finance and the Twelfth Finance Commission", *The Indian Economic Journal* Vol. 53, IEA.
27. Mohan, Rakesh (2008), *op.cit.,* p. 2115.
28. Pattnaik, R.K., Bose, D., Bhattacharyya, I., Chander, Jai (2005), *Public Expenditure and Emerging Fiscal Policy Scenario in India*, www.rbi.org.in.
29. Panagariya, Arvind (2005), "India's Trade Reforms, India Policy Forum 2004", *National Council of Applied Economic Research,* New Delhi, pp. 1-57.

9

Conclusions and Suggestions

The strategy of fiscal consolidation initiated in the early 1990s was a mix of measures towards revenue augmentation through tax reforms and expenditure compression. Given the limited improvement in revenue mobilization, the fiscal consolidation during the first half of the 1990s was essentially achieved through expenditure containment. The sharp cuts in expenditure were effected as part of the stabilization package in 1991, attempts to curb expenditure growth in successive Central Government budgets in the 1990s were found to be mostly irregular and illogical in nature. It is only in the second generation of economic reforms that expenditure reform has become an integral part of the overall fiscal reform. Expenditure Reform Commission set up by the Government suggested a host of measures to curb built-in growth in expenditure and to bring about structural changes in the composition of expenditure. Some of these measures have been implemented by the Government.

Despite, the wide range of measures, the expenditure compression was mainly effected in the capital expenditure. A major initiative towards institutionalizing an expenditure management system was through constitution of Expenditure Reform Commission to look into various areas of expenditure correction. These included creation of national food stock along with cost minimization of buffer stock operations, rationalization of fertilizer subsidies through phased dismantling of controls, imposing a ceiling on Government staff strength through a two-year ban on new recruitment. With a view to promoting transparency and curbing the growth of contingent Government liabilities, a Guarantee Redemption Fund has been set up as a part of expenditure management strategy.

Systematic and comprehensive efforts to reform the tax system in India started only after market based economic reforms were initiated in 1991. Government proposed to implement various suggestions made by the Chelliah Committee on tax reforms. Tax Reform Committee recommended moderate direct tax rates with reduced tax deduction and exemptions, ways of improving compliance of direct taxes and strengthening enforcement, revamping of tax administration and computerization, simplification and rationalization of customs tariffs with a view to reducing the multiplicity and dispersion of rates and to eliminate exemptions which have become unnecessary, reducing the level of tariff rates and simplification and rationalization of the structure of excise duties for better tax compliance and administration, the scope of extending the MODVAT Scheme.

With double digit inflation, fiscal deficit, the precarious foreign exchange, and current account position in 1990-91, the fiscal stabilization programme was directed inter alia at drastically cutting the budget deficit and tightening monetary policy with the objective of reducing inflation and achieving external sector viability. Reforms in the public sector enterprises have also been introduced in the form of disinvestment and autonomy etc. Priorities in reforms include raising return on investments in PSUs and infusing professionalisation in management. Reform of PSUs including privatization and phasing out of unviable units have not gathered as much momentum as had been hoped for. Disinvestment has been piecemeal and the funds so raised are being used to reduce budget deficits, rather than strengthen the PSUs.

India has adopted a rule-based fiscal framework with the enactment of the FRBM Act, 2003 by the Central Government and the framing of FRBM Rules, 2004, thereby marking a new beginning in the fiscal consolidation process. Under the FRBM Act, 2003 the Central Government is committed to eliminate revenue deficit and reduce fiscal deficit to 3 percent of GDP by end-March 2009.

The rise in the share of income tax has, however, not sufficient to make-up fully for the loss from the tariff reforms. In sum, reforms so far have succeeded in making a small dent on India's tax structure by reducing the weight of custom and excise duties and raising that of direct taxes. The shift away from foreign trade taxes and excise duties appears to have taken place at the cost of overall revenue growth. The rise in the relative share of direct taxes has resulted partly from the decline in the revenue from customs and excise duties. The non-tax revenue of the Centre as a proportion to GDP recorded some rise, poor cost recovery for the services provided by the Government have been responsible for this trend.

However, in the light of the study few important points may be mentioned so as to make fiscal stability a long-lasting feature. Undertaking fiscal adjustment often requires difficult decisions involving increasing Government revenue and reducing spending. This can be achieved by a progressive reduction in public debt and through higher revenues. The possibility of achieving higher revenues through increased rate of taxes is both undesirable and non-feasible. Higher tax revenues can be achieved only through buoyancy and expansion of the tax base. It must be emphasized, however, that improvements in tax policy are more likely to be successful when they are accompanied by measures to strengthen tax administration.

An explicit and sustained political commitment, a team of capable officials dedicated to tax administration reform, relevant training for staffs, additional resources for the tax administration, changes in incentives for both tax payers and tax administrators are the essential elements required for successful tax administration reform. It is important to remember that "tax administration is tax policy". Making the transition to information-based tax administration, online filing of tax returns, and compiling and matching information are key to administration reform. Tax administrators should also assist tax payers in a timely fashion and help them to reduce their compliance cost.

Thus, a tax system becomes desirable which should be responsive to GDP growth and its revenue generating capacity should be high, from the point of view of its efficiency, thus leaving the allocation of resources essentially undisturbed, taxes should be levied in a fair and equitable manner, a simple transparent tax system is relatively easy to administer and promotes compliance, and the ratio of tax revenue to GDP should increase at appropriate level.

Following taxes may be helpful in raising revenues of the Central Government:

1. The personal income tax can be increased at least by broadening the base and strengthening the administration while at the same time ensuring that the main aim of the administration would be to collect increasing revenues without harassment that the exacting illegal payments will be drastically cut down. The base of income tax can be widened by:
   - Removing many exemptions that are unjustified and reducing the magnitude of some of the concession;
   - Bringing into the tax net a large number of income earners who are evading tax;
   - Introducing such acceptable simplified procedures as the estimated income scheme; and
   - Introducing a minimum profits tax on all business income other than income of professionals.
2. On the corporation tax, base broadening involves getting rid of the tax concessions and preferences. In particular, the exemption for profits from exports, free trade zones, and technology parks, as well as exemptions for area-based development and for infrastructure should be phased out.
3. Sales tax/VAT should be broadly based tax on final domestic consumption that does not tax intermediated consumption or export, and one that does not differentiate

by source of production (foreign and domestic). Because of its efficiency and revenue security the ideal instrument to achieve this objective is a VAT at a single rate, with crediting provisions and zero rating of exports.

4. Wide-ranging exemptions are a big problem with excise duties. Therefore, one of the most important base-broadening measures should be to reduce the exemptions. In particular, the exemptions given to small scale industry have not only eroded the tax base but have inhibited the growth of firms into an economically efficient size. Similarly, various exemptions given to project imports have significantly eroded the tax base. This has infused the tax system with selectivity and discretion. The rate structure should be rationalized by converting the remaining items subject to specific duties to ad valorem and by unifying the rates towards a single CENVAT.
5. If a moderate level of protection is thought desirable to encourage local industry, a low uniform custom duty, when properly coordinated with a VAT and excises, is the preferred instrument. Duty drawback or suspension schemes are needed to relieve exporters of the anti-export bias caused by custom duties on inputs. Exemptions from customs duties should be limited and clearly defined to avoid abuse. With the rates of custom duties coming down, it would be necessary to subject at most all imports to some import duty. That would also be economically a rational policy.

Likewise, expenditure reduction measures have to be pragmatic, adequate to achieve the intended stabilization, but nonetheless economically, politically, and socially feasible. Several types of expenditure measures can be adopted quickly to contain a deteriorating fiscal situation. Sustainable expenditure reform, however, requires a review of underlying Government policies, the composition of spending, the coverage of activities by the public sector, and the modes of delivery of public services. Similar to the importance of tax administration in tax reform, efficient spending reduction usually requires improvements in systems of budget design, preparation and execution. There are no hard and fast rules about how public expenditure should be cut. This will depend partly on the factors driving the growth in spending, as well as on the social and political constraints facing policymakers. However, some guidelines may be suggested:

1. Avoid across-the broad cuts. Across-the-board cuts often seem attractive, this approach allows each individual operating ministry to decide how to cut its budget-whether to delay the purchase of goods and services, run down stocks, cut back on temporary staff, etc. and it appears to imply equal hardship for all and is thus seen as equitable.
2. It is essential to identify specific programs for reductions. Some programmes should be dropped, pruned or consolidated, as economic development is there such as subsidies etc.
3. Wage restraint in the public sector can be a major source of savings. But there is limit for wage freezing. Cutbacks in civil services numbers are more appropriate since it has expanded more to absorb a growing labour force.
4. Target social programmes narrowly.
5. By raising fees and charges.
6. Public enterprises should, in general, not be a drain on the budget. If they are in deficit, pricing structures should be adjusted, the scope of activities redefined, their employment policy reassessed, and their capital programme rationalized. Preferably, they should be privatized and fully exposed to a competitive market environment.
7. Expenditure restructuring relating to both its size and sectoral allocations aimed at removing inefficiencies arising from misallocation, design and implementation of scheme, and delivery of services.
8. Rationalizing subsidies by reducing their overall volume, increasing their transparency by making them explicit, and

improving their targeting.

Following measures may be suggested to eliminate wasteful expenditure:

1. The elimination of unproductive or very low-priority services.
2. Privatization of activities that can and should be carried out in the private sector.
3. The introduction of a mere commercial approach to public activities, including competitive tendering, the contracting out of some services to the private sector, and the use of commercial accounting techniques to set the basis for full cost recovery.
4. The wider use of balance sheets to improve the analysis of the long-term implications of existing and new expenditure.
5. The stimulation of market discipline, including separate assessment of its application to the Government's role as purchaser and provider of services for example, in health care.
6. For those services that are to remain in the public sector, measures designed to improve managerial performance, efficiency and effectiveness, including establishing cost centres_ which combine under a unified management, the costing interlinked activities, setting objectives, output requirements, and inputs for each centre, more developed managerial authority for the centres, and the linking of manager's salaries to performance.

It may be concluded that viable and effective fiscal adjustment may be restored, if the above suggestions are taken into consideration and implementation in an earnest and proper manner.

Bibliography

Bibliography

Articles and Books

Acharya, Shankar (1988), "India's Fiscal Policy", in R.E.B. Lucas and G.F. Papanek (eds.), *The Indian Economy: Recent Development and Future Prospects*, Oxford University Press, New Delhi.

—(2001), "India's Macroeconomic Management in the 1990s", *Indian Council for Research on International Economic Relations (ICRIER)*, New Delhi.

—(2003), "Back to the Past?", *Economic and Political Weekly*, March 15, Mumbai..

—(2005), "Thirty Years of Tax Reform in India", *Economic and Political Weekly*, May 14, Mumbai.

—(2008), "India's Macroeconomic Performance and Policies Since 2000", *ICRIER*, New Delhi.

Ahluwalia, M.S. (2002), "Economic Reforms-A Policy Agenda for the Future" in Raj Kapila and Uma Kapila (ed.) *A Decade of Economic Reforms in India*, Academic Foundation, Delhi.

—(2002), "Economic Reforms in India Since 1991: Has Gradualism Worked?", *The Journal of Economic Perspectives*, Vol. 16, No. 3.

—(2002), "India's Vulnerability to External Crisis: An Assessment", in Montek S. Ahluwalia, S.S. Tarapore and Y.V. Reddy (eds.), *Macroeconomics and Monetary Policy: Issues for a Reforming Economy: Essays in Honour of C. Rangarajan*, Oxford University Press, New Delhi.

Ahmed, E. and N. Stern (1983), "The Evaluation of Personal Income Taxes in India", *Development Economics Research Centre*, Discussion Paper No. 36, University of Warwick.

—(1984a), "The Evaluation of Different Sources of Government Revenue in India", *Development Economics*

Research Centre, Discussion Paper No. 37, University of Warwick.

—(1991), *The Theory and Practice of Tax Reform in Developing Countries*, Cambridge University Press, Cambridge.

Ahuja, H.L. (2007), *Macro Economics Theory and Policy*, S. Chand and Company Ltd., New Delhi.

Ali, W.N., and Goswami, C.K. (2003), "Direct Taxes A Study of Problem And Impact of Tax Reform Measures With Special Reference to Dr. Raja. J. Chelliah Committees Report", in P.T. Chaudhari (ed.), *Tax Reform in India*, Shree Niwas Publications, Jaipur.

Asha, P. (1986), "Trends in Growth and Pattern of Subsidies in Budgetary Operations of Central Government", *Reserve Bank of India Occasional Papers*, Vol. 7, No. 2, December.

Atkinson, A.B. and Striglitz, J. (1987), *Lectures in Public Economics*, McGraw Hill London and New York.

Bagchi, Amaresh (1972a), "Dissecting the Tax Structure", *Economic and Political Weekly*, January 15, Mumbai.

—(1988), "Fiscal Policy for Financing Development The Indian Experience", in Uma Kaplia (ed.) *Indian Economy Since Independence*, SYNAPSE Publication, New Delhi, pp. 243-272.

—(1988), "Recent Initiatives in Enforcement and Trends in Income Tax Revenues: An Appraisal", *Economic and Political Weekly*, January 16, Mumbai.

—(2002), "Vision of the Kelkar Papers: A Critique", *Economic and Political Weekly*, December 21, Mumbai.

—(2006), "India's Fiscal Management Post-Liberalization", *Economic and Political Weekly*, September 30, Mumbai.

Bagchi, Amaresh and P. Nayak (1994), "A Survey of Public Finance and the Planning Process: The Indian Experience", in Amaresh Bagchi and N. Stern (ed.), *Tax Policy and Planning in Developing Countries*, Oxford University Press, New Delhi.

Bardhan, Pranad (1962), "Tax Payer Psychosis in India", *Economic and Political Weekly*, March 10, Mumbai.

——(2004), "Disjunctures in the Indian Reform Process: Some Reflections", in Kaushik Basu (ed.), *India's Emerging Economy-Performance and Prospects in the 1990s and Beyond*, Oxford University Press, New Delhi.

Baru, S. (1993), "New Economic Policy: Efficiency, Equity and Fiscal Stabilization", *Economic and Political Weekly*, April 21, Mumbai.

Basu, Kaushik (1983), "The Budget: A Critique of its Rationale", *Economic and Political Weekly*, March 19, Mumbai.

Bhargava, K.P. (2003), "Deteriorating Fiscal Management of States in India: Remedial Measures Needed", in Anil Kumar Thakur and Md. Abdus Salam (ed.), *Indian Public Finance and The Twelfth Finance Commission*, Deep and Deep Publications, New Delhi.

Bhatt, V.V. (1972), "Taxation and Economic Development", *Economic and Political Weekly*, June 24, Mumbai.

Bhattacharya, B.B. (1984), *Public Expenditure, Inflation and Growth: A Macro econometric Analysis for India*, Oxford University Press, New Delhi.

Buchanan, M. James and Flowers, R. Merily (1975), "Fiscal Neutrality and Economic Efficiency" in James M. Buchanan and Merilyn R. Flower (ed.) *The Public Finances*, Richard D. Irwin,Inc., U.S.A.

Buiter, W. and Patel, U (1997), "Solvency and Fiscal Correction in India: An Analytical Discussion", *Public Finance: Policy Issues for India*, Oxford University Press, New Delhi.

Cashin, Paul., Olekalns, Nilss and Sahay, Ratna (2001), "Tax Smoothing, Financial Repression and Fiscal Deficits in India", in Tim Callen, Patricia Reynolds and Christopher Towe (eds.) *India At the Crossroads-Sustaining Growth and Reducing Poverty*, International Monetary Fund, Washington, D.C.

Cerra, V. and Saxena, S.C. (2002), "What Caused the 1991 Currency Crisis in India?", *IMF Staff Papers,* Vol. 49, No. 3, Washington, D.C.

Chakravarty, S. (2004), "Reforms of Tax Administration in India-A Quiet Revolution", *Asian Development Bank (ADB), India-Economic Bulletin*, Volume II, Number 3, October, New Delhi.

Chandrashekhar, C.P. (1995), "The Macroeconomics of Imbalance and Adjustment" in P. Patnaik (ed.), *Macroeconomics,* Oxford University Press, New Delhi.

Chelliah, R.J. (1967), "Fiscal Policy Must be Reoriented", *Economic and Political Weekly,* May 20, Mumbai.

—(1969), *Fiscal Policy in Underdeveloped Countries*, 2nd edition, Allen Urwin Publications, London.

—(1980), "Case for an Expenditure Tax", *Economic and Political Weekly,* January 26, Mumbai.

—(1991), "The Growth of Indian Public Debt–Dimensions of the Problem and Corrective Measures", *IMF Working Paper,* WP/91/72, July, Washington, D.C.

—(1992), 'Growth of Indian Public Debt', in B. Jalan (ed.), *The Indian Economy,* Viking Publications, New Delhi.

—(1996), *Towards Sustainable Growth: Essays in Fiscal and Financial Sector Reforms in India*, Oxford University Press, New Delhi.

—(2005), "Malady of Continuing Fiscal Imbalance", *Economic and Political Weekly*, July 30, Mumbai.

Chelliah, R.J., Aggarwal, P.K., Ghoshal R., Gupta, A. and Rao M.G. (1981), *Trends and Issues in Indian Federal Finance*, Allied Publishers Private Ltd, Delhi.

Chelliah, R.J. and Lall, R.N. (1978), "The Incidence of Indirect Taxation in India,1973-74", *National Institute of Public Finance and Policy*, New Delhi.

Chelliah, R.J. and Rao, K.V. (2002), Rational Ways of Increasing Tax Revenues in India, *National Institute of Public Finance and Policy (NIPFP), Discussion Paper No.4*, January, New Delhi.

Chona, Jag M. (1980), "Expenditure of the Central Government: Some Issues", *Economic and Political Weekly,* July 27, Mumbai.

Correa, R. (2006), "Reinventing Fiscal Policy", *Economic and Political Weekly*, June 10, Mumbai.

Dev, M.S. and Mooij, J. (2002), "Social Sector Expenditures in the 1990s-Analysis of Central and State Budget", *Economic and Political Weekly*, March 2, Mumbai.

Desai,V.A. (2001), "A Decade of Reform", *Economic and Political Weekly*, December 15, Mumbai.

Dholakia, A (2005), "Measuring Fiscal Performance of States: An Alternative Approach", *Economic and Political Weekly*, July 30, Mumbai.

Dwivedi, D.N. (1994), "India's Fiscal Policy and Its Performance", in D.N. Dwivedi (ed.), *Readings in Indian Public Finance*, Wiley Eastern Limited, New Delhi.

D'souza, E. (1996), "Budgetary Policy and Economic Growth", *Economic and Political Weekly*, September 21, Mumbai.

Edwards, S. (2004), "Public Sector Deficits, Macroeconomic Stability, and Economic Performance", in Anne, O. Krueger and Sajjid Z. Chinoy (ed.) *Reforming India's External, Financial and Fiscal Policies,* Oxford University Press, New Delhi.

Feldstein, Martin (2004), "Budget Deficits and National Debt"', 8th L.K. Jha Memorial Lecture organised by *Reserve Bank of India*, January 12.

Guha, A (2007), "Company Size and Effective Corporate Tax Rate: Study on Indian Private Manufacturing Companies", *Economic and Political Weekly*, May 19, Mumbai.

Guhan, S. (1986), "Fiscal Policy, Projections and Performance", *Economic and Political Weekly,* April 12, Mumbai.

Gulati, I.S. (1961a), "An Analysis of the Central Government Expenditure", *Economic and Weekly*, April 1, Mumbai.

——(1972), "Wanchoo Report: A Critique", *Economic and*

Political Weekly, July 8, Mumbai.

Gupta, D.A. (2005), "Recent Individual Income Tax Reform", *Economic and Political Weekly,* April 2, Mumbai.

Gupta, K.P., and Chand, D. (2003), "Tax Reforms in India", in P.T. Chaudhari (ed.), *Tax Reforms in India* , Shree Niwas Publication, Jaipur.

Gupta, J.R. (2007), *Public Economics in India Theory and Practice*, Atlantic Publications Ltd., New Delhi.

Hausmann, R. and Purfield, C. (2004), "The Challenge of Fiscal Adjustment in a Democracy: The Case of India", *IMF Working Paper*, WP/04/68, September, Washington, D.C.

Heller, P. (2004), "India: Today's Fiscal Policy Imperatives Seen in the Context of Longer-Term Challenges and Risks", *Paper presented at IMF-NIPFP Conference on Fiscal Policy*, January, New Delhi.

Heller, P. and Rao, M. Govinda (2006), "A Sustainable Fiscal Policy for India: An International Perspective", *RBI Ocaasional Papers,* Vol. 28, No. 1.

Herd, Richard and Leibfritz (2008), "Fiscal Policy in India: Past Reforms and Future Challenges", *Economics Department Working Papers No. 595, OECD*, France.www.oecd.org.

Holani, U (2003), "Indirect Taxes Reforms", in P.T. Chaudhari(ed.), *Tax Reforms in India* , Shree Niwas Publication, Jaipur.

Howes, S., and Murgai, R. (2004), "Subsidies and Salaries: Issues in the Restructuring of Government Expenditure in India", *Paper presented at IMF-NIPFP Conference on Fiscal Policy*, January, New Delhi.

Jadhav, N.D. (1994), *Monetary Economics for India*, Macmillan India Limited, Delhi.

Jadhav N.D. and Balwant Singh (1990), "Fiscal-Monetary Dynamic Nexus in India", *Economic and Political Weekly*, January 20, Mumbai.

Jain, M.M. (1969), "Income Elasticity of Indian Tax Structure:

1955-56 to 1965-66", *Economic and Political Weekly*, May 3, Mumbai.

Jena, P.R. and Rao, M.G. (2005), "Balancing Stability, Equity and Efficiency", *Economic and Political Weekly,* July 30, Mumbai.

Jha, R. (2003), "Fiscal Consolidation", *Economic and Political Weekly,* March 22-29, Mumbai.

Jha, Shikha (1989), "Indirect Tax in India: An Incidence Analysis", *Economic and Political Weekly,* April 15, Mumbai.

Jha, Shikha and Srinivasan, P.V. (1988), "Indirect Taxes in India: An Incidence Analysis", *Mimeo*, National Institute of Public Finance and Policy, New Delhi.

Joshi, R. and Kapoor, S. (2004), *Business Environment*, Kalyani Publication, New Delhi.

Joshi, V. and Little, I.M.D. (1993), "Macroeconomic Stabilisation in India, 1991-93 and Beyond", *Economic and Political Weekly*, December 4, Mumbai.

——(1994), *India: Macroeconomics and Political Economy*, Oxford University Press, New Delhi.

Kaldor, N., (1956), *Indian Tax Reform: Report of a Survey*, Ministry of Finance, Government of India, New Delhi.

Kapila, U. (2004-05), *Indian Economy Since Independence*, Academic Foundation, New Delhi.

Kapila, U. and Kapila, R. (2002), "The Role of Fiscal Policy in Reinvigorating Growth", in Uma Kapila and Raj Kapila (ed.), *Economic Development in India,* Vol. 49, Academic Foundation, New Delhi.

——(2002), "Indian Economy: Review of Development", in Uma Kapila and Raj Kapila (ed.), *Economic Development in India,* Vol. 50, Academic Foundation, New Delhi.

Karan, N. and Dholakia, R.K. (2005), "Consistent Measurement of Fiscal Deficit and Debt of States in India", *Economic and Political Weekly*, June 18, Mumbai.

Karnik, A. (2002a), "Fiscal Responsibility and Budget Management Bill: Offering Credible Commitments",

Economic and Political Weekly, January 19, Mumbai.

——(2002b), "Fiscal Policy and Growth", *Economic and Political Weekly*, March 2, Mumbai.

Kelkar, V. (2002), "Economic Reforms Agenda Micro, Meso and Macro Economic Reforms" in Raj Kapila and Uma Kapila(ed.), *A Decade of Economic Reforms in India*, Academic Foundation, Delhi, pp. 69-77.

Khundrakpam, J.K. (1998), "Sustainability of Central Government Debt", *Reserve Bank of India, Occasional Papers*, Volume 17(1).

Kimmel, H.L. (1959), *Federal Budget and Fiscal Policy 1789-1958*, The Brookings Institution, Washington, D.C.

Kletzer, M. Kenneth (2004), "Liberalizing Capital Flows in India: Financial Repression, Macroeconomic Policy and Gradual Reforms", *National Council of Applied Economic Research (NCAER) Conference on the Indian Economy*, March, New Delhi.

Kochhar, K. (2004), "Macroeconomic Implications of the Fiscal Imbalances", *Paper presented at IMF-NIPFP Conference on Fiscal Policy*, January, New Delhi.

Kochhar, K. and Khatri, Y. (2002), "India's Fiscal Situation in International Perspective", *IMF Staff Seminar*, October, India.

Kopits, George R. (2001), "Fiscal Policy Rules for India?", *Economic and Political Weekly*, March 2, Mumbai.

Kothari, S.S. (2001), *Reform of Fiscal And Economic Policies For Growth In Developing Countries With Special Reference To India*, Macmillan India Ltd, New Delhi.

Krueger, O.A. and Chinoy, S. (2004), *Reforming India's External, Financial and Fiscal Policies*, Oxford University Press, New Delhi.

Krueger, O.A. (2002), "Priorities for Further Reforms", in Anne O.Krueger (ed.), *Economic Policy Reforms and the Indian Economy*, Oxford University Press, New Delhi.

Kumar, N. (2002), "Economic Reforms and Their Macro-Economic Impact" in Raj Kapila and Uma Kapila (ed.), *A*

Decade of Economic Reforms in India, Academic Foundation, Delhi.

Kumar, N. and Mittal, R. (2002), *Public Finance: Theory and Practice*, Anmol Publication Pvt.Ltd., New Delhi.

Kumar, R.T. (2001), "Regional Development Criteria and Horizontal Devolution under the Finance Commission Awards", *Economic and Political Weekly*, December 15, Mumbai.

Kumar, V. (1988), *Tax System in India and Role of Income Tax*, Deep and Deep Publications, New Delhi.

Lahiri, Ashok K. (2000), "Budget Deficits and Reforms", *Economic and Political Weekly*, April 29, Mumbai.

Lahiri, Ashok K. and Kannan, R. (2004), "India's Fiscal Deficit and their Sustainability in Perspective", in Edward M. Favaro and Ashok K. Lahiri (eds), *Fiscal Policies and Sustainable Growth in India*, Oxford University Press, New Delhi.

Mahore, Y.R. (2003), "Twelfth Finance Commission and Indebtedness of States", in Anil Kumar Thakur and Md. Abdus Salam (ed.), *Indian Public Finance And The Twelfth Finance Commission,* Deep and Deep Publications, New Delhi.

Mody, R.J. (1991), "On Defining the Fiscal Deficit", *Economic and Political Weekly*, September 17, Mumbai.

——(1992), "Fiscal Deficit and Stabilization Policy", *Economic and Political Weekly*, February 15, Mumbai.

Mohan, Rakesh (2000), "Fiscal Correction for Economic Growth", *Economic and Political Weekly*, June 10, Mumbai.

——(2005), "Fiscal Challenges of Population Aging: The Asian Experience", *Global Demographic Change: Economic Impact and Policy Challenges*, Federal Reserve Bank of Kansas City.

——(2006), "Economic Reforms in India: Where are We and Where do We Go?", *Paper presented at a Public Seminar Organized by the Institute of South Asia Studies*,

Singapore.

——(2008), "Growth Record of the Indian Economy, 1950-2008: A Story of Sustained Savings and Investment", *Economic and Political Weekly*, May 10, Mumbai.

Mohanty, K.M. and Sharma, K.G. (2003), "Tax Reforms in India: A Fact Sheet", in P.T. Chaudhari (ed.) *Tax Reform in India*, Shree Niwas Publications, Jaipur.

Mohanty, M.S. (1995), "Budget Deficits and Private Savings in India: Evidence on Ricardian Equivalence", *Reserve Bank of India, Occasional Papers*, Vol. 16, No.1, March.

——(1997), "Macro-Economic Stability, Growth and Fiscal Reform- The Indian Perspective", *Economic and Political Weekly*, February 8, Mumbai.

Muhleisen, M. (1998), "Tax Revenue Performance in the Post-Reform Period in India: Selected Issues", *IMF Staff Country Report*, No. 98/112, October.

Mukhopadhyay, Hiranya and Das, Kuntal Kumar (2003), "Horizontal Imbalances in India: Issues and Determinants", *Economic and Political Weekly*, April 5, Mumbai.

Mundle, S. and Rao, G.M. (2004),"Issues in Fiscal Policy", in Bimal Jalan (ed), *The Indian Economy Problems and Prospects*, Penguin Group, New Delhi.

Mishra, V. (2001), "Fiscal Deficits and Fiscal Responsibility Act", *Economic and Political Weekly*, February 24, Mumbai.

Nayak, Pulin B. (1991), "On the Crisis and its Remedies", *Economic and Political Weekly*, August 24, Mumbai.

Nayyar, Deepak (1993), "Indian Economy at the Crossroads: Illusions and Realities", *Economic and Political Weekly*, April 10, Mumbai.

Pattnaik, R.K; Bose, D; Bhattacharyya, I and Chander, Jai (2005), "Public Expenditure and Emerging Fiscal Policy Scenario in India", *Paper presented in the 7th Workshop on Public Finance organised by Banca d' Italia*, 31 March-2 April 2005 at Perugia, Rome.

Pattnaik R.K., Raj, Deepa S. and Chander, Jai (2006), "Fiscal Policy Indicators in a Rule-Based Framework: An Indian Experience", *Paper presented in the 8th Workshop on Public Finance organised by Banca d' Italia*, 30 March- 1 April 2006 at Perugia, Rome.

Pinto, B. and Zahir F. (2004), "Why Fiscal Adjustment Now?", *Economic and Political Weekly*, March 6, Mumbai.

Poirson, H. (2006), "The Tax System in India: Could Reform Spur Growth?", *IMF Working Paper* No. WP/06/93, April.

Pokharna, V. (2003), "Growth And Structure Of Income Tax in India", in P.T. Chaudhari (ed.), *Tax Reform in India*, Shree Niwas Publication, Jaipur.

Prasad, C.S. (2005), *India: Economic Policies and Performance*, New Century Publications, New Delhi.

—(2008), *Economic Survey of India: 1947-48 to 2008-09*, New Century Publications, New Delhi.

Prasad, C.S., Mathur, V. and Chatterjee, Anup (2007), *Sixty Years of the Indian Economy: 1947 to 2007*, New Century Publications, New Delhi.

Prasad, K.N. (2003), *Indian Economy Before And Since Reform*, Atlantic Publications, New Delhi.

Premchand, A. and Chattopadhyay, S. (2002),"Fiscal Adjustment and Expenditure Management", *National Institute of Public Finance and Policy*, Discussion Paper No. 3, January, New Delhi.

Purohit, C.M., Kumar, S.C. and Pradhan, G. (1992), *Fiscal Policy For The National Capital Region*, Vikas Publication, New Delhi.

Radha Krishna, R. (2008), "Indian Development Report (2008)", *Indira Gandhi Institute of Development Research*, Oxford University Press, New Delhi.

Rajaraman, Indira, Bhide, Shashank and Pattnaik R.K. (2005), *A Study of Debt Sustainability at State Level in India,* Reserve Bank of India, Mumbai.

Rajaraman, Indira, and Kanwarjit Singh (1995), "Report on

Presumptive Direct Taxation", *National Institute of Public Finance and Policy*, New Delhi.

Rajaramanan, Indira (2005), "Fiscal Developments and Outlook in India", *National Institute of Public Finance and Policy, Working Paper* No.15, March, New Delhi.

Rajaraman, Indira and Majumdar, D. (2005), "Equity and Consistency Properties of TFC Recommendations", *Economic and Political Weekly*, July 30, Mumbai.

Rakshit, Mihir (1991), "The Macroeconomic Adjustment Programme: A Critique", *Economic and Political Weekly*, August 24, Mumbai.

——(2000), "On Correcting Fiscal Imbalances in the Indian Economy: Some Perspectives", *Money and Finance, ICRA Bulletin*, July-September.

——(2005), "Some Analytics and Empirics of Fiscal Restructuring in India", *Economic and Political Weekly*, July 30, Mumbai.

——(2004), "Some Macroeconomics of India's Reform Experience", in Kaushik Basu (ed.), *India's Emerging Economy Performance and Prospects in the 1990s and Beyond*, Oxford University Press, New Delhi.

Raman Janeyulu, M. (2003), "Impact of Tax Revenue on Economic Growth in View of Twelfth Finance Commission", in Anil Kumar Thakur and Md. Abdus Salam (ed.) *Indian Public Finance and The Twelfth Finance Commission*, Deep and Deep Publications, New Delhi.

Rangarajan, C., Basu A. and Jadhav, N. (1989), "Dynamics of Interaction between Government Deficit and Domestic Debt in India", *Reserve Bank of India, Occasional Papers*, Vol. 10 (3), September.

Rangarajan, C. (2004), "Fiscal Deficit, External Balance and Monetary Growth–A Study of the Indian Economy", in R.Kannan (ed.) *Select Essay on Indian Economy by C. Rangarajan*, Academic Foundation, New Delhi.

Rangarajan, C. and Srivastava, D.K. (2003), "Dynamics of

Debt Accumulation in India: Impact of Primary Deficit, Growth and Interest Rate", *Economic and Political Weekly*, November 15, Mumbai.

—(2005, "Fiscal Deficits and Government Debt: Implications for Growth and Stabilisation", *Economic and Political Weekly*, July 2, Mumbai.

—(2008), "Reforming India's Fiscal Transfer System: Resolving Vertical and Horizontal Imbalances", *Economic and Political Weekly*, June 7, Mumbai.

Rao, G. (2007), "Fiscal Adjustment: Rhetoric and Reality", *Economic and Political Weekly*, April 7, Mumbai.

Rao, M. Govinda and Jena P.R. (2005), "Balancing Stability, Equity and Efficiency", *Economic and Political Weekly*, July 30, Mumbai.

Reddy, Y.V. (2002), "Restructuring of Public Finances and Macro-Economic Stability", in Raj Kapila and Uma Kapila (ed.) *A Decade of Economic Reforms in India*, Academic Foundation, New Delhi.

Rao, M. Govinda and Sen T.K. (1993), "Government Expenditure in India: Level, Growth and Composition", *Mimeo, National Institute of Public Finance and Policy*, August, New Delhi.

Rao, M. Govinda and Tulsidhar, V.B. (1991), "Public Expenditure in India: Emerging Trends", *National Institute of Public Finance and Policy, Working Paper* No. 4, June, New Delhi.

Rao, M.J.M. (2000), "Fiscal Deficits, Interest Rates and Inflation, Assessment of Monetisation Strategy", *Economic and Political Weekly*, July 22, Mumbai.

Reddy, Y.V. (2000), "Fiscal and Monetary Policy Interface–Recent Developments", *Presentation at the Workshop on Budgeting and Financial Management in the Public Sector*, August, Harvard University.

Reynolds, P. (2001), "Fiscal Adjustment and Growth Prospects in India", in Tim Callen, Patricia Reynolds and Christopher Towe (eds.), *India at the Crossroads:*

Sustaining Growth and Reducing Poverty, IMF, Washington D.C.

Sarma, E.A.S. (2004), "Quality of Government Expenditure: A Review", in Edward M Favaro and Ashok K. Lahiri (eds.), *Fiscal Policies and Sustainable Growth in India*, Oxford University Press, New Delhi.

Sarma, A. and Gupta, Manish (2002), "A Decade of Fiscal Reforms in India", *International Studies Program, Working Paper 02-04*, Georgia State University Andrew Young School of Policy Studies, U.S.A.

Sarma, Y.S.R. (1982), "Government Deficit, Money Supply and Inflation", *Reserve Bank of India, Occasional Papers*, Vol. 3 (1).

Shah, A and Parikh S.K. (2002), "Second Generation Reforms" in Raj Kapila and Uma Kapila (ed.), *A Decade of Economic Reforms in India*, Academic Foundation, New Delhi.

Shome, Parthasarthy (2002), "Indian Fiscal Policy in the 1990s: An Overview", in *India's Fiscal Matters*, Oxford University Press, New Delhi.

Shome, Parthasarathy, Sen, T.K. and Gopalakrishnan, S. (1996), "Public Expenditure Policy and Management in India: A Consideration of the Issues", *National Institute of Public Finance and Policy, Working Paper No.8*, New Delhi.

Singh, B.M.P. (2004), *Indian Economy Today: Changing Contours*, Deep and Deep Publications, New Delhi.

Singh, K.N. (2004), "Tax Reform in India", in Anne O Krueger and Sajjid Z. Chinoy (ed.), *Reforming India's External, Financial, and Fiscal Policies*, Oxford University Press, New Delhi.

Srinivasan, T.N. (2002), "India's Fiscal Situation: Is a Crisis Ahead", in Anne O. Krueger (ed.), *Economic Policy Reforms and the Indian Economy*, Oxford University Press New Delhi.

Srivastava, D.K. (2005), *Issues in Indian Public Finance*, New

Century Publications. New Delhi.

Srivastava, D.K. (2005), "Indian Public Finance and the Twelfth Finance Commission", *The Indian Economic Journal,* Vol .53, No. 2, IEA, Patna.

Sury, M.M. (2007), *Fiscal Policy Developments in India-1947 to 2007*, New Century Publications, New Delhi.

Thakur, K. A. (2003), "Twelfth Finance Commission and Trends of Centre and State Finance", in Anil Kumar Thakur and Md. Abdus Salam (ed.), *Indian Public Finance and the Twelfth Finance Commission*, Deep and Deep Publications, New Delhi.

Thimmaiah, G. (2002), "Evaluation of Tax Reforms in India", in M. Govinda Rao (ed.) *Development, Poverty, and Fiscal Policy*, Oxford University Press, New Delhi.

Vaish, M.C. (1999), *Macroeconomic Theory*, Vikas Publication House, New Delhi.

Virmani, Arvind (2005), "India's Economic Growth History: Fluctuations, Trends, Break Points and Phases", *Indian Council for Research on International Economic Relations*, January, New Delhi.

Williamson, J. (2004), "IMF and Fiscal Policy", *Economic and Political Weekly*, July 3, Mumbai.

World Bank, (1998), "Public Expenditure Management Handbook", *The World Bank-The International Bank for Reconstruction and Development*, Washington, D.C., U.S.A.

—(2003), *Fiscal Policy in India: Sustaining Reform, Reducing Poverty*, World Bank and Oxford University Press, New Delhi.

Reports/Publications of Reserve Bank of India:

Reserve Bank of India, (1985), Report of the Committee to Review the Working of the Financial System, Chairman: Sukhamoy Chakravarty, Bombay.

—(1999), *Report on Currency and Finance*, 1998-99, Mumbai.

——(2002), *Report on Currency and Finance*, 2000-01, Mumbai.
——(2003), *Report on Currency and Finance*, 2001-02, Mumbai.
——(2006), *Report on Currency and Finance*, 2004-05, Mumbai.
——*Annual Report*, Various issues.

Reports/Publications of the Government of India

Government of India, (1955), *Report of the Taxation Enquiry Commission* (3 vols.), Ministry of Finance, New Delhi.
——(1971), *Direct Taxes Enquiry Committee; Final Report*, Ministry of Finance, New Delhi.
——(1986), *'Administered Price Policy', Discussion Paper*, Ministry of Finance, New Delhi.
——(1988), *Report of the Ninth Finance Commission.*
——(1991), *Interim Report of the Tax Reforms Committee*, Ministry of Finance, New Delhi.
——(1992a), *Tax Reforms Committee: Final Report*, Ministry of Finance, New Delhi.
——1993, *Economic Survey,* Department of Economic Affairs, Ministry of Finance, New Delhi.
——(2004), *Report of the Task Force on Implementation of the Fiscal Responsibility and Budget Management Act, 2003*, Ministry of Finance, New Delhi.
——(2004), *Report of the Twelfth Finance Commission (2005-10)*, Government of India, New Delhi.

Index

Index